STANDARD GRADE STUDY

Chemistry

W. A. C. Sharp

A Handbook of Practical Advice and Practice Questions

Hamilton Publishing

STANDARD GRADE STUDY-MATE

First Published 1991
© W. A. C. Sharp 1991
ISBN 0 946164 16 9

All rights reserved. No part of this publication may be reproduced, stored in a retrieval system, or transmitted, in any form or by any means, electronic, mechanical, photocopying, recording or otherwise, without prior written permission from the publisher.

British Library Cataloguing in Publication Data
Sharp, W.A.C.
    Standard grade study-mate—Chemistry.
    1.   Scotland. Secondary schools. Curriculum subjects: Chemistry
    I. Title
    540
    ISBN 0946164169

Published by **The Hamilton Publishing Co. Ltd,**
12 Colvilles Place, Kelvin, East Kilbride G76 0SN

Produced in Great Britain by
M & A Thomson Litho Ltd, East Kilbride, Scotland

Introduction

Standard Grade Chemistry will be one of a number of subjects which you need to master at the end of your fourth year in school. Chemistry, like many of the other subjects, involves 'jargon', words that are not used in everyday life.

Chemicals are all around us and are used by people who have no knowledge of chemistry. Maybe you say 'Please pass the en ay see el, Dad!', but more likely you will say 'Pass the salt'. You may tell someone that your sister has fallen into the 'Aitch two oh', but most people would have called it the water! If someone who had not studied chemistry overheard you reading aloud some of the equations in Chapter Seven of this book, they would perhaps think that you were talking a foreign language. One of the aims of this book is to help you master the 'language' of chemistry. The first twelve chapters contain concise revision notes of all the *knowledge and understanding* that you will require for Standard Grade Chemistry.

Chemistry is not just about knowing things. Being able to apply this knowledge is called *problem solving*. Only one chapter, Chapter Thirteen, is devoted to this, but you will find plenty of questions on problem solving throughout the book. The secret of mastering problem solving is to get plenty of practice in it. Questions about knowledge and understanding and problem solving are found together in the exams which you sit. You will find them similarly presented in the practice questions in this book. Problem solving questions are identified by the abbreviation **PS**.

Unfortunately all of your school courses end in exams! As in all subjects, chemistry exams have changed a lot over the years. Advice is given on tackling different types of questions which are now asked in Standard Grade Chemistry exams. Included in the *practice questions* are many of the 'grid' type. In the answer section at the end of the book, help is given on how you should approach these types of questions.

Reference is often made to the *Data Booklet*, published by the Scottish Examinations Board. As this is so commonly used in schools, it has not been reproduced here. It is assumed that you have been given a copy of this by your school.

This *Standard Grade Study-Mate* has all you need to know to help you make the grade in Chemistry. *Good Luck!*

WACS

Acknowledgments

The Author and Publisher would like to thank the following for permission to reproduce copyright material in this book:

The Scottish Examination Board for the extracts on pages 1, 3 and 4 from the 1990 Standard Grade Chemistry examination paper, and the table of solubilities on page 48 from the *Data Booklet*;

ICI for the photograph on page 46;

The Building Research Establishment, Fire Research Station, for the photograph at the top of page 85 (BRE Crown Copyright 1991);

Strathclyde Police for the poster on page 105.

Contents

Preparing for the Exam
1

CHAPTER ONE
Chemical Reactions (Topics 1 and 2)
5

CHAPTER TWO
Atoms and Molecules (Topics 3 and 4)
14

CHAPTER THREE
Symbols, Formulae and Equations
21

CHAPTER FOUR
Hydrocarbons (Topics 5 and 6)
26

CHAPTER FIVE
Ions (Topic 7)
38

CHAPTER SIX
***Acids, Alkalis and Chemical Calculations
(Topics 8 and 9)***
44

CHAPTER SEVEN
Making Electricity (Topic 10)
57

CHAPTER EIGHT
Metals (Topic 11)
64

CHAPTER NINE
More about Metals (Topics 12 and 13)
75

CHAPTER TEN
Plastics and Synthetic Fibres (Topic 14)
84

CHAPTER ELEVEN
Fertilisers (Topic 15)
92

CHAPTER TWELVE
Carbohydrates and Related Substances (Topic 16)
100

CHAPTER THIRTEEN
Problem Solving
108

Answers to Practice Questions
119

Appendix: The Periodic Table
134

Index
135

Preparing for the Exam

This book provides a summary of all the *knowledge and understanding* in the sixteen topics of Standard Grade Chemistry. It will also provide you with help to develop your skills in *problem solving*.

Practical abilities are not covered, although they are referred to. Practical abilities will be taught and assessed by your class teacher.

HOW YOU WILL BE ASSESSED

Standard Grade Chemistry is assessed both during the course in your school and in an external exam which you will take at the end of your fourth year.

Element	Assessment
Knowledge and understanding	School exams and external exam
Problem solving	School exams and external exam
Practical abilities	School assessment only

As you can see, a lot of your success in Standard Grade Chemistry can depend on your school assessments. However, a good performance in the external exam is important, especially if your school grades were not very good. In this book you will find plenty of advice which should help you to prepare for the external exam.

In the external exam there are two papers: *General* and *Credit*. In each of the papers there will be questions on *knowledge and understanding* and on *problem solving*. Many of the problem solving questions will be applications of your knowledge.

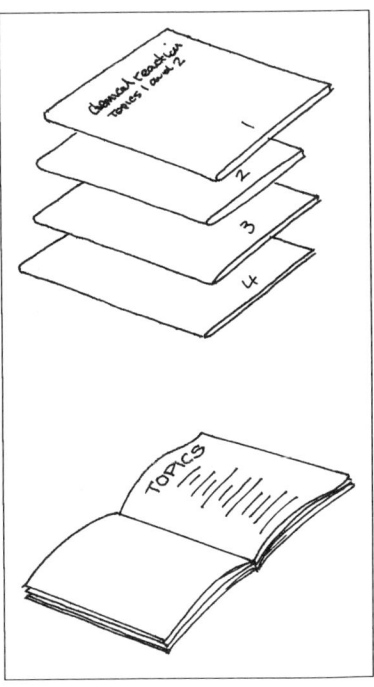

GETTING ORGANISED

In your school you will probably have made your own chemistry notes. The work in this book will be very similar to your own work.

Organise your school work by putting your notebooks in order and numbering them. Write on the cover of each notebook the names of the topics they contain. If you have loose-leaf notes, then see that they are in the sequence in which you worked through the topics, and make sure that each topic has a title at the start.

If you find a few things here which are *not* in your own notes, then don't go complaining to your class teacher! You may have been absent for a time or you may have gone at a slower pace in some of the topics. If you know *everything* in your school notes and *everything* in this book, then you should achieve a Grade 1. If you miss out parts of some topics, then perhaps you will have to settle for less.

There may be a few differences between your school notes and some of the notes in this book. Every chemistry book you read will give a different temperature for the Haber process, and different values for the boiling ranges for kerosine. However, there is no doubt that powders react faster than lumps, or that mercury is a liquid. If you are concerned about differences, then ask your chemistry teacher to advise you.

GENERAL AND CREDIT

The work has not been separated into *General* and *Credit* as you will sit *both* of these papers. Quite simply Credit work is more difficult than General work. In problem solving you will have to handle more information in Credit questions than in General questions. You should aim to do well in *both* papers. However, if by chance you do well in the Credit paper and badly in the General paper, this will not count against you.

STUDYING CHEMISTRY

Organise your notes. This will make revising an easier task for you.

Do not learn by reading. A pencil and paper are essential for studying chemistry. You can never learn to draw cyclobutane by looking at it. Draw and redraw formulae, diagrams, tables and flowcharts. Your best writing is not needed for revision and you should put the paper you have used into the bin when your revision session is over.

Take your own time. There are 16 topics of unequal lengths. Aim to revise each topic several times. Don't waste time on the easy work — yes, there is easy work! Spend more time on the work involving chemical calculations, formation of ions, cells, electrolysis, redox and the structure of polymers. A chart of your work plan will be a help — remember to include rest days and breaks.

Decide for yourself how long a period of revision is best for you. Fifteen minutes is probably too short. An hour is almost certainly too long.

Avoid distractions. It may be tempting to watch your favourite TV programme whilst trying to learn about isomers, or to study and sunbathe at the same time. However, the less distractions that you have the better.

Your notes are your own. Write as many extra comments and references into your notes as you wish. You may have written about catalysts in Topic 2. Beside this you may want to write 'See Haber process, Topic 15, or catalytic converters, Topic 5'. Such additions of your own are called 'cross-references'.

THE EXAM

In each paper the same number of marks, usually 30, will be given for knowledge and understanding and for problem solving.

Two kinds of questions are asked. *Part 1* contains questions in which you must select a letter (or letters) in a grid. The questions in *Part 2* require you to write your own answers.

Part 1

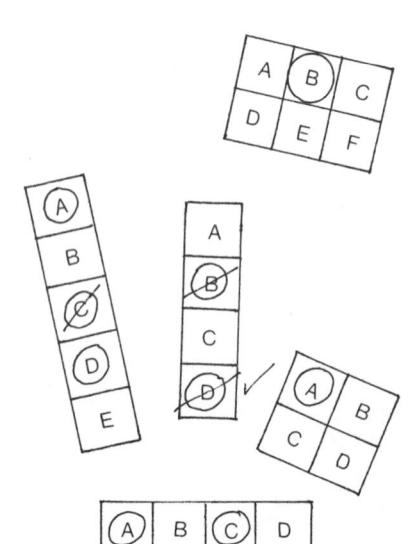

At the start of Part 1 you will find advice on how to answer the questions. As well as reading this advice, you should also be careful in reading the questions themselves.

You may be told how many correct answers to select.

'Identify the **two** substances which . . .'

Or you may be asked to identify for yourself how many answers to choose.

'Identify the statement(s) which can be applied to . . .'

In all these questions it is important that you select the correct number of letters. You will lose marks if you circle too many or too few.

If you make a mistake and want to change it, then make it clear which answer(s) you have finally selected.

Look for words in **bold type**. You may not always be asked to identify a correct statement. However, the examiner is not trying to trick you. Important words such as **two**, **incorrect** or **both** will be emphasised.

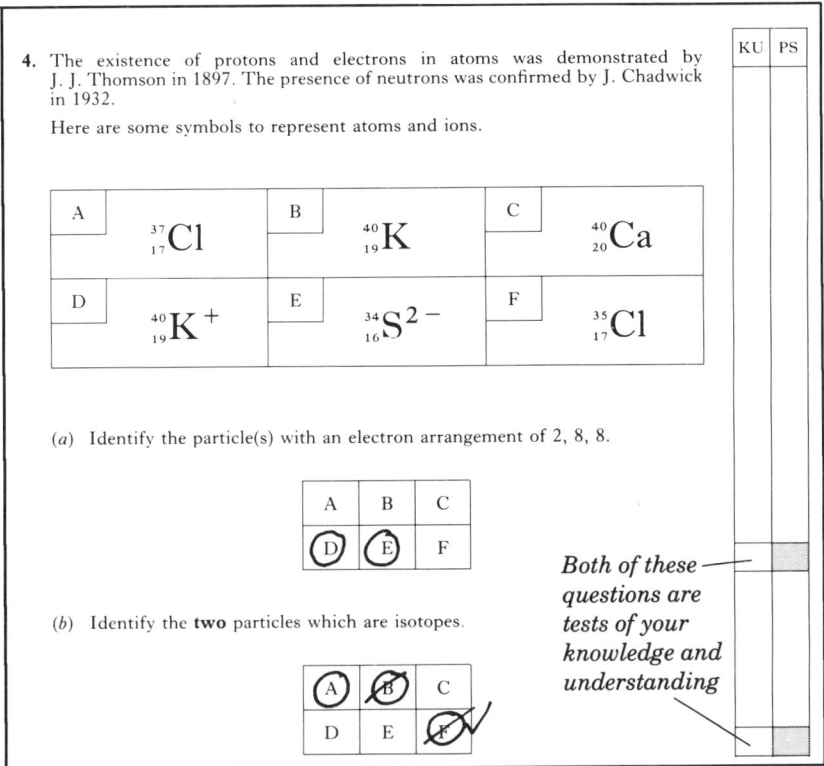

(a) You must decide for yourself how many letters to circle. The electron arrangements of the atoms (A, B, C, F) can be found in the Data Booklet. D, a positive ion, has one electron less than the atom while E, a negative ion, has two electrons more than the atom.
The correct answers are D and E.
(b) You are told that there are **two** correct answers. They are A and F. As you can see, several changes have been made but it is clear that A and F are the answers that have finally been decided on.

Part 2

In Part 2 the number of marks will be indicated. The number of marks and the space provided for the answers are a guide as to how much you should write.

Answer exactly what you are asked. If you are asked to '**Name** the element which is a liquid metal', then give the name, mercury, and not the symbol, Hg. If you are asked for a '**word equation**', then do not write a chemical equation. Do not write equations or formulae with charges unless you are asked to.

Always '**show your working clearly**' in calculations. If you have made a mistake somewhere, you will still get marks for the parts which are correct. A wrong answer on its own will always get no marks.

There is a lot of reading in some questions. There are a lot of clues contained in the words. Drawings often contain help. They may remind you that copper(II) oxide is a solid or that hexane burns. Look for hints.

Your diagrams are not meant to be works of art. They should, however, be realistic and whatever you draw must work. A stencil will help you, and a ruler should be used for straight lines. There are no sausage-shaped test tubes or pear-shaped beakers in your chemistry lab. Labels should be accurate, with names of substances rather than formulae, with lines touching the correct part of the diagram.

When presenting information, use the methods asked for in the question. Make sure that you draw a **line graph** if that is what is asked for, and not a bar graph. You may lose marks if you get it wrong.

Remember that you may get different grades for knowledge and understanding and problem solving. If you have a bad memory and do badly in knowledge and understanding, you may still do well in problem solving. Make sure that you can look up information in the *Data Booklet*, construct tables and both draw and use graphs.

15. The following results were obtained from an industrial plant which produces ammonia, NH_3, for the fertiliser industry.

$$N_2(g) + 3H_2(g) \rightleftharpoons 2NH_3(g)$$

Conversion to ammonia/%	95	90	83	77	70	60	48
Temperature/°C	200	300	400	500	600	700	800

(a) Plot the results from the table in the form of a **line graph**. Label each axis clearly.

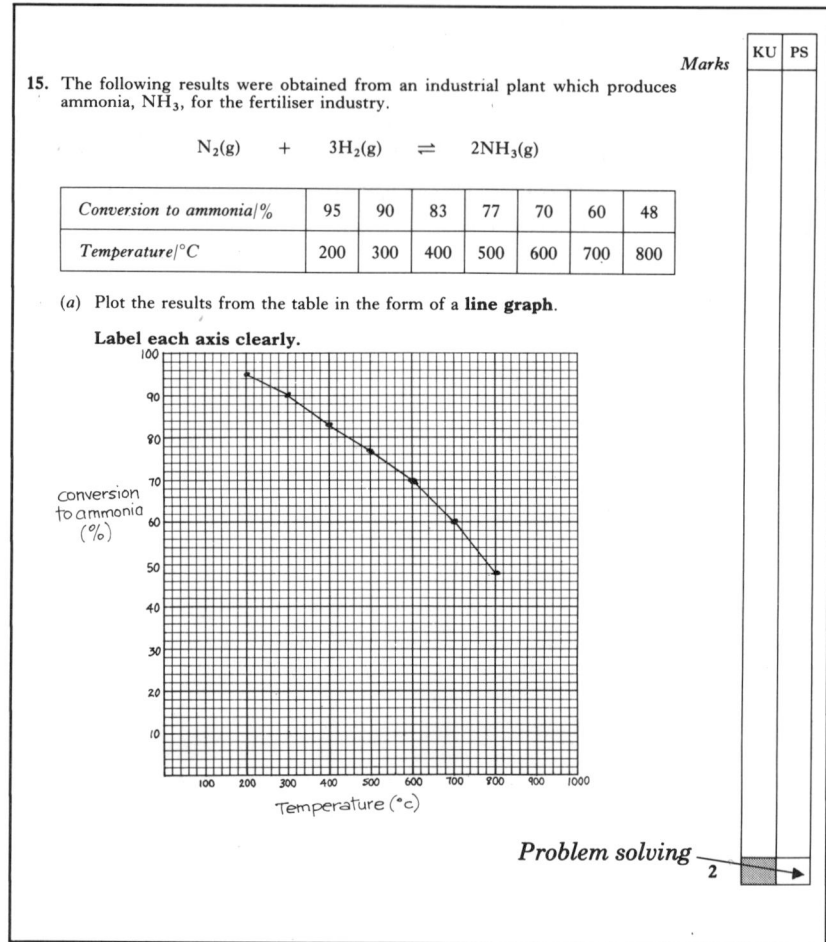

Problem solving — 2

(a) Marks are given for correct figures on each axis, labels and units. **Line graph** has been emphasised. You will lose marks for points which have not been accurately plotted. You will usually find another piece of graph paper at the end of the exam book. Use this if you make a mess of the first one.

15. (Continued)

(b) Making use of the graph, calculate the amount of ammonia produced at 450 °C, when 280 kg of nitrogen reacts with excess hydrogen.

(b) From the graph, at 450°C the conversion to ammonia is 80%.

$N_2 + 3H_2 \rightleftharpoons 2NH_3$
1 mole of N_2 gives 2 moles of NH_3
28 g of N_2 gives 2 × 17 g of NH_3
280 kg of N_2 gives 340 kg of NH_3
mass of ammonia = 80% of 340 kg

$$= 340 \times \frac{80}{100} = 272 \, kg$$

NH_3
N 1 × 14 = 14
H 3 × 1 = 3
fm = 17

All working has been shown. This means that marks can be earned even if the final answer is wrong. Take care that the correct units (kg in this question) are used.

CHAPTER ONE
Chemical Reactions

In chemistry there are two common kinds of changes: **physical changes** and **chemical reactions**.

PHYSICAL CHANGES

There are three **states** of matter: solid, liquid and gas. A physical change is a change of state. Physical changes can usually be reversed easily. A melted ice lolly can be refrozen in the freezer. Steam from a boiling kettle will condense on a cold window.

The following are physical changes:

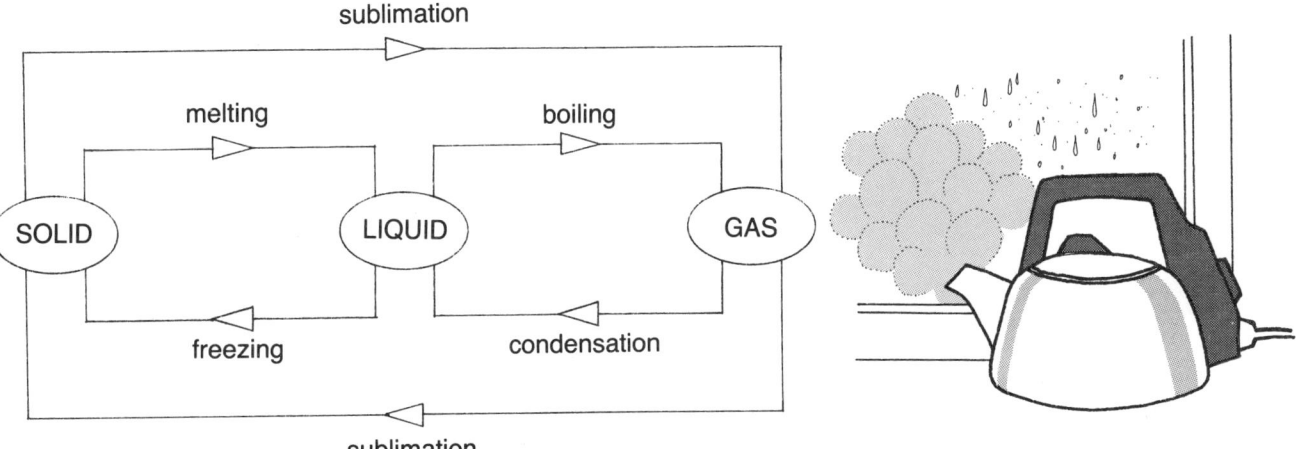

In a physical change there is no new substance forming, only a change of state. Physical changes always occur at a fixed temperature.

Substance	Melting point (°C)	Boiling point (°C)	State at room temp. (25°C)
water	0	100	liquid
oxygen	−218	−183	gas
iron	1537	2747	solid

CHEMICAL REACTIONS

In a chemical reaction a new substance is formed. It may be very difficult or even impossible to reverse a chemical reaction. Imagine trying to 'unburn' petrol or to 'unrust' iron.

Signs of Change

New substances which form in chemical reactions may be in a different state. Adding some tablets to water might cause bubbles of gas to form. This is called **effervescence**.

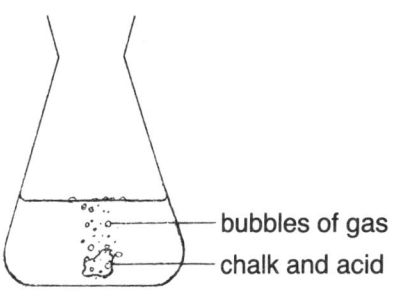

CHAPTER ONE • *Chemical Reactions*

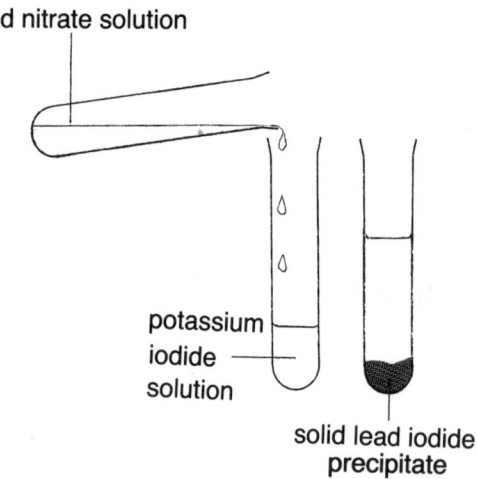

Sometimes when two solutions are mixed a solid forms. This solid is called a **precipitate**. In one of your practical techniques you may have added colourless lead nitrate solution to colourless potassium iodide solution and formed a yellow precipitate of lead iodide.

These changes in appearance or colour are signs of new substances forming. Chemical reactions are taking place.

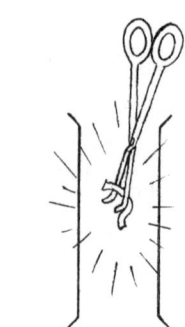

magnesium buring in oxygen

Other Signs of Change

When magnesium reacts with oxygen to form magnesium oxide, a great deal of *heat* and *light* are given out.

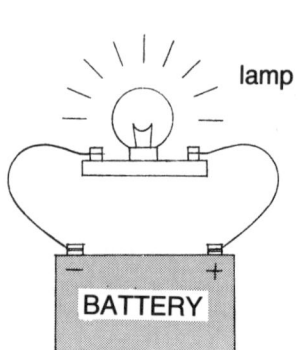

In a battery, zinc reacts with other chemicals to produce *electricity*.

Even if there are no flames or flashes in a chemical reaction, energy may still be given out. When an acid reacts with an alkali a thermometer is needed to detect the temperature change.

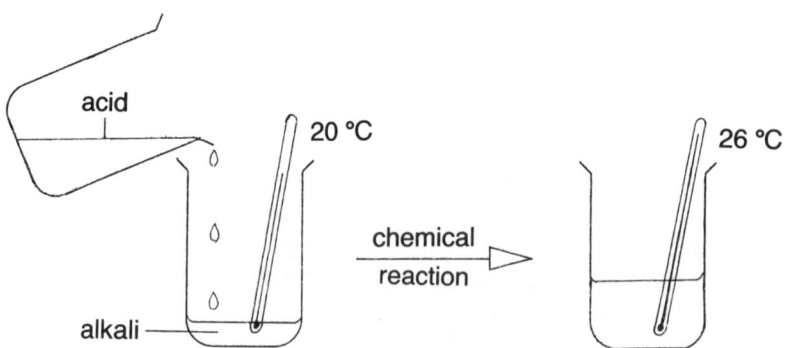

Energy has been given out in all of the chemical reactions described. Other reactions may require energy to be put in before they can take place. For example, many substances need to be heated before they will decompose (break up). In the kitchen both baking and cooking involve heating and chemical reactions.

Every chemical reaction is accompanied by an energy change.

ELEMENTS — THE BUILDING BLOCKS

Elements are the simplest substances in chemistry. Each element has a **symbol**. The names of the elements and their symbols are to be found in the periodic table.

CHAPTER ONE • *Chemical Reactions*

Most elements are metals and are very similar in appearance. Many of the metals have similar properties.

If a substance is an element, then its name will appear in the periodic table. Hydrogen and oxygen are elements. Water and salt are not elements, their names do not appear in the periodic table.

Compounds

Although there are only about one hundred elements there are many millions of **compounds**. A compound contains two or more elements joined together. The chemical name for a compound gives a clue to the elements in it.

The ending *-ide* indicates that the compound contains only two elements.

Compound	Elements present
zinc ox*ide*	zinc and oxygen
calcium sulph*ide*	calcium and sulphur
magnesium nitr*ide*	magnesium and nitrogen

There are exceptions to this rule: hydroxides contain hydrogen and oxygen and another element (calcium hydroxide contains calcium, hydrogen and oxygen); and cyanides contain carbon and nitrogen and another element (potassium cyanide contains potassium, carbon and nitrogen).

When a name ends in *-ate* or *-ite* this indicates the presence of oxygen in addition to the other elements.

Compound	Elements present
copper carbon*ate*	copper, carbon and oxygen
potassium phosph*ate*	potassium, phosphorus and oxygen
sodium sulph*ite*	sodium, sulphur and oxygen

Mixtures

The substances in a **mixture** have not reacted together.

Water is a *compound* of hydrogen and oxygen, not a mixture of hydrogen and oxygen. A *mixture* of the gases hydrogen and oxygen is also a gas but with quite different properties from those of water. Oxygen can be breathed, but water cannot. Hydrogen burns, but water certainly does not!

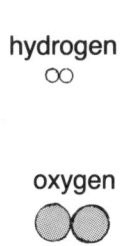
hydrogen

oxygen

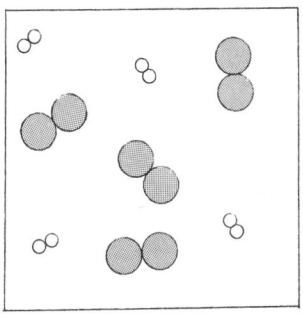
mixture

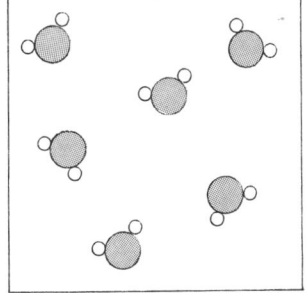
compound

CHAPTER ONE • *Chemical Reactions*

A mixture of two substances has properties rather like those of the individual substances. A mixture can be separated again if the right method can be found.

Separating Mixtures

Filtration separates an insoluble solid from a liquid.

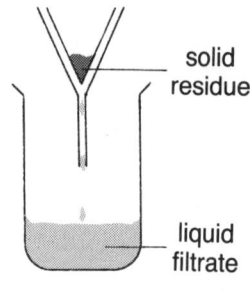

Distillation separates a liquid from a liquid or a liquid from a solution.

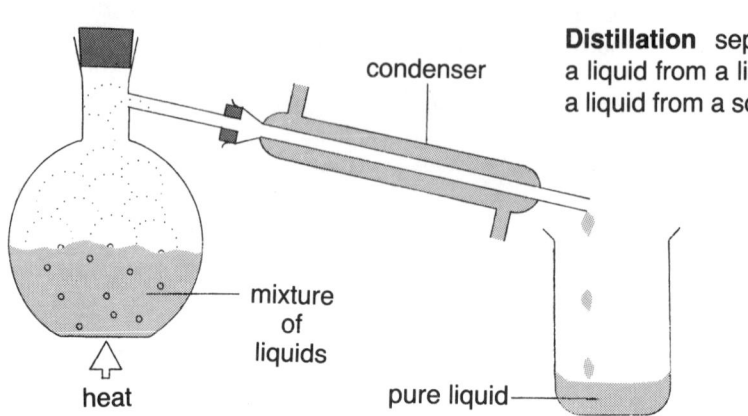

Chromatography separates mixtures of colours into individual colours.

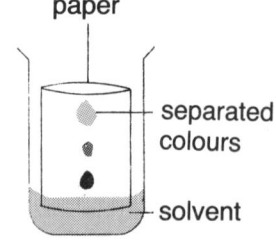

Solutions

A liquid with a substance dissolved in it is called a **solution**. The liquid is called the **solvent**. The substance added to the liquid is called the **solute**. The solute can be solid, liquid or gas.

Lemonade is a solution of carbon dioxide (gas), sugar (solid) and flavouring (liquid) in water.

Solutions in water are called **aqueous** solutions. A solution in which no more solute can be dissolved is called a **saturated** solution.

Concentration

You will often meet the idea of **concentration**. The concentration of a solution tells you how much solute is dissolved in it. A lot of solute in a solution means that the solution will be **concentrated**. Little solute means the solution is **dilute**.

Later it will be shown that concentration is given by figures such as 1 mol/*l* and 0.1 mol/*l*. The bigger the number, the more concentrated the solution.

SPEED OF REACTIONS

Here are some examples showing how the rates of chemical reactions can be increased, and how this can be seen.

CHAPTER ONE • *Chemical Reactions*

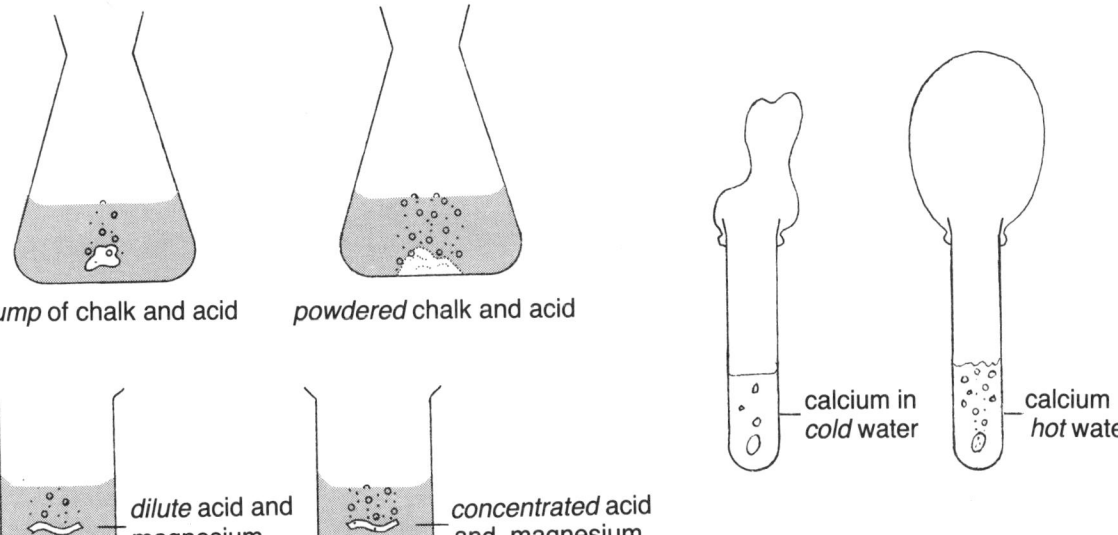

The speed (or rate) of a chemical reaction can be increased by:
- using *powders* instead of lumps of solids;
- increasing the *temperature* of the reactants;
- increasing the *concentration* of the reactants.

Catalysts

Another way in which the speed of a reaction can be altered is by using a **catalyst**. A catalyst speeds up the rate of a reaction but is not used up itself.

For example, when a liquid called hydrogen peroxide is heated, it slowly decomposes to give oxygen. However, adding powdered manganese dioxide, a catalyst, produces oxygen much more quickly without heating. When oxygen has stopped coming off there is still as much catalyst left as there was at the start. If the powder is filtered and dried, its mass will be the same as it was at the beginning of the experiment.

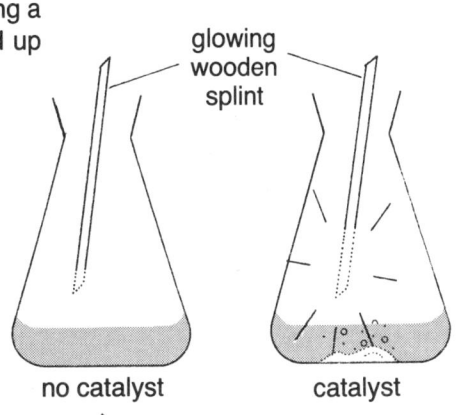

Uses of Catalysts

Many catalysts are metals such as nickel, platinum and iron. They are used for making margarine, polythene, ammonia, sulphuric acid and many other substances.

Cars are now being fitted with catalytic converters. These convert harmful chemicals in the exhaust into other substances which are harmless.

In Chapter Twelve you will learn about biological catalysts called enzymes.

CHAPTER ONE • *Chemical Reactions*

The Idea of Fairness

When powdered chalk was added to acid it reacted much faster than lumps of chalk did. But how can we be sure that this is a **fair comparison**?

The conditions that can be changed in a reaction are called **variables**. In this experiment the variables are:

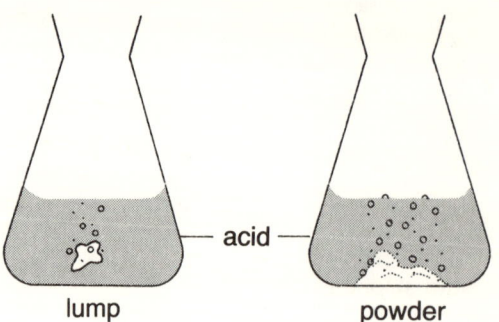

- the *temperature* of the acid;
- the *concentration* of the acid;
- the *size* of the chalk lumps;
- the *volume* of acid;
- the *mass* of chalk.

If only *one* of the variables is changed, e.g. the size of the chalk lumps, then the test is a fair one. If the results of two experiments are to be compared, then only *one* variable must be changed at a time.

Practice Questions

1. In chemistry there are two common changes, physical and chemical.

A	B	C
burning a match	dissolving sugar	melting ice
D	**E**	**F**
milk going sour	meths and water mixing	water forming from hydrogen and oxygen
G	**H**	**I**
steam condensing	iron rusting	sand and salt mixing

   (a) Which **four** boxes refer to chemical changes?
   (b) Which **two** boxes refer to solutions forming?
   (c) Which box refers to a **compound** forming from its elements?
   (d) Which box refers to a change which is the **opposite** of boiling?

CHAPTER ONE • *Chemical Reactions*

2. State the symbols of the following elements.

(a) carbon (b) neon (c) iron
(d) chlorine (e) sodium (f) chromium
(g) copper (h) tungsten (i) helium

3. Name the following elements.

(a) P (b) N (c) Ar
(d) K (e) Pt (f) Br
(g) Ca (h) Au (i) B

4. Name the elements in the following compounds.

(a) magnesium oxide (b) zinc chloride
(c) potassium hydroxide (d) copper carbonate
(e) barium iodide (f) potassium sulphite
(g) calcium hydroxide (h) sodium cyanide

5. Name the compounds formed between the following elements.

(a) zinc and chlorine (b) iron and oxygen
(c) sodium and fluorine (d) copper, sulphur and oxygen
(e) hydrogen and oxygen (f) magnesium and nitrogen

6. A mixture of iron and sulphur is different from the compound iron sulphide.

Explain to someone who has not studied chemistry the difference between a mixture and a compound.

7. You are given a mixture of sand and salt.

Describe how you could separate them. You must finish with dry samples of each.

8. A technician has to make up a chemical for a chemistry class to use. To make this he must dissolve solid copper sulphate in water.

(a) What are the names of the solute and solvent that he uses?
(b) What should he write on the label of the bottle?

9. Mixtures of substances can be separated in different ways.

A	B	C	D
filtration	sea water	iron and sulphur	distillation

E	F	G	H
lemonade	water	chromatography	oil and water

(a) Which box shows a method of separating mud and water **without** heating?
(b) Which **two** boxes show solutions?
(c) Which box shows a mixture of two solids?
(d) Which box shows a method for separating salt from water?

11

CHAPTER ONE • *Chemical Reactions*

PS 10. Draw a **labelled** diagram of the apparatus you would use to filter muddy water. Your labels should include 'residue' and 'filtrate'.

11. The rate of a chemical reaction can be changed in a number of ways.

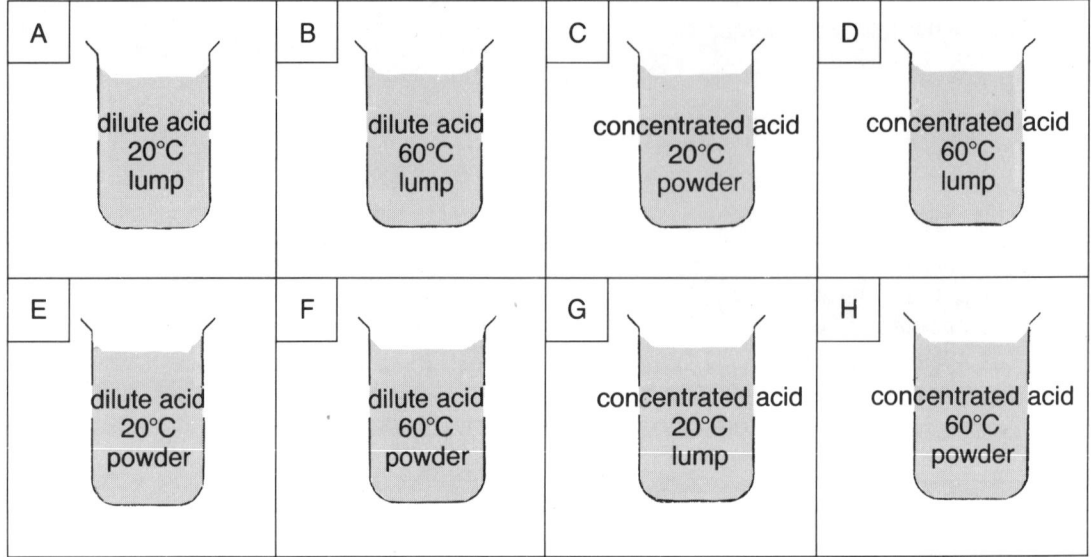

PS (a) In which experiment will the speed of the reaction be **greatest**?
(b) In which experiment will the speed of the reaction be **slowest**?
(c) Which **two** experiments could be chosen to show that changing the concentration of the acid altered the speed of the reaction?
(There are several possible pairs of experiments.)

PS 12. Lumps of ice were added to the acid in experiment **A** in question 11 above. This slowed down the rate of the reaction. Give **two** reasons why this should be.

13. A group in a chemistry class carried out a practical investigation. This was intended to show that sugar lumps really do take longer to dissolve than the more usual ground sugar.

PS (a) Describe the experiment you could carry out to prove this.
PS (b) Name **three** variables which should be kept constant.

14. Catalysts are used in many different chemical reactions.

A	B	C
remains unchanged in a reaction	weighs less at the end of a reaction	cooling reactants
D	**E**	**F**
increasing the concentration of reactants	burning magnesium	manufacture of margarine

CHAPTER ONE • *Chemical Reactions*

(a) Which box describes what happens to a catalyst in a chemical reaction?
(b) Which box gives a use of a catalyst?
(c) A catalyst can speed up a reaction.
    Which box gives **another** way of speeding up a reaction?

15. In an experiment, a group of pupils added exactly 2.00 g of powdered manganese dioxide catalyst to 20 cm³ of hydrogen peroxide solution. Here is their report.

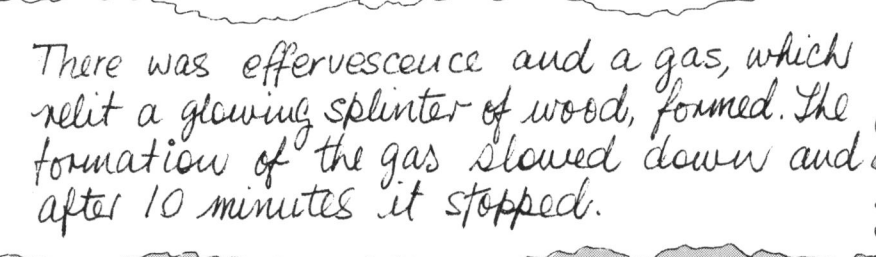

There was effervescence and a gas, which relit a glowing splinter of wood, formed. The formation of the gas slowed down and after 10 minutes it stopped.

The group carefully filtered the remaining solid, left it to dry and then reweighed it.

(a) What evidence is there in their report that a chemical reaction has taken place?

(b) Suggest the reason why the formation of the gas slowed down.

(c) What was the name of the 'remaining solid'?

(d) Manganese dioxide is a catalyst. What mass of dry solid would you expect the group to find?
    Explain your answer.

CHAPTER TWO

Atoms and Molecules

THE PERIODIC TABLE

Elements are classified by their arrangement in the **periodic table**. The horizontal rows of elements are called **periods**; the vertical columns are called **groups**.

	Groups																	0
	I	II		H									III	IV	V	VI	VII	He
	Li	Be			Transition metals								B	C	N	O	F	Ne
	Na	Mg											Al	Si	P	S	Cl	Ar
Periods	K	Ca	Sc	Ti	V	Cr	Mn	Fe	Co	Ni	Cu	Zn	Ga	Ge	As	Se	Br	Kr
	Rb	Sr	Y	Zr	Nb	Mo	Tc	Ru	Rh	Pd	Ag	Cd	In	Sn	Sb	Te	I	Xe
	Cs	Ba	La	Hf	Ta	W	Re	Os	Ir	Pt	Au	Hg	Tl	Pb	Bi	Po	At	Rn
	Fr	Ra	Ac															

Ce	Pr	Nd	Pm	Sm	Eu	Gd	Tb	Dy	Ho	Er	Tm	Yb	Lu
Th	Pa	U	Np	Pu	Am	Cm	Bk	Cf	Es	Fm	Md	No	Lr

Radioactive and man-made elements

The elements in each group show similarities to the others in the group in their properties.

- All of the metals in Group I react violently with water and have to be stored under oil. They are called **alkali metals**.
- The elements in Group II all burn brightly.
- Group VII elements are called **halogens**.
- The Group 0 elements are called **noble gases**.

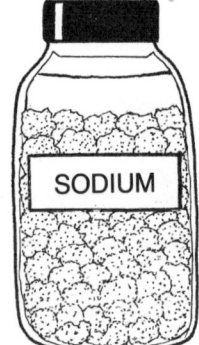
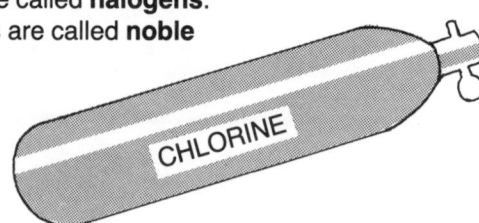

Group 0 elements do not feature much in chemistry as they are all very unreactive gases. This can, however, be an advantage. Helium is less dense than air and is safer for filling weather ballons than explosive hydrogen. Light bulbs are filled with argon rather than air so that the filament will last longer.

Most of the elements are metals. In the middle of the table is a large group called the **transition metals**. This group contains many useful metals such as iron and copper. The transition metals also include precious metals like gold and silver, and the only liquid metal, mercury. Here, too, are found the catalysts such as platinum nickel and iridium.

The last elements in the table are 'man-made' and are radioactive. Many of these man-made elements take the names of countries or scientists, e.g. Americium, Curium and Einsteinium.

CHAPTER TWO • *Atoms and Molecules*

ATOMIC STRUCTURE

Elements are made up of very small particles called **atoms**. Atoms themselves are made up of even smaller particles: **protons**, **neutrons** and **electrons**.

The diagram shows where these particles are arranged in an atom of lithium. Protons and neutrons are found in the **nucleus**, the centre of the atom. Electrons are found moving in paths outside of the nucleus and at a distance from it.

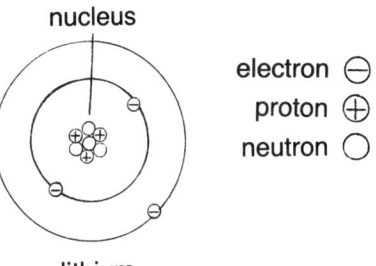

lithium

Atomic particle	Mass	Electrical charge	Where particle found in atom
proton	1	+	nucleus
neutron	1	0	nucleus
electron	almost 0	−	outside nucleus

There are equal numbers of protons and electrons in an atom. Because of this, individual atoms have no overall charge. Atoms are neutral.

Atoms are described by their atomic number and mass number. The **atomic number** is the number of protons in the atom. The **mass number** is the number of protons *and* neutrons in the atom. For example, an atom of sodium would be described as follows:

The elements are arranged in the periodic table in order of their atomic numbers.

Atoms of different elements have different atomic structures and may have very different chemical properties.

mass number (11 protons, 12 neutrons) → $^{23}_{11}$Na ← symbol
atomic number (11 protons)

Electron Arrangement

The chemical properties of elements are determined by their **electron arrangement**. Electrons are arranged in layers around the nucleus. The layers, or shells, are different **energy levels**.

For example,

- boron has five electrons arranged 2, 3;
- sulphur has 16 electrons arranged 2, 8, 6.

You will *not* be asked to work out the electron arrangement of elements with more than eight electrons in their outer levels. In any case, the electron arrangements of *all* the elements can be found in the *Data Booklet for Standard Grade Chemistry* (SEB).

Level	Number of electrons
1	2
2	8
3	8 (this level *can* take up to 18)
4	8 (this level *can* take up to 32)

Outer Electrons

The **group number** of an element is given by the *number of electrons in the outer level*. All the elements in Group I have one electron in their outer level. All those in Group II have two electrons in their outer level, etc.

It is the number of electrons in the outer level which determines the chemical properties of an element.

Ions and Atoms

An **ion** is a charged atom. An atom can become charged by *gaining* or *losing* electrons. The number of electrons in an ion will be greater or less than in a neutral atom:

- *more* electrons than protons in a *negative* ion;
- *less* electrons than protons in a *positive* ion.

CHAPTER TWO • *Atoms and Molecules*

The table shows the numbers of atomic particles in some atoms and ions.

	Protons	Neutrons	Electrons	
Na	11	12	11 (2, 8, 1)	same number of protons and electrons
F^-	9	10	10 (2, 8)	one electron more than the number of protons
Mg^{2+}	12	12	10 (2, 8)	two electrons less than the number of protons

There is more information about ions in Chapter Five.

Isotopes

The number of neutrons in atoms of the same element can vary. Atoms of an element with different numbers of neutrons, and thus with different mass numbers, are called **isotopes**. For example, there are two isotopes of carbon: $^{12}_{6}C$ and $^{14}_{6}C$.

Isotope	Protons	Neutrons	Electrons
$^{12}_{6}C$	6	6	6 (2, 4)
$^{14}_{6}C$	6	8	6 (2, 4)

The two carbon isotopes have the same chemical properties, and the two isotopes exist together in nature.

All elements are made up of mixtures of isotopes.

Relative Atomic Mass

The **relative atomic mass** of an element is the *average mass number* of all its isotopes. The units are atomic mass units or 'amu'.

In the *Data Booklet*, with the exception of chlorine, the relative atomic masses are given as being the mass numbers of the commonest isotope.

Atoms of different elements vary both in size and mass.

BONDS

Molecules are groups of atoms held together by **bonds**. The bonds in molecules are called **covalent bonds**. Covalent bonds are formed by two atoms sharing a pair of electrons. Molecules are formed between elements which are both non-metals.

The chemical **formula** of a compound or element represents the number of atoms of the elements in the molecule. Here are some examples.

Molecule	Formula	Atoms present
H | H – C – H | H	CH_4	1 carbon, 4 hydrogen
F – F	F_2	2 fluorine
H – O – H	H_2O	1 oxygen, 2 hydrogen

From the molecules in the table above, it can be seen that:

- carbon atoms form four bonds;
- fluorine atoms form one bond;
- oxygen atoms form two bonds;
- hydrogen atoms form one bond.

CHAPTER TWO • *Atoms and Molecules*

The number of bonds which an atom forms is called its **valency** or combining power. For a *metal* element its valency is the *number of electrons in the outer shell*. For a *non-metal* element its valency is the *number of electrons by which it is short of a full outer shell*.

Group number	I	II	III	IV	V	VI	VII	0
Number of electrons in outer shell	1	2	3	4	5	6	7	8
Valency	1	2	3	4	3 (8–5)	2 (8–6)	1 (8–7)	0

As a full outer shell usually contains eight electrons, the valency of a non-metal element is 8 — group number.

Covalent Bonds

The electrons in the outer level of an atom can be represented as follows.

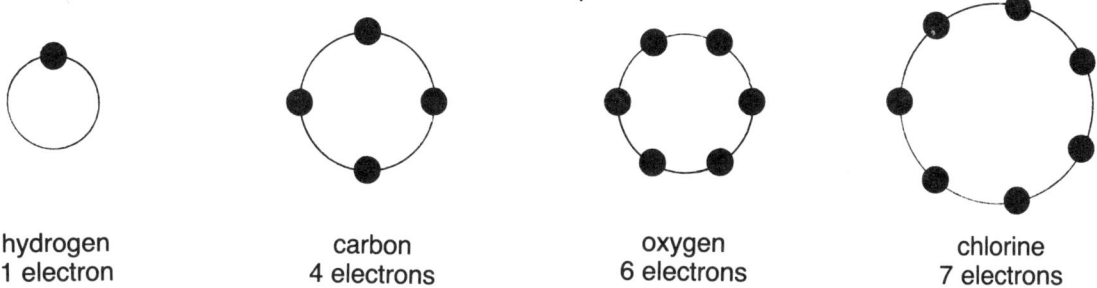

hydrogen — 1 electron
carbon — 4 electrons
oxygen — 6 electrons
chlorine — 7 electrons

The electrons in the inner energy levels need not be shown when representing bonds. Only the outer electrons of an atom are involved in bonding.

The simplest molecule is that of hydrogen which forms when two hydrogen atoms share their electrons, as follows:

(H) and (H) join to give (H:H) with a molecular formula H_2.

The molecule of hydrogen can be represented with electrons as: H ∻ H

Or without electrons as: H – H

Here are other examples of molecules.

Substance	Atoms	Molecule	Molecular formula
hydrogen oxide			H_2O
nitrogen hydride			NH_3
oxygen chloride			OCl_2

17

CHAPTER TWO • *Atoms and Molecules*

Structural Formula

The **structural formula** of a compound represents the bonds in the compound as lines. The electrons in the bond are not shown.

Here is an example of how to draw the structural formula of the compound formed between nitrogen and hydrogen:

$$\begin{array}{c} H - N - H \\ | \\ H \end{array}$$

If electrons are to be shown, then they can be represented thus:

$$\begin{array}{c} \cdot\cdot \\ H \div N \div H \\ \cdot | \cdot \\ H \end{array}$$

Molecules which contain only two atoms are called **diatomic molecules**. Seven elements, when uncombined, are made up of diatomic molecules. When uncombined with other elements, they are written:

$$H_2 \quad N_2 \quad O_2 \quad F_2 \quad Cl_2 \quad Br_2 \quad I_2$$

Compounds such as hydrogen chloride (HCl) and carbon monoxide (CO) also form diatomic molecules.

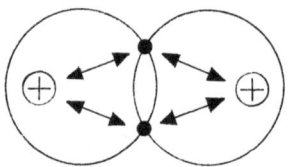

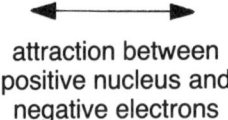

attraction between positive nucleus and negative electrons

Atoms are held together in molecules by their shared electrons being attracted by the nuclei of *both* atoms.

Molecules often have three-dimensional shapes. However, their structural formulae are always drawn as if they were flat.

Three-dimensional molecules

Practice Questions

1. Elements are arranged in groups in the periodic table.

A	B	C	D
sodium	iron	argon	chlorine
E	F	G	H
fluorine	lithium	nitrogen	zinc

CHAPTER TWO • *Atoms and Molecules*

(a) Which element is a noble gas?
(b) Which **two** elements are alkali metals?
(c) Which **two** elements are transition metals?
(d) Which **two** elements are halogens?
(e) Which **three** elements are in the second period?
(f) Which **four** elements are gases?

2. (a) Copy **and label** the diagram of an atom. Use the labels 'electrons' and 'nucleus'.

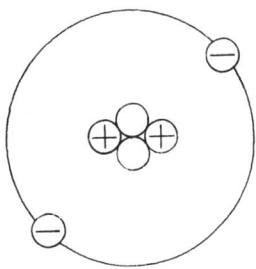

(b) Explain why the atom is neutral.
(c) Which element is represented by the diagram?

3. Lithium and sodium are in the same group in the periodic table. Explain what it is about their atomic structures that makes them belong to the same group.

4. Copy and complete the following table.

Particle	Charge	Mass	Where particle found in atom
proton		1	in nucleus
	0		
		almost 0	

5. Copy and complete the following table.

Atom	Number of protons	Number of neutrons	Number of electrons
$^{4}_{2}He$			
$^{19}_{9}F$			
$^{27}_{13}Al$			
	15	16	

6. Copy and complete the following table.

Ion	Number of protons	Number of neutrons	Number of electrons
$^{23}_{11}Na^+$			
$^{19}_{9}F^-$			
$^{24}_{12}Mg^{2+}$			
$^{32}_{16}S^{2-}$			

CHAPTER TWO • Atoms and Molecules

7. (a) Give the electron arrangement of the following atoms and ions.
   (i) O^{2-} (ii) Ne (iii) Na^+ (iv) Mg^{2+}

   (b) From your anwers to (a) above, what do you notice about the number of electrons in the outer shell of positive and negative ions?

8. The two main isotopes of chlorine are $^{35}_{17}Cl$ and $^{37}_{17}Cl$.

   (a) Using the words 'mass number' and 'neutrons', explain why the above atoms are said to be isotopes.

   (b) The relative atomic mass of chlorine is 35.5. Explain why the relative atomic mass is not a whole number.

9. The structural formulae of molecules of some elements and compounds are given below.

   State the chemical formula of each of the following molecules.

   (a)
   ```
        H
        |
    H - C - H
        |
        H
   ```
   (b)
   ```
        Cl
        |
   Cl - C - Cl
        |
        Cl
   ```
   (c) H – F

   (d) H – H

   (e)
   ```
   H - N - H
       |
       H
   ```
   (f) H – S – H

   (g)
   ```
   H - P - H
       |
       H
   ```
   (h)
   ```
        Cl
        |
   Cl - C - F
        |
        F
   ```

10. The structural formula of hydrogen oxide can be represented as:

$$H - O - H$$

Draw the structural formulae of the compounds formed between the following elements.

(a) hydrogen and fluorine
(b) fluorine and oxygen
(c) nitrogen and hydrogen
(d) carbon and hydrogen

11. Redraw the structural formulae of the compounds in question 10 showing the **outer** electrons of the atoms.

CHAPTER THREE
Symbols, Formulae and Equations

SYMBOLS

Each element is given a symbol using the letters of the alphabet. As there are more elements than letters of the alphabet, some symbols are given more than one letter.

If there is only one letter in the symbol, a capital letter is used, for example hydrogen H, oxygen O.

Where two letters form the symbol, then the first is a capital letter and the second a small letter, for example bromine Br, zinc Zn.

Not all the symbols take the first letter of the English name of the element. Many elements were first named in languages other than English, for example tungsten W (wolfram), iron Fe (ferrum), mercury Hg (hydrargyrum).

It is important to write symbols correctly. Co is the symbol for the element cobalt whereas CO is a poisonous compound called carbon monoxide.

WRITING FORMULAE

The formulae of covalent compounds can be obtained from their structural formulae. The formulae of many compounds can also be written using the instructions which follow. All the compounds in the examples below contain only two elements.

1. The chemical formula of a compound is written by swapping over the valencies of the two atoms.

   The number '1' is always left out of formulae.

   sodium oxide
   valency 1   2
   formula Na_2O

   nitrogen fluoride
   valency 3   1
   formula NF_3

2. When both elements have the same valency no numbers are added.

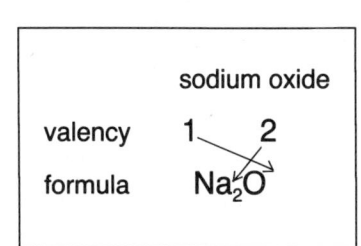

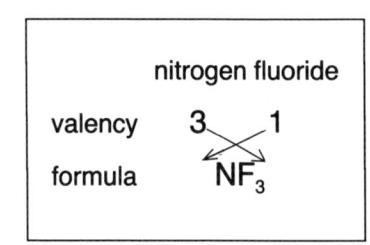

   magnesium oxide
   valency 2   2
   formula MgO

   aluminium nitride
   valency 3   3
   formula AlN

3. The name of the compound may include 'mono' (meaning 1), 'di' (2), 'tri' (3), 'tetra' (4) or 'penta' (5). If it does, then the above rules are not followed. The formula must be written from the 'clues' in the name, for example:

carbon *mono*xide	CO
carbon *di*oxide	CO_2
*di*nitrogen *tetr*oxide	N_2O_4
sulphur *di*oxide	SO_2

CHAPTER THREE • *Symbols, Formulae and Equations*

4. The transition metals can each have many different valencies Manganese, for example, can have valencies of 2, 3, 4, 6 and 7. A Roman numeral (I, II, III, IV, etc.) is used to indicate which valency should be used in writing the formula. Here are some examples.

   iron(II) chloride $FeCl_2$ (iron valency 2)
   iron(III) oxide Fe_2O_3 (iron valency 3)
   vanadium(V) oxide V_2O_5 (vanadium valency 5)

WORD EQUATIONS

A chemical reaction can be described by a **word equation**. The chemicals at the start of a reaction are called **reactants** and those at the finish are called **products**. Here is an example.

Copper(II) chloride solution reacts with *zinc* to form *zinc chloride* solution and *copper* metal.

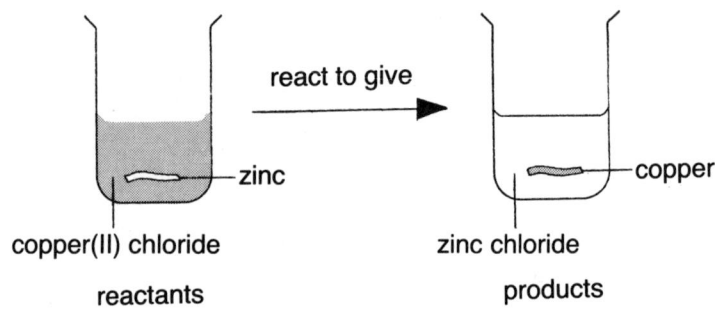

copper(II) chloride   zinc chloride
reactants   products

The word equation is:

     copper(II) chloride + zinc → zinc chloride + copper

This is not the same as an equation which you might meet in your maths class. In an equation in chemistry:

     '+' means 'and' or 'reacts with';
     '→' means 'gives' or 'changes into'.

Here are other examples of word equations:

     magnesium + oxygen → magnesium oxide
     zinc + hydrochloric acid → zinc chloride + hydrogen
     hydrogen peroxide → oxygen + water

There is a lot of information missing from a word equation. In the first example above, it is not stated that the magnesium must be heated.

A word equation is simply a list of the names of all the reactants and products in the reaction. Some detective work may be needed to find which elements are present in compounds. In the examples above, it can be seen that 'water' is 'hydrogen oxide' and that 'hydrochloric acid' is 'hydrogen chloride'.

CHEMICAL EQUATIONS

A **chemical equation** gives the chemical formulae of the reactants and products instead of their names.

     iron + sulphur → iron(II) sulphide
     Fe + S → FeS

CHAPTER THREE • Symbols, Formulae and Equations

hydrogen + chlorine → hydrodgen chloride
$$H_2 + Cl_2 \rightarrow HCl$$

magnesium + hydrochloric acid → magnesium chloride + hydrogen
$$Mg + HCl \rightarrow MgCl_2 + H_2$$

In the two equations above in which the element hydrogen appears, it is written as 'H_2'. Hydrogen is one of seven elements which occur as diatomic molecules. Always write the symbol for the element hydrogen as H_2 in a chemical equation. The other six elements, N_2, O_2, F_2, Cl_2, Br_2 and I_2, are also written in this way. All the other elements have their symbols written as if they were monatomic.

STATE EQUATIONS

More information can be given by adding **state symbols** to a chemical equation:

(s) solid
(l) liquid
(g) gas
(aq) solution (in water or 'aqueous').

Here is an example of a chemical equation with state symbols.

calcium carbonate + hydrochloric acid → calcium chloride + water + carbon dioxide
$$CaCO_3(s) + HCl(aq) \rightarrow CaCl_2(aq) + H_2O(l) + CO_2(g)$$

This chemical equation says:

'When *solid* calcium carbonate is added to hydrochloric acid (a *solution* of hydrogen chloride in water) a *solution* of calcium chloride, water (a *liquid*) and carbon dioxide *gas* are formed'.

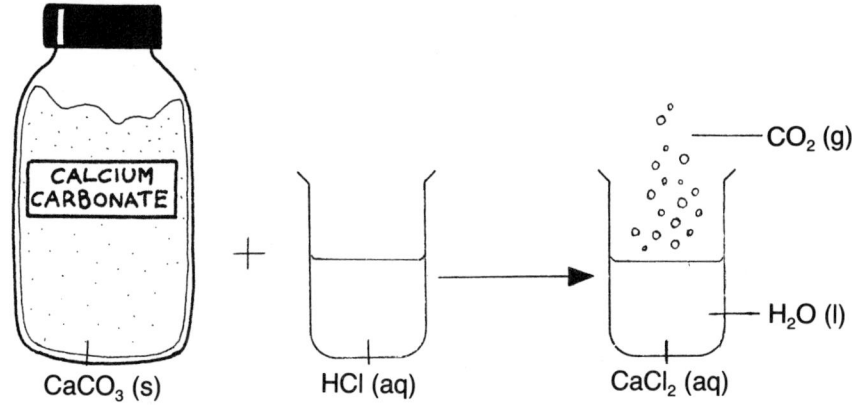

BALANCING CHEMICAL EQUATIONS

Here is the chemical equation for the reaction of hydrogen and chlorine.

$$H_2 + Cl_2 \rightarrow HCl$$

Here is the same equation written with the structural formulae of the compounds.

$$H - H + Cl - Cl \rightarrow H - Cl$$

It can be seen from the structural formulae that there are enough nydrogen atoms and chlorine atoms in the molecules of hydrogen and chlorine to form *two* molecules of hydrogen chloride, so it could be rewritten like this:

$$H - H + Cl - Cl \rightarrow H - Cl + H - Cl$$

or in a shorter form:
$$H_2 + Cl_2 \rightarrow 2HCl$$

CHAPTER THREE • *Symbols, Formulae and Equations*

This **balanced equation** states that:
'*1 molecule of hydrogen* reacts with *1 molecule of chlorine* to form *2 molecules of hydrogen chloride*'.

Here is an example for sodium reacting with sulphur to form sodium sulphide.

Word equation: sodium + sulphur → sodium sulphide
Unbalanced equation: Na + S → Na_2S
Balanced equation: 2Na + S → Na_2S

In balancing a chemical equation, numbers are always put in front of formulae. Formulae themselves must *never* be altered in order to balance an equation.
Here are other examples of balanced equations. In each case the unbalanced equation has been written first.

methane + oxygen→carbon dioxide + water   hydrogen + oxygen→ water
$CH_4 + O_2$ → $CO_2 + H_2O$ $H_2 + O_2$ → H_2O
$CH_4 + 2O_2$ → $CO_2 + 2H_2O$ $2H_2 + O_2$ → $2H_2O$

You will be expected to write word equations from descriptions of experiments in both the General and Credit exams. Unbalanced chemical equations with symbols and formulae will also be required in the General exam, and for the Credit exam you should, in addition, be able to write balanced chemical equations.
Symbols, formulae and equations are the 'language' of chemistry. Although they may account for only a few marks in your exams, it is essential that you master the 'language' if you are going to study chemistry further.

Practice Questions

1. Write the chemical formulae of the following:

    (a) sodium chloride
    (b) fluorine oxide
    (c) magnesium sulphide
    (d) aluminium oxide
    (e) carbon monoxide
    (f) carbon disulphide
    (g) dinitrogen tetroxide
    (h) copper(II) chloride
    (i) iron(III) oxide
    (j) mercury(II) bromide

2. Name the reactants and products for each of the following chemical reactions. Give your answers in the form of a **table** with the headings 'reactants' and 'products'.

    (a) Sodium reacts with chlorine to form sodium chloride.
    (b) Magnesium reacts with copper(II) bromide to give copper and magnesium bromide.
    (c) Magnesium oxide is formed when magnesium is burned.
    (d) Chlorine reacts with sodium iodide to give iodine and sodium chloride.
    (e) Calcium carbonate decomposes when heated to give calcium oxide and carbon dioxide.

3. Write the **word equations** for the reactions in (a) to (e) in **2** above.

CHAPTER THREE • *Symbols, Formulae and Equations*

4. Copy the equations below and complete them by putting the names of the missing chemicals in the boxes.

   (a) aluminium + chlorine → ☐
   (b) zinc + hydrochloric acid → zinc chloride + ☐
   (c) lead(II) nitrate + potassium iodide → potassium nitrate + ☐
   (d) sodium + ☐ → sodium oxide
   (e) ☐ + copper(II) chloride → iron(II) chloride + copper

5. Write **balanced** chemical equations for the following.
   (Not all the equations will require to be balanced.)

   (a) zinc + sulphur → zinc sulphide
   (b) iron + copper(II) chloride → iron(II) chloride + copper
   (c) calcium + chlorine → calcium chloride
   (d) carbon + oxygen → carbon dioxide
   (e) sodium + sulphur → sodium sulphide
   (f) aluminium + sulphur → aluminium sulphide
   (g) magnesium + oxygen → magnesium oxide
   (h) hydrogen + oxygen → water
   (i) hydrogen + chlorine → hydrogen chloride
   (j) magnesium + hydrochloric acid → magnesium chloride + hydrogen

6. Copy and balance the following equations.

   (a) $CH_4 + O_2 \rightarrow CO_2 + H_2O$
   (b) $H_2 + F_2 \rightarrow HF$
   (c) $Mg + CO_2 \rightarrow MgO + C$
   (d) $Al + Fe_2O_3 \rightarrow Fe + Al_2O_3$
   (e) $Fe + HCl \rightarrow FeCl_2 + H_2$

7. Write **balanced state** equations for the following reactions.

   (a) Magnesium metal reacting with steam to form solid magnesium oxide and hydrogen gas.
   (b) Powdered iron and sulphur reacting to form solid iron(II) sulphide.
   (c) A solution of copper(II) chloride reacting with magnesium to give a solution of magnesium chloride and copper metal.
   (d) Calcium oxide powder reacting with hydrochloric acid (hydrogen chloride solution) to form calcium chloride solution and water.

CHAPTER FOUR
Hydrocarbons

FUELS

A **fuel** is a chemical which gives out energy when it burns. Burning is also called combustion. In combustion a substance combines with oxygen and gives out energy. A chemical reaction in which energy is given out is called an **exothermic** reaction.

When a chemical reaction takes place, bonds are broken in the reactant molecules. New bonds then form to make the product molecules.
- Energy is put in to break bonds.
- Energy is released when bonds are formed.

In an exothermic reaction such as combustion *more* energy is given out in forming bonds than was put in to break bonds.

Fossil Fuels

Most fuels are derived from coal, oil or natural gas. These are called the **fossil fuels**.

Coal was formed over a period of millions of years. Decayed plant material was changed into coal by high pressures and temperatures.

Oil and natural gas were derived from the decayed remains of the bodies of sea organisms. Oil and natural gas were formed over a long period of time in a similar way to coal.

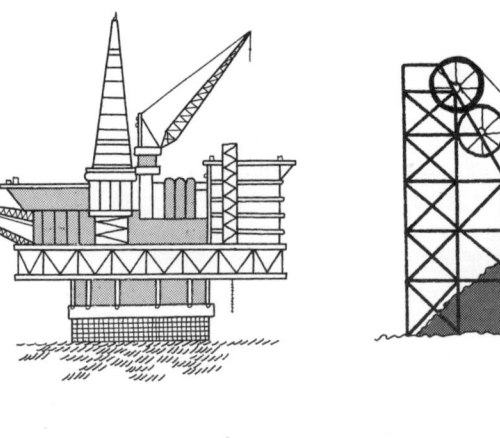
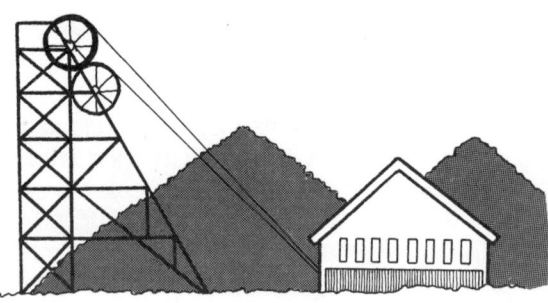

Coal is mainly composed of carbon whereas oil and natural gas are mixtures of **hydrocarbons**. Hydrocarbons are compounds made up of the elements carbon and hydrogen only.

Because one day our reserves of fossil fuels will be used up, these resources are said to be **finite**. Methods of using alternative sources such as solar, wind, wave and tidal power are being developed.

Oil

Crude oil is a mixture of many hydrocarbons. Its exact composition depends on where the oil is found. Crude oil is separated into **fractions**, which are not pure substances but mixtures of hydrocarbons whose boiling points are close together.

CHAPTER FOUR • *Hydrocarbons*

Separation of crude oil into fractions is carried out in an oil refinery in a process called **fractional distillation**. The separation of crude oil into fractions depends on its different constituents having different boiling points.

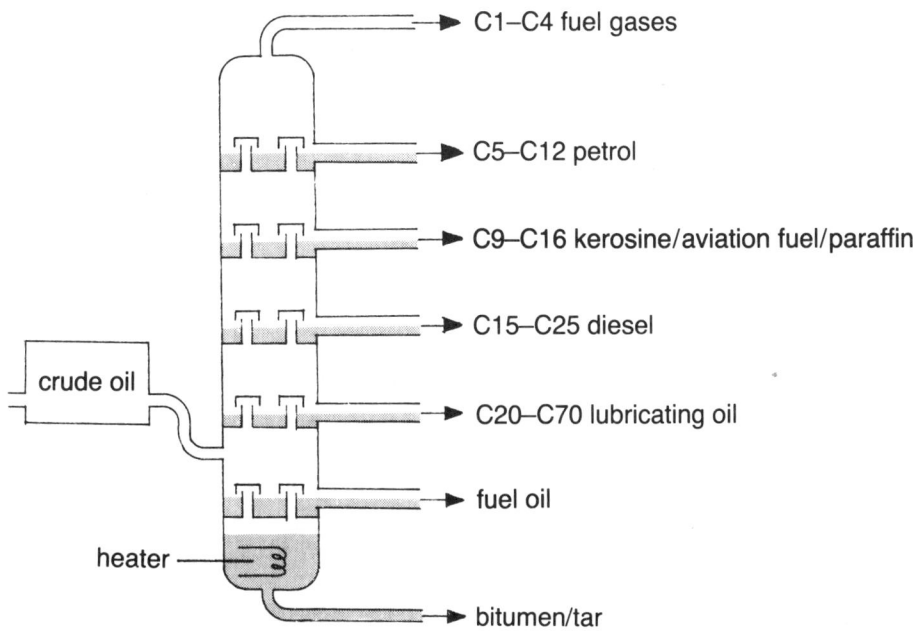

When crude oil is heated the fractions begin to boil. As the temperature at the bottom of the column is much greater than at the top, the fractions can be removed from the column where they reach the point at which it is cool enough for them to condense.

The fractions of oil have many similarities, they are all hydrocarbons and they all burn. The fractions differ both in the size and in the mass of their molecules. Their properties also vary in ways which are summarised in the following table.

Fraction	Properties
'light' – small molecules with short chains of atoms	gases or liquids which are easy to boil evaporate easily catch fire easily (flammable) low boiling points light in colour
'heavy' – larger molecules with longer chains of atoms	liquids which are more difficult to boil, or waxes or solids do not evaporate easily difficult to set on fire higher boiling points darker in colour viscous

A thick oily liquid is said to be **viscous**. The **viscosity** of a liquid is a measure of how 'runny' it is. Syrup is viscous, water is not viscous.

The ease with which a liquid catches fire is called its **flammability**. Liquids which catch fire easily are **flammable**. Fuels with low boiling points are highly flammable, their vapours are easily set on fire.

CHAPTER FOUR • *Hydrocarbons*

BURNING FUELS

Air is a mixture of gases. Its composition is shown in the pie chart.

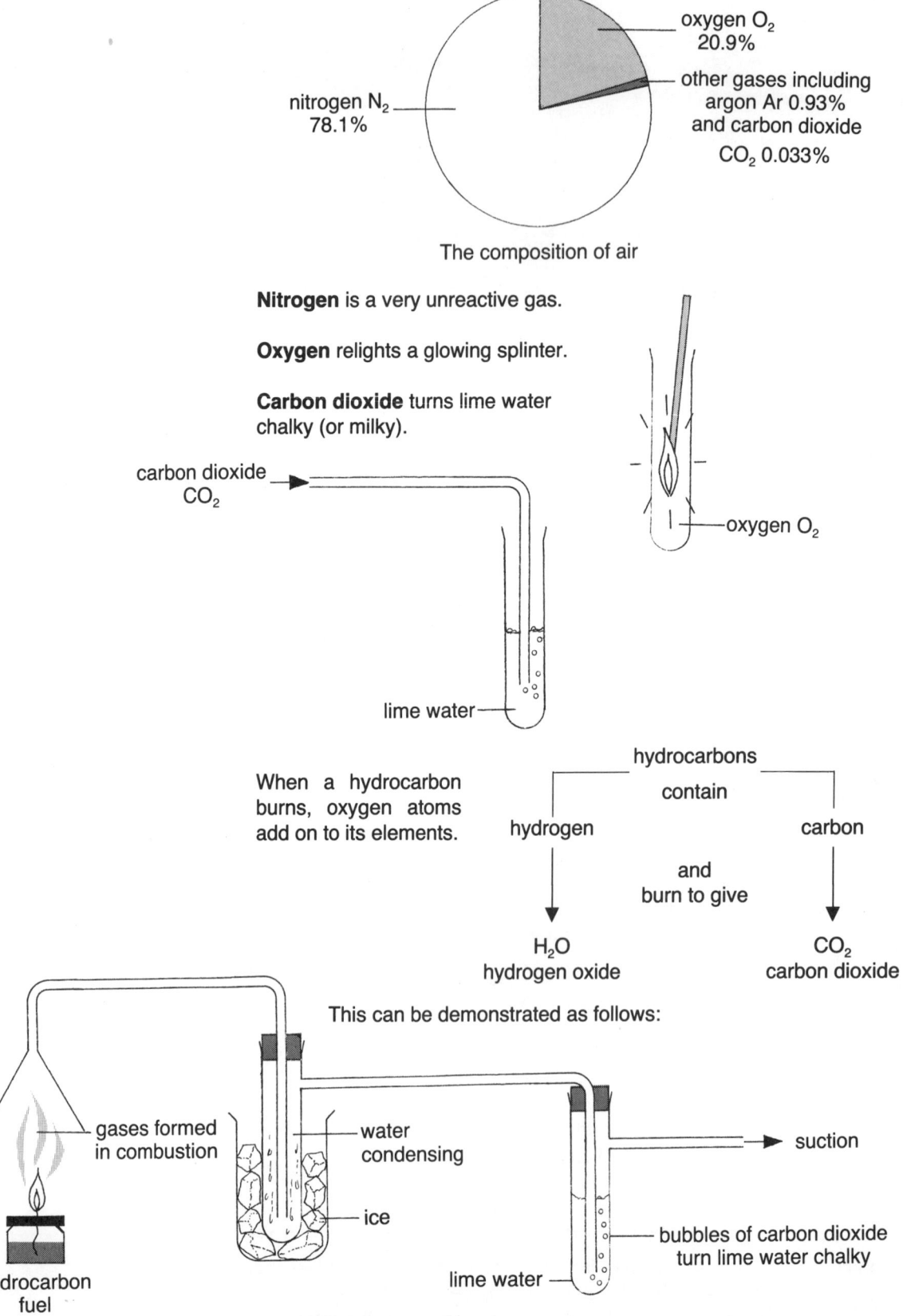

The composition of air

Nitrogen is a very unreactive gas.

Oxygen relights a glowing splinter.

Carbon dioxide turns lime water chalky (or milky).

When a hydrocarbon burns, oxygen atoms add on to its elements.

hydrocarbons contain hydrogen and carbon

and burn to give

H_2O hydrogen oxide

CO_2 carbon dioxide

This can be demonstrated as follows:

If insufficient oxygen is present when a hydrocarbon fuel burns, then either carbon monoxide (a poisonous gas) or carbon (soot) may form.

CHAPTER FOUR • *Hydrocarbons*

Pollution

Gases present in air but which do not naturally occur are called pollutants and cause **air pollution**. Almost all of these pollutants are harmful.

Carbon monoxide (CO) is one gas which can pollute air. Sulphur dioxide (SO_2) and nitrogen dioxide (NO_2) are others.

Sulphur dioxide forms when the small amounts of sulphur in fossil fuels burn. Removing sulphur and sulphur compounds from fuels or from the chimney gases is now considered a priority, as oxides of sulphur combine with water to form acids which cause widespread damage.

The motor car is another cause of air pollution. Petrol is ignited in a car engine by a spark from the sparking plug. The enormous energy of the spark is enough to cause normally inactive nitrogen in the air to combine with oxygen and form oxides of nitrogen. Another pollutant is lead which is found in small amounts in the exhaust of cars which use petrol containing lead compounds. These lead compounds have been added to petrol to improve the performance of the car engine.

Car manufacturers have introduced a number of changes which will help to reduce air pollution from car exhausts. These are: *more efficient engines*, reducing the amount of *carbon monoxide* produced; *lead-free petrol*, so removing *lead* from the exhaust gases; *catalytic converters* in exhausts which reduce the *oxides of nitrogen* and *carbon monoxide*. *Platinum* and *rhodium* are examples of metals used as catalysts.

Water and land pollution is another problem. Oil spillages at sea can cause serious damage to the environment and wildlife.

HYDROCARBONS

There are many thousands of hydrocarbon compounds. This large number of compounds is possible because carbon atoms have the ability to form chains. Hydrocarbons are arranged into families or series according to their structural formulae. Three of these families are **alkanes, cycloalkanes** and **alkenes**.

Alkanes

The fractions of crude oil are mostly made up of compounds belonging to a family of hydrocarbons called the alkanes.

Name	Structural formula	Shortened structural formula	Molecular formula
methane	H | H – C – H | H	CH_4	CH_4
ethane	H H | | H – C – C – H | | H H	CH_3CH_3	C_2H_6
propane	H H H | | | H – C – C – C – H | | | H H H	$CH_3CH_2CH_3$	C_3H_8
butane	H H H H | | | | H – C – C – C – C – H | | | | H H H H	$CH_3CH_2CH_2CH_3$ or $CH_3(CH_2)_2CH_3$	C_4H_{10}

CHAPTER FOUR • *Hydrocarbons*

The molecular formulae of the next four compounds are:
C_5H_{12} pentane; C_6H_{14} hexane; C_7H_{16} heptane; C_8H_{18} octane.

The first part of the name of each compound states the number of carbon atoms in the molecule:

    meth–   1 carbon atom;
    eth–   2 carbon atoms.

The second part of the name, the ending *–ane*, indicates that the compound belongs to the alkane series.

All of the members of the alkane series have similar chemical properties. A series of compounds such as the alkanes, in which all the members have the same name ending and similar chemical properties, is called a **homologous series**.

The **general formulae** of the alkanes is C_nH_{2n+2}. If $n=1$ the formula is CH_4. If $n=2$ the formula is C_2H_6.

The first four alkanes are gases. The other alkanes listed above are liquids. From pentane to octane the boiling points of the liquids increase as the number of carbon atoms in the molecules increases.

The table illustrates how the properties of some alkanes change as the number of carbon atoms in their molecules increases.

Name	Formula	Melting point (°C)	Boiling point (°C)	Properties or uses
methane	CH_4	–183	–164	'North Sea' gas or 'natural' gas
butane	C_4H_{10}	–138	0	cigarette lighter fuel
pentane	C_5H_{12}	–130	36	liquid which boils easily
heptane	C_7H_{16}	–91	98	component of petrol
octadecane	$C_{18}H_{38}$	28	306	solid which melts easily
tricontane	$C_{30}H_{62}$	66	445	waxy solid

Cycloalkanes

A second homologous series is the cycloalkanes.

Name	Structural formula	Molecular formula
cyclopropane	(triangular ring of 3 C atoms, each with 2 H)	C_3H_6
cyclobutane	H–C–C–H / H–C–C–H (square ring, each C with 2 H)	C_4H_8
cyclopentane	(pentagonal ring of 5 C atoms, each with 2 H)	C_5H_{10}

CHAPTER FOUR • *Hydrocarbons*

A cycloalkane molecule is a ring of carbon atoms. The general formula for the cycloalkanes is C_nH_{2n}. This is different from that of the alkanes. If $n = 6$ then the molecular formula is C_6H_{12}. This compound is called cyclohexane.

Alkenes

A third homologous series of hydrocarbons is called the alkenes. Alkene molecules, like alkane molecules, contain chains of carbon atoms. The general formula of the alkenes is C_nH_{2n}, the same general formula as the cycloalkanes.

In alkene molecules *two* of the carbon atoms in the molecule are joined by a 'double bond' as shown in the models.

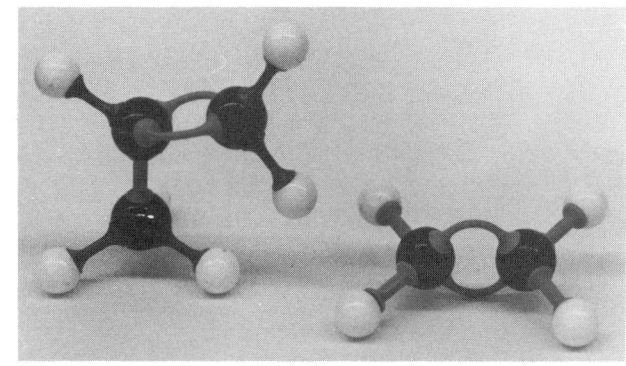

Name	Structural formula	Shortened structural formula	Molecular formula
ethene	H H | | C = C | | H H	$CH_2=CH_2$	C_2H_4
propene	H H H | | | C = C – C – H | | H H	$CH_2=CH\ CH_3$	C_3H_6
butene	H H H H | | | | C = C – C – C – H | | | H H H	$CH_2=CH\ CH_2CH_3$	C_4H_8

The molecular formula of pentene is C_5H_{10}, hexene is C_6H_{12}.

Molecules are always drawn on paper as if they were two-dimensional, even though this is unrealistic. As the models show, molecules are three-dimensional.

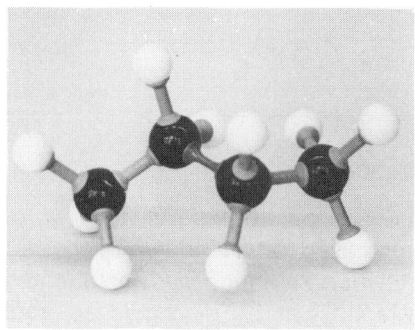

Butane   Cyclopentane   Butene

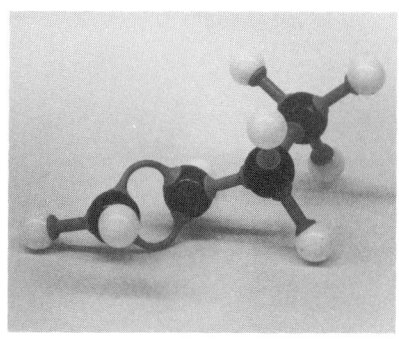

31

CHAPTER FOUR • *Hydrocarbons*

Isomers

As molecules are drawn in two dimensions, care must be taken to notice whether two structural formulae represent the same compound or different compounds. Here is an example.

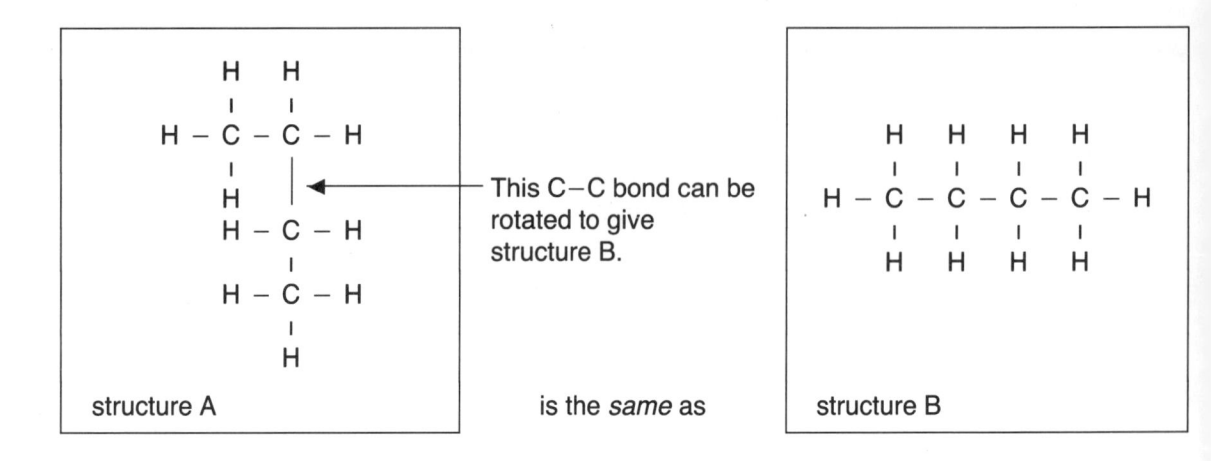

structure A ← This C–C bond can be rotated to give structure B. — is the *same* as — structure B

However...

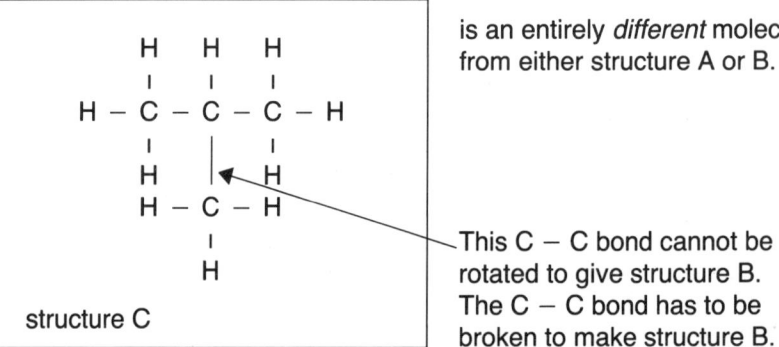

structure C — is an entirely *different* molecule from either structure A or B.

This C – C bond cannot be rotated to give structure B. The C – C bond has to be broken to make structure B.

Compounds which have the *same* molecular formulae but *different* structural formulae are called **isomers**.

Here are models of the molecules of the two isomers above.

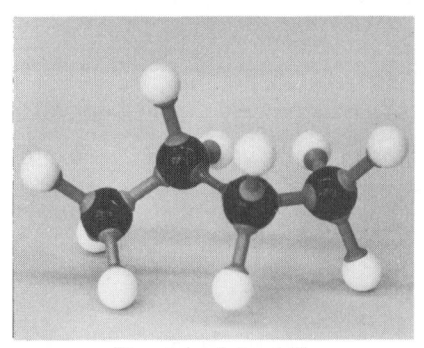

Structure A (and B)

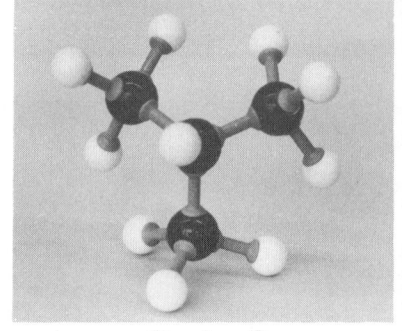

Structure C

Saturated and Unsaturated Hydrocarbons

Alkenes contain a double bond and are called **unsaturated** hydrocarbons. Alkanes and cycloalkanes are called **saturated** hydrocarbons.

A chemical test will distinguish between saturated and unsaturated hydrocarbons. Alkanes and cycloalkanes can be distinguished from alkenes by adding brown bromine solution.

CHAPTER FOUR • *Hydrocarbons*

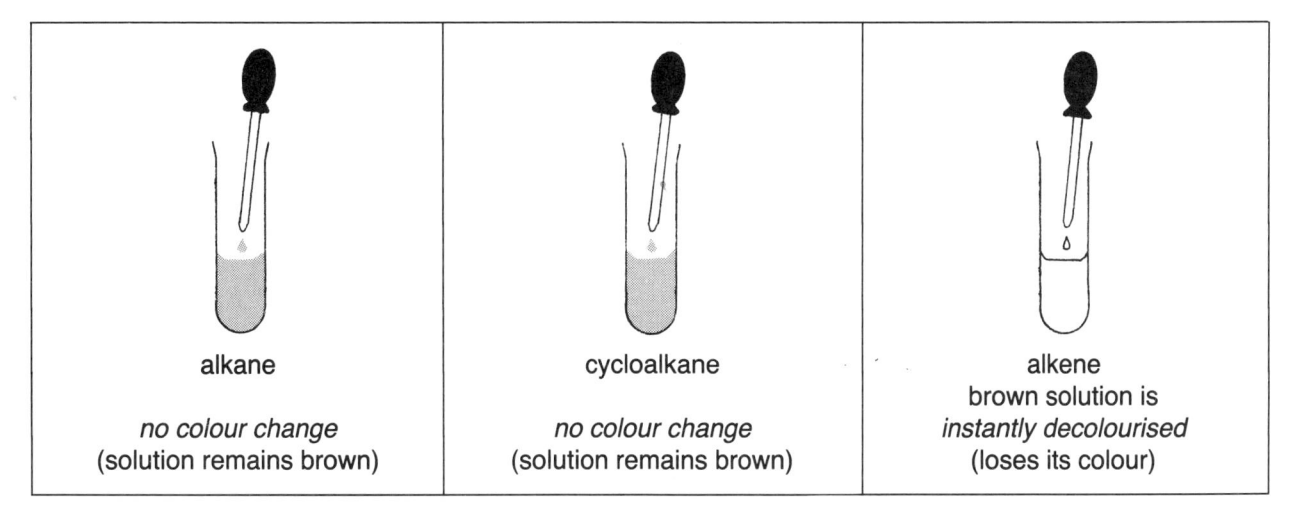

alkane	cycloalkane	alkene
no colour change (solution remains brown)	*no colour change* (solution remains brown)	brown solution is *instantly decolourised* (loses its colour)

When ethene reacts with bromine the following reaction occurs:

$$\begin{array}{c} H \quad H \\ | \quad | \\ C = C \\ | \quad | \\ H \quad H \end{array} + Br_2 \rightarrow \begin{array}{c} H \quad H \\ | \quad | \\ Br - C - C - Br \\ | \quad | \\ H \quad H \end{array}$$

                    brown   colourless

The reaction of bromine with an unsaturated hydrocarbon is called an **addition** reaction. When hydrogen adds on to an alkene molecule the corresponding alkane molecule is formed. This is also an addition reaction.

$$\begin{array}{c} H \quad H \\ | \quad | \\ C = C \\ | \quad | \\ H \quad H \end{array} + H_2 \rightarrow \begin{array}{c} H \quad H \\ | \quad | \\ H - C - C - H \\ | \quad | \\ H \quad H \end{array}$$

                    hydrogen   ethane

Alkenes can be used for the manufacture of plastics.

Cracking

There are far more of the compounds with long chain molecules in the fractions of oil than are required. These long chain molecules can be made into shorter chains and more useful compounds by a process called **cracking**. Paraffin contains long chain alkane molecules and can be cracked as follows:

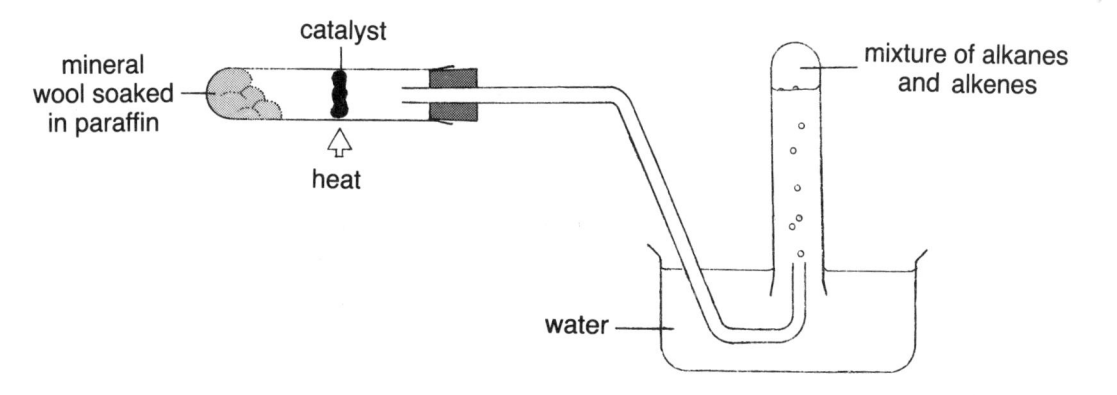

CHAPTER FOUR • *Hydrocarbons*

It is not necesary to use a catalyst. Heat alone will crack paraffin. However, a catalyst enables cracking to take place at a lower temperature or to take place at a greater rate. This is important in industry.

Some of the cracked compounds which form are unsaturated. Here is an example of the type of products which may be produced by cracking nonane.

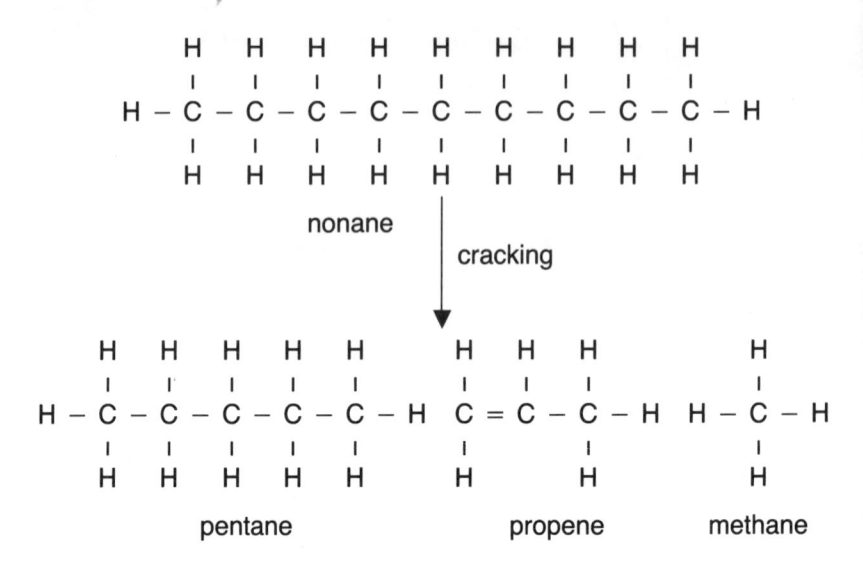

```
      H   H   H   H   H   H   H   H   H
      |   |   |   |   |   |   |   |   |
  H - C - C - C - C - C - C - C - C - C - H
      |   |   |   |   |   |   |   |   |
      H   H   H   H   H   H   H   H   H
                      nonane
                            │ cracking
                            ▼

  H   H   H   H   H        H   H   H            H
  |   |   |   |   |        |   |   |            |
H-C - C - C - C - C - H    C = C - C - H    H - C - H
  |   |   |   |   |        |       |            |
  H   H   H   H   H        H       H            H
         pentane                propene       methane
```

Practice Questions

1. When crude oil is distilled, fractions are obtained which vary greatly in their properties and uses.
   Here are the names of some fractions and the temperature ranges over which they boil.

A	B	C
gasoline 40 °C–180 °C	natural gas < 0 °C	light gas oil 230 °C–305 °C
D	E	F
kerosine 180 °C–230 °C	lubricating oil 405 °C–515 °C	heavy gas oil 305 °C–405 °C

Which box (or boxes) could represent:

(a) the fraction whose molecules contain the **least** number of carbon atoms?
(b) a fraction which boils **less** easily than C?
(c) a fraction which is **more** viscous than F?
(d) the liquid fraction which is **most** flammable?

CHAPTER FOUR • *Hydrocarbons*

2. Air is a mixture of gases including 79% nitrogen, 20% oxygen, less than 1% argon and traces of carbon dioxide.
   Nitrogen is a largely unreactive gas, it gives no result with common chemical tests. Oxygen relights a glowing splinter and carbon dioxide can be identified by lime water which it turns chalky. Argon is a totally unreactive gas.

   Present the above information in the form of a table with **three** headings.

3. Give the names of the products of complete combustion of the substances in the table.

Fuel	Combustion products
hydrogen carbon carbon monoxide methane ethene	

4. Hydrocarbons can be represented by molecular and structural formulae.

A	B	C
CH_4	H H | | C = C | | H H	C_5H_{12}

D	E	F
H H \ / C / \ H–C——C–H | | H H	H H H | | | H – C – C = C | | H H	C_5H_8

G	H	I
H H | | H – C – C – H | | H – C – C – H | | H H	H H | | H – C – C – H | | H H	H | H – C – H | H

   Which box (or boxes) could represent:
   (a) the structural formula of an alkene?
   (b) the structural formula of a cycloalkane?
   (c) isomers?
   (d) a substance which is **neither** an alkane or an alkene or a cycloalkane?
   (e) pentane?

CHAPTER FOUR • *Hydrocarbons*

5. Hydrocarbons are obtained from the fractional distillation of crude oil. Two common groups of hydrocarbons are alkanes and alkenes.

A	B	C
H H | | H – C – C – H | | H H	C_3H_6	C_4H_{10}
D	**E**	**F**
methane	H H H | | | C = C – C – H | | H H	ethene

(a) Which **three** boxes show alkanes?
(b) Which box gives the structural formula of a compound with the general formula C_nH_{2n}?
(c) Which box gives the molecular formula of an **alkane**?
(d) Which box represents an alkene with **two** carbon atoms?
(e) Which **three** boxes could show **unsaturated** hydrocarbons?

6. (a) Draw the structural formula of the alkene with **four** carbon atoms and state its name.
   (b)
   $$H-\overset{\underset{|}{H}}{\underset{|}{C}}-\overset{\underset{|}{H}}{\underset{|}{C}}-\overset{\underset{|}{H}}{\underset{|}{C}}-\overset{\underset{|}{H}}{C}=\overset{\underset{|}{H}}{C}$$

   (i) Give the molecular formula of the above alkene and state its name.

   PS (ii) Draw the structural formula of the cycloalkane which has the **same** molecular formula.

7. The following two compounds are both gases and both have the same molecular formula.

   $$H-\overset{\underset{|}{H}}{\underset{|}{C}}-\overset{\underset{|}{H}}{\underset{|}{C}}-\overset{H}{C}=\overset{H}{\underset{|}{C}}$$ $$H-\overset{\underset{|}{H}}{\underset{|}{C}}-\overset{H}{\underset{|}{C}}-H$$ over $$H-\overset{\underset{|}{H}}{\underset{|}{C}}-\overset{H}{\underset{|}{C}}-H$$

   compound A   compound B

   (a) State the name of compounds A and B.
   PS (b) Describe a chemical test which you could carry out to distinguish them.
   (c) What name is given to such compounds with the same molecular formula and different structural formulae?

CHAPTER FOUR • *Hydrocarbons*

8. Draw a **labelled** diagram of the apparatus which you would use to crack a liquid hydrocarbon such as paraffin and collect the product which is a mixture of gases.

9. When butane gas is passed over a heated catalyst it cracks as follows:

$$C_4H_{10} \rightarrow C_2H_6 + \text{compound X}$$

   (a) Give the molecular formula and the name for compound X.
   (b) Draw the structural formula of the compounds which form when compound X reacts with (i) hydrogen, (ii) bromine.
   (c) What name is given to the type of reactions occurring in (b)?

CHAPTER FIVE

Ions

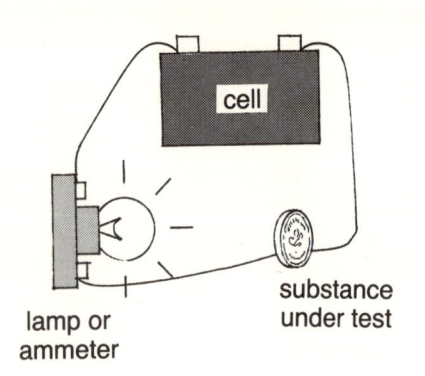

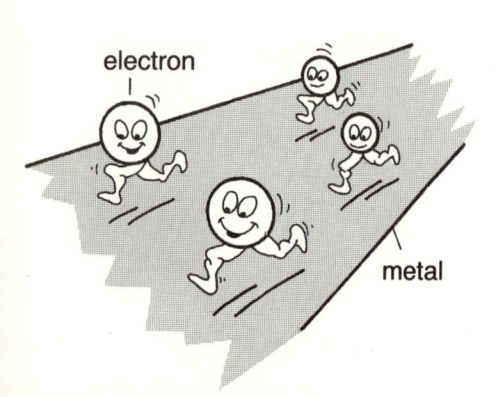

ELECTRICAL CONDUCTIVITY

The diagram shows how the electrical conductivity of a substance can be tested. If the substance under test is a conductor of electricity, the lamp will light or there will be a reading on the ammeter.

Both **conductors** and **insulators** are important. Conductors carry electrical current in wires. Insulators do not conduct electricity and are used as sleeves on wires and casings for appliances.

Here is a summary of the electrical conductivity of substances.

Conductors	Non-conductors
metals	non-metals
carbon (graphite)	solid metal compounds
solutions of metal compounds	non-metal (covalent) compounds
molten metal compounds	in any state

Electricity travels along metals and carbon as an electric current. An electric current in a wire is a flow of electrons and is measured in amperes (A).

IONS

The conductivity of molten metal compounds and solutions of metal compounds shows that metal compounds are not covalent. Metal compounds are not made up of molecules but are made up of charged atoms or **ions**. The conductivity of ionic compounds comes from a movement of ions, not electrons.

A battery or cell supplies a direct current (DC) in which electrons always move in the same direction.

The conductivity of an ionic solution is shown.

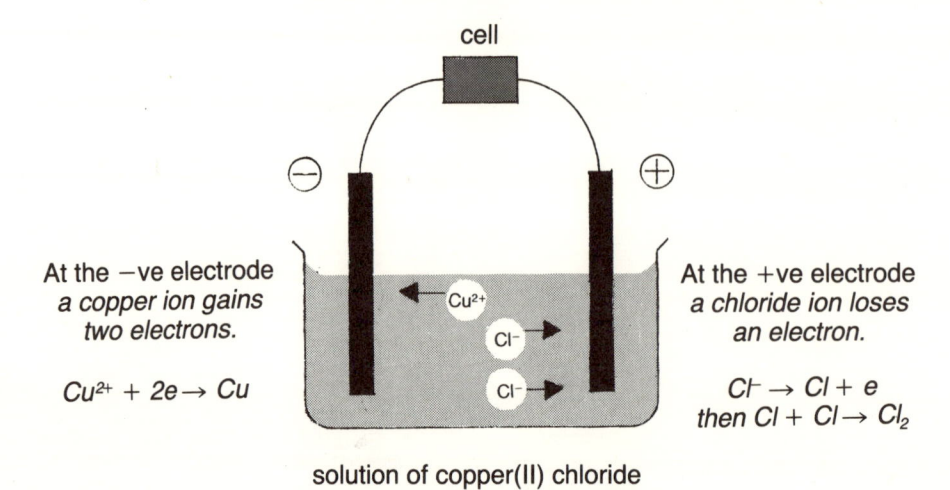

At the −ve electrode a copper ion gains two electrons.

$$Cu^{2+} + 2e \rightarrow Cu$$

At the +ve electrode a chloride ion loses an electron.

$$Cl^- \rightarrow Cl + e$$
$$\text{then } Cl + Cl \rightarrow Cl_2$$

solution of copper(II) chloride or molten copper(II) chloride

This experiment shows that metal ions have a positive charge and non-metal ions have a negative charge.

CHAPTER FIVE • *Ions*

Formation of Ions from Atoms

A *positive ion* forms when a *metal atom loses its outer electrons*.

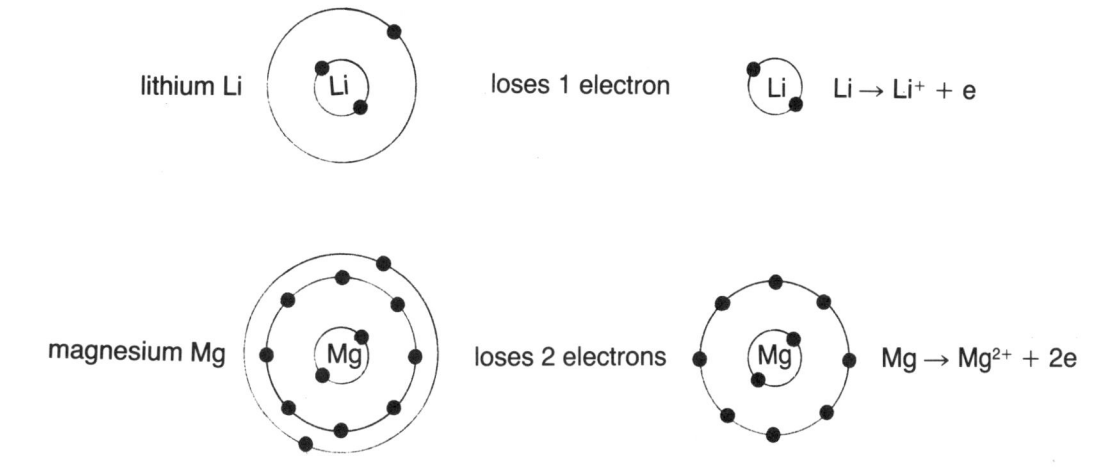

lithium Li — loses 1 electron — Li → Li$^+$ + e

magnesium Mg — loses 2 electrons — Mg → Mg^{2+} + 2e

The opposite happens when non-metal atoms form ions.
A *negative ion* forms when a *non-metal atom gains enough electrons to have a full outer shell*.

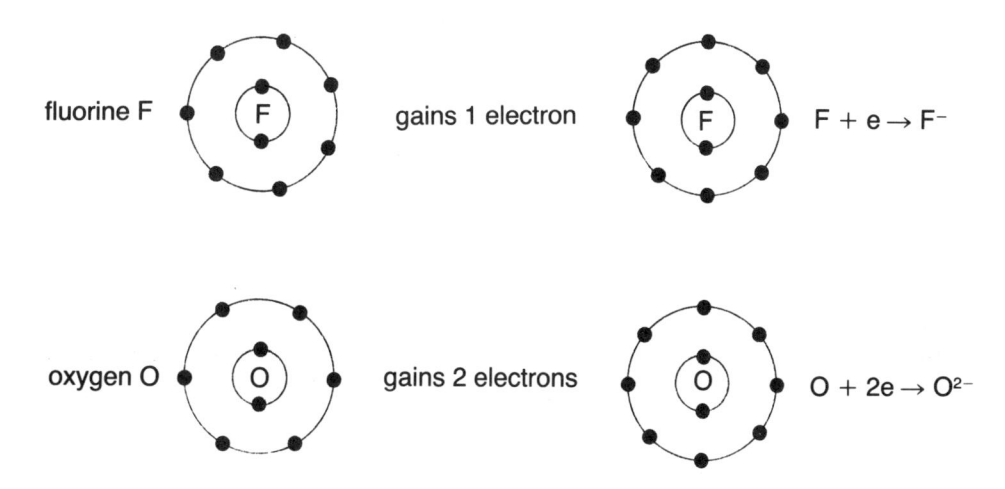

fluorine F — gains 1 electron — F + e → F$^-$

oxygen O — gains 2 electrons — O + 2e → O^{2-}

In each case the atoms reach the same electron arrangement as the nearest noble gas. Usually this means having eight electrons in the outer level.

Ionic Formulae

The formula of ionic compounds can be written to include charges, for example:

sodium chloride	Na$^+$Cl$^-$
magnesium oxide	Mg^{2+}O^{2-}
calcium fluoride	Ca^{2+}(F$^-$)$_2$

In each of the examples the total number of positive and negative charges in the formula are equal.

NETWORK SOLIDS

Ionic compounds do not form molecules. Instead they form **networks** or **lattices**. These grow naturally as **crystals**.
In ionic networks each ion is tightly held by its oppositely charged neighbours, and the network is difficult to break down. Ionic compounds have high melting and boiling points and are solids at room temperature.

ionic crystal

CHAPTER FIVE • *Ions*

There are no such strong forces of attraction between neighbouring covalent molecules. Covalent compounds may be solids but they are often liquids or gases. Covalent substances which have very high melting points contain a network of covalently bonded atoms. Examples of these are diamond (carbon) and sand (silicon dioxide).

Electrolysis

Ions which are tightly held in the network of the solid are set free to move when dissolved in water or melted. Solid ionic compounds do not conduct electricity as the ions are unable to move.

A solution of an ionic compound or a molten ionic compound is called an **electrolyte**. When an electric current flows through an electrolyte **electrolysis** occurs. In electrolysis the compound decomposes.

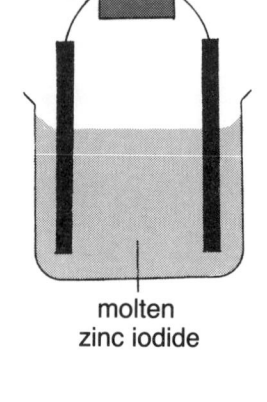

At the *negative* electrode *metal ions gain electrons.*
At the *positive* electrode *non-metal ions lose electrons.*

For example, when molten zinc iodide is electrolysed:

negative electrode $\quad\quad Zn^{2+} + 2e \rightarrow Zn$
positive electrode $\quad\quad\quad\quad\quad I^- \rightarrow I + e$
$\quad\quad\quad\quad\quad\quad\quad\quad\quad\quad$ then $I + I \rightarrow I_2$

Equations which show electrons being gained or lost in electrolysis are called **discharge equations** or ion electron equations.

Covalent compounds, which do not contain ions, do not undergo electrolysis.

Colours of Ionic Compounds

Ionic compounds are often coloured.

- *Copper(II)* compounds are *blue*.
- *Nickel* compounds are *green*.
- *Chromate* compounds are *yellow*.

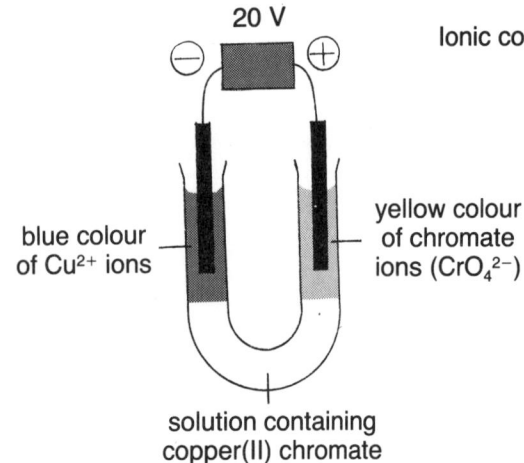

This enables the movement or **migration** of ions in electrolysis to be seen.

Blue copper(II) ions are seen to move towards the negative electrode showing that *copper(II) ions have a positive charge*.

Yellow chromate ions are seen to move towards the positive electrode showing that *chromate ions have a negative charge*.

Solvents

Although water is a covalent liquid, it is unusual in being a slight conductor of electricity. Water contains a very small number of ions.

Many ionic compounds dissolve in water. Covalent compounds do not dissolve in water but can dissolve in covalent solvents such as hexane or propanone.

Soap

Soap is a covalent compound part of whose molecule is ionic. It can be thought of as being like a snake with an ionic 'head' and a covalent 'tail'.

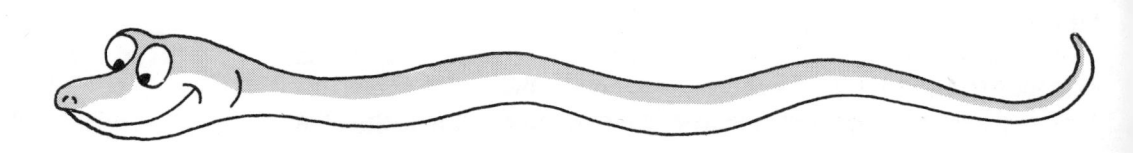

CHAPTER FIVE • *Ions*

This means that soaps and soapless detergents are able to dissolve in *both* water *and* covalent solvents.

When a mixture of oil and water is shaken and allowed to stand, the two liquids separate. However, if soap is added to the mixture, they mix permanently. This 'solution' of oil in water containing soap is called an **emulsion**.

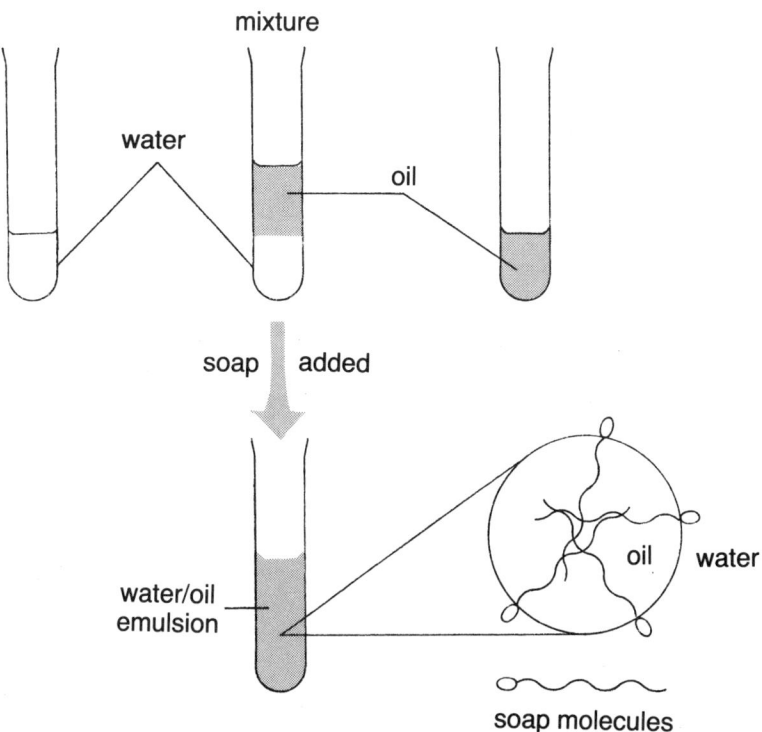

More about Ions

Not all ionic compounds contain only two elements. Those which have the name ending 'ate' or 'ite' also contain oxygen.

Here are examples of ions containing more than one kind of atom.

The formulae of these and other ions are listed in the *Data Booklet*.

Ion	Formula	Valency
ammonium	NH_4^+	1
hydroxide	OH^-	1
nitrate	NO_3^-	1
carbonate	CO_3^{2-}	2
sulphate	SO_4^{2-}	2

More about Formulae

To write the formula of a compound containing ions with more than one atom, each part of the name of the compound should be treated as one unit. The formulae are written by using the rule of 'swapping' over valencies. In the first example, the carbonate ion has been put in brackets to make the two units clear. It is really only necessary to use a bracket if a number subscript has to be added.

Charges may be added to formulae. It may be helpful to put a bracket round *each* of the ions although it is again only necessary when a number subscript has to be added.

ammonium carbonate
1   2
$(NH_4)_2(CO_3)$

aluminium carbonate
3   2
$Al_2(CO_3)_3$

aluminium sulphate
3   2
$(Al^{3+})_2(SO_4^{2-})_3$

ammonium chloride
1   1
$(NH_4^+)Cl^-$

CHAPTER FIVE • *Ions*

Practice Questions

1. Elements and compounds can be divided into two sets, conductors of electricity and insulators.

A carbon (graphite)	B copper	C mercury
D sodium chloride crystals	E petrol	F sulphur
G molten lead(II) bromide	H copper(II) sulphate solution	I sodium

   (a) Which **three** boxes represent **solids** which are conductors of electricity?
   (b) Which **two** boxes represent conductors of electricity through which **ions** flow?
   (c) Which box represents a liquid which conducts electricity by a **flow of electrons**?
   (d) Which box represents an ionic **solid**?

2. Carbon dioxide is a **gas** made up of molecules of CO_2. Magnesium oxide is a **network solid** made up of Mg^{2+} ions and O^{2-} ions.

   Explain why carbon dioxide is a gas whereas magnesium oxide is a solid.

3. A pupil wrote the following in her notebook.

   Ionic solids such as sodium chloride do not conduct electricity. They do conduct when they are melted or dissolved in water. They conduct only when their ions are free to move.

   Draw a diagram showing the arrangement of the ions in an ionic crystal, and use it to explain the note which the girl wrote.

CHAPTER FIVE • *Ions*

4. When a copper(II) chloride solution was electrolysed, it decomposed to form copper (metal) and chlorine (gas).

    (a) Write the formula for copper(II) chloride showing charges.
    (b) Write the discharge equations for this electrolysis showing the formation of (i) copper, (ii) chlorine.

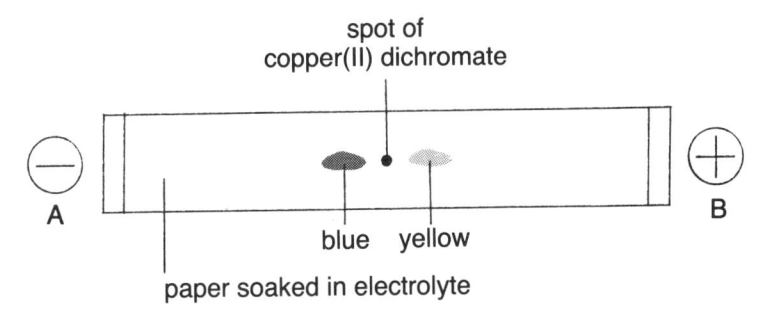

5.

The experiment shown above is about ion migration. Copper(II) dichromate solution was spotted on to a piece of wet paper. The terminals A and B were connected to a source of 20 V direct current and the experiment was left for ten minutes.
A blue colour was seen moving towards A and a yellow colour was seen moving towards B.

   (a) What does this experiment indicate about the charges on the two ions in copper(II) dichromate?
   (b) Why did the blue colour move towards A?
   (c) Why was a 'direct' current used?
   (d) Suggest why the paper was soaked in an 'electrolyte' and not simply water.

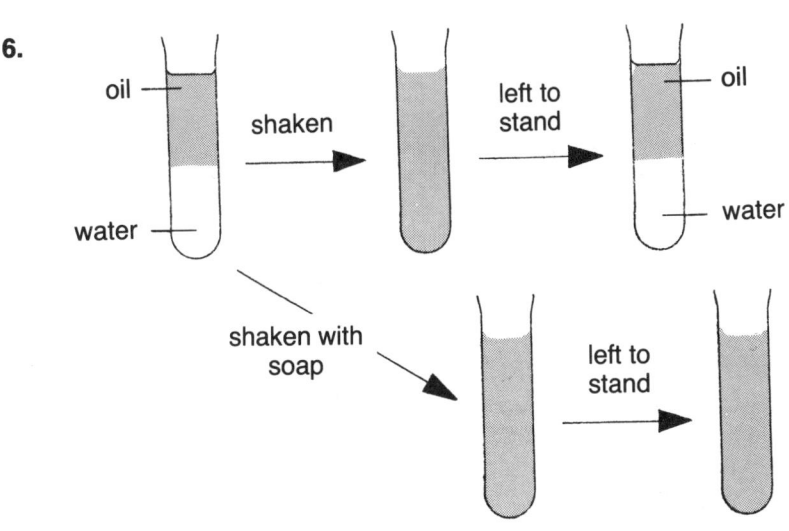

6.

Soap molecules can be thought of as having an ionic 'head' and a covalent 'tail'. Use this idea to explain how oil and water and soap form an emulsion. Diagrams might help with your explanation.

7. Write the formulae for the following compounds.
    (a) sodium nitrate
    (b) potassium hydroxide
    (c) ammonium chloride
    (d) ammonium hydroxide
    (e) copper(II) sulphate
    (f) sodium carbonate
    (g) lithium carbonate
    (h) ammonium sulphate
    (i) iron(III) nitrate
    (j) aluminium sulphate

8. Rewrite the formulae in **7** above showing the charges on the ions.

CHAPTER SIX

Acids, Alkalis and Chemical Calculations

THE pH SCALE

An aqueous solution can be **acidic**, **neutral** or **alkaline**. The degree of acidity or alkalinity is measured by the pH scale and can be measured by using indicator paper, liquid 'Universal' indicator or a pH meter.
In an *acid solution* there are *more H^+ ions than OH^- ions*.
A *neutral solution* contains the *same number of H^+ ions and OH^- ions*.
In an *alkaline solution* there are *more OH^- ions than H^+ ions*.

Ions present		Solution
large number of OH^- ions	14	sodium hydroxide
		ammonium hydroxide
		sodium carbonate
		sodium hydrogen carbonate
small number of OH^- ions		
equal number of OH^- and H^+ ions	7	water, salt solutions
small number of H^+ ions		lemonade
		fruit juice
		ethanoic acid (vinegar)
large number of H^+ ions	0	hydrochloric acid

(more alkaline ↑ neutral ↓ more acidic)

Acid solutions contain a much greater concentration of H^+ ions than water. Alkaline solutions contain a greater concentration of OH^- ions than water. When an acidic or an alkaline solution is diluted with water the pH of the solution moves towards 7.
The table lists some common acids and alkalis.

Acids	hydrochloric acid	HCl
	nitric acid	HNO_3
	sulphuric acid	H_2SO_4
	phosphoric acid	H_3PO_4
	ethanoic acid	CH_3COOH
Alkalis	sodium hydroxide	NaOH
	potassium hydroxide	KOH
	calcium hydroxide	$Ca(OH)_2$
	ammonium hydroxide	NH_4OH

CHAPTER SIX • *Acids, Alkalis and Chemical Calculations*

Electrolysis of Acid Solutions

When acid solutions are electrolysed, **hydrogen** gas forms at the negative electrode.

$$H^+ + e \rightarrow H$$
$$\text{then } H + H \rightarrow H_2$$

A mixture of hydrogen and air explodes with a pop when ignited. This is a test for the hydrogen formed.

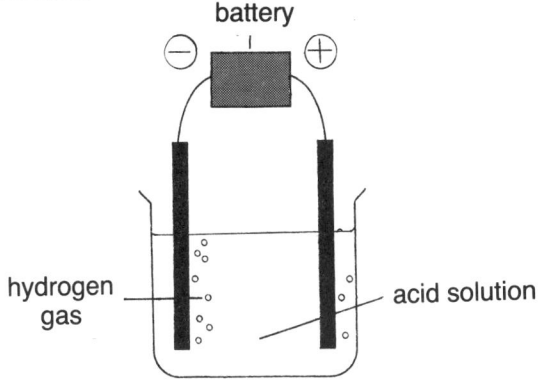

MAKING ACIDS AND ALKALIS

Many acids and alkalis are formed from the oxides of elements.

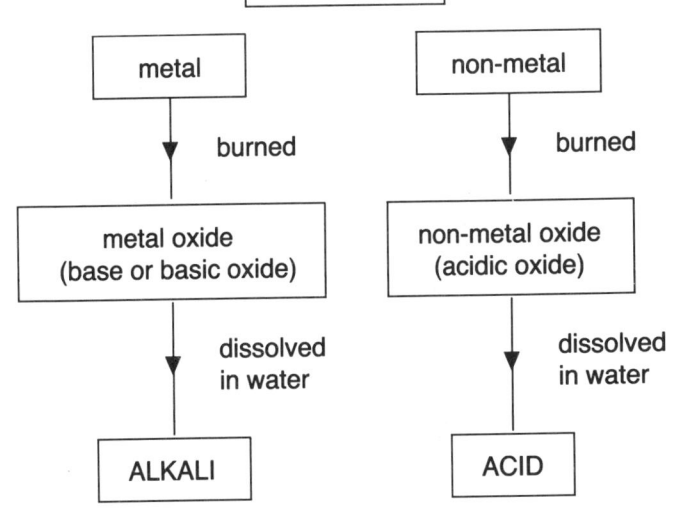

Not all metal oxides dissolve in water to form alkalis. The table of solubilities in the *Data Booklet* indicates which metal oxides dissolve.

Here are examples of alkalis and acids forming.

Sodium forms sodium oxide which then forms the alkali sodium hydroxide.

sodium + *oxygen* → *sodium oxide*
sodium oxide + *water* → *sodium hydroxide*

Carbon forms carbon dioxide which then forms the acid carbonic acid.

carbon + *oxygen* → *carbon dioxide*
carbon dioxide + *water* → *carbonic acid*

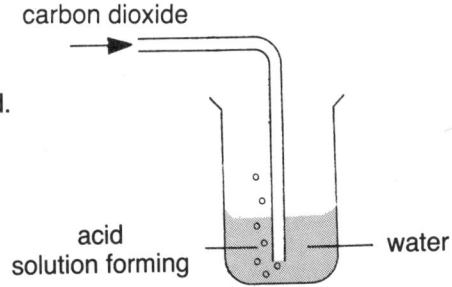

Acid Rain

Many fuels contain traces of sulphur. When sulphur burns it pollutes the atmosphere with sulphur dioxide which dissolves in rain water to form **acid rain**.

Acid rain damages structures made from many materials. Buildings made from limestone or marble (calcium carbonate) slowly react with acid rain and become eroded. In many buildings a lot of fine detail has been lost over the years.

Acid rain also has a damaging effect on many metals, plant and animal life. Iron is one of the metals which is affected by acids and rusting is accelerated by contact with acid rain.

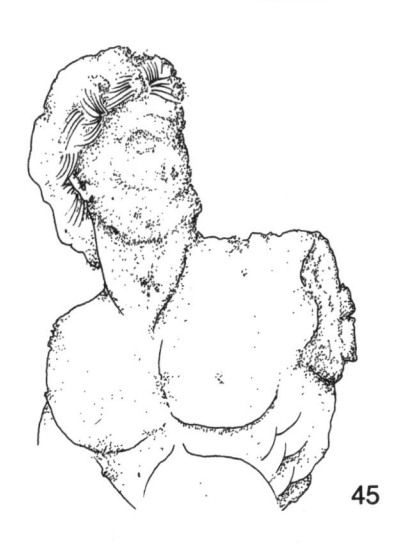

CHAPTER SIX • *Acids, Alkalis and Chemical Calculations*

NEUTRALISATION

Acids react with substances such as metals, bases, carbonates and alkalis. Substances such as these are called **antacids**. In such reactions acids are **neutralised**.

The antacid tablets which chemists sell neutralise acidity in the stomach.

Lime is an antacid which farmers dig into the soil to reduce its acidity. Lime can also be added to lakes and rivers which have become acidic. This encourages the return of living things which cannot tolerate acidity.

Alkalis and Acids

Water is formed when an acid is neutralised by an alkali. The volume of antacid solution required to neutralise an acid solution can be found by using an indicator which changes colour when the pH reaches 7.

$$\text{acid (pH} < 7) \quad \text{alkali (pH} > 7) \quad \text{neutral (pH} = 7)$$
$$H^+(aq) \quad + \quad OH^-(aq) \quad \rightarrow \quad H_2O(l)$$

As well as water another compound, called a **salt**, is formed. The pH of salt solutions is 7.

Naming Salts

The first part of the name of a salt is taken from the metal in the antacid. Salts take the second part of their names from the acid used.

Acid	Salt
hydrochloric acid sulphuric acid nitric acid phosphoric acid ethanoic acid	– chloride – sulphate – nitrate – phosphate – ethanoate

For example:

$$\textit{sodium } \text{hydroxide} \quad + \quad \textit{nitric } \text{acid} \quad \rightarrow \quad \text{water} \quad + \quad \textit{sodium nitrate}$$
$$\text{NaOH} \quad + \quad HNO_3 \quad \rightarrow \quad H_2O \quad + \quad NaNO_3$$

A salt is formed when the hydrogen ion, H^+, in an acid is replaced by a metal ion or an ammonium ion, NH_4^+.

Here are examples of salts:

sodium chloride (common 'salt')   NaCl
calcium nitrate $Ca(NO_3)_2$
ammonium sulphate $(NH_4)_2 SO_4$

CHAPTER SIX • *Acids, Alkalis and Chemical Calculations*

Carbonates and Acids

Carbon dioxide gas is formed, along with water and a salt, when an acid is neutralised by a carbonate.

sulphuric acid + copper(II) carbonate → water + copper(II) sulphate + carbon dioxide
H_2SO_4 + $CuCO_3$ → H_2O + $CuSO_4$ + CO_2

This equation can be written in a simpler way:

$2H^+(aq) + CO_3^{2-}(s) → H_2O(l) + CO_2(g)$

The ions which have been missed out are called **spectator ions**.

Many carbonates are insoluble in water and react with acids to form soluble salts. Here is how a salt solution can be made from an acid and an insoluble carbonate.

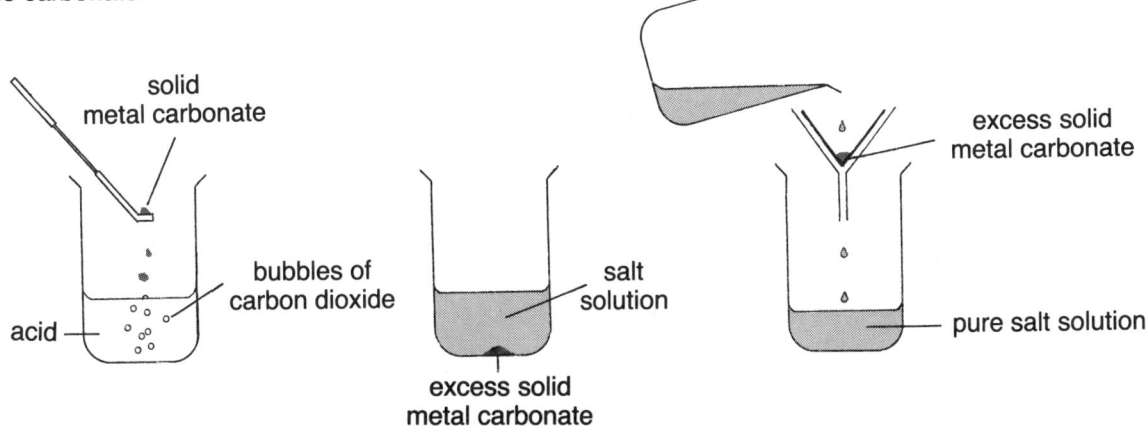

As long as the reaction is taking place, bubbles of carbon dioxide will be seen forming. When the acid has been neutralised the bubbling will stop. Excess carbonate, which is insoluble, can then be removed by filtering, leaving a solution of the salt.

Metal Oxides and Acids

Metal oxides, many of which are insoluble solids, neutralise acids to form salts. It is usually necessary to heat the acid.

sulphuric acid + magnesium oxide → water + magnesium sulphate
H_2SO_4 + MgO → H_2O + $MgSO_4$

Omitting the spectator ions, this can be written:

$2H^+(aq) + O^{2-}(s) → H_2O(l)$

A salt solution can be made by adding a base to an acid by the same method described for a carbonate. When the acid has been neutralised the excess insoluble base will lie at the bottom of the beaker. Excess oxide can then be removed by filtering, leaving a solution of the salt.

Metals and Acids

Some metals react with acids to form hydrogen and a salt.

magnesium + sulphuric acid → hydrogen + magnesium sulphate
Mg + H_2SO_4 → H_2 + $MgSO_4$

Water does *not* form when a metal reacts with an acid. Salts formed when metals react with acids are named in the same way as those formed in the other neutralisation reactions.

Metals such as sodium and potassium react violently with acids.

The metals chosen to make hydrogen are those known as the **'mazit'** metals: magnesium, aluminium, zinc, iron and tin.

CHAPTER SIX • *Acids, Alkalis and Chemical Calculations*

Summary of Neutralisation Reactions

acid + alkali → salt + water
acid + carbonate → salt + water + carbon dioxide
acid + metal oxide → salt + water
acid + metal → salt + hydrogen

Neutralisation by an alkali is the method which should always be chosen to make sodium, potassium and ammonium salts. Reacting an acid and a carbonate is the most convenient way of making other soluble salts. The end of the reaction can easily be seen and no heating is required. Metal carbonates are also much cheaper than metals and the reaction forms carbon dioxide rather than hydrogen which is a flammable gas.

INSOLUBLE SALTS

If two solutions react to form a precipitate then the reaction is called a **precipitation** reaction. The precipitate is an insoluble solid.

Insoluble salts can be formed by mixing together two solutions. One solution must contain the metal part, positive ion, of the salt and the other the non-metal part, the negative ion.

The table of solubilities in the *Data Booklet* (reproduced below) enables appropriate solutions to be chosen. The table shows how some compounds behave in water.

	bromide	carbonate	chloride	iodide	nitrate	phosphate	sulphate	oxide	hydroxide
aluminium	—	i	—	—	vs	i	vs	i	i
ammonium	vs	vs	vs	vs	vs	vs	vs	—	—
barium	vs	i	vs	vs	vs	i	i	reacts	vs
calcium	vs	i	vs	vs	vs	i	s	reacts	s
copper(II)	vs	i	vs	—	vs	i	vs	i	i
iron(II)	vs	i	vs	—	vs	i	vs	i	i
lead(II)	s	i	s	i	vs	i	i	i	i
lithium	vs	vs	vs	vs	vs	i	vs	reacts	vs
magnesium	vs	i	vs	vs	vs	i	vs	i	i
nickel	vs	i	vs	vs	vs	i	vs	i	i
potassium	vs	vs	vs	vs	vs	vs	vs	reacts	vs
silver	i	i	i	i	vs	i	s	i	i
sodium	vs	vs	vs	vs	vs	vs	vs	reacts	vs
tin(II)	vs	i	vs	s	—	i	vs	i	i
zinc	vs	i	vs	vs	vs	i	vs	i	i

vs means very soluble   (a solubility greater than 10 g/*l*)
s   means soluble   (a solubility of between 1 and 10 g/*l*)
i   means insoluble   (a solubility of less than 1g/*l*)
—   indicates that data is unavailable

Oxides which react with water form alkalis.

Making Copper(II) Carbonate

The table of solubilities shows that copper(II) carbonate is insoluble in water. Copper(II) carbonate can be made by mixing a solution of *any* soluble copper compound with a solution of *any* soluble carbonate.

Here are examples of solutions which could be mixed to form copper(II) carbonate (the chemical equations are also given for the third example):
copper(II) sulphate solution and sodium carbonate solution
copper(II) nitrate solution and potassium carbonate solution
copper(II) chloride solution and sodium carbonate solution

$CuCl_2(aq)$ + $Na_2CO_3(aq)$ → $CuCO_3(s)$ + $2NaCl(aq)$
or $Cu^{2+}(aq)$ + $CO_3^{2-}(aq)$ → $Cu^{2+}CO_3^{2-}(s)$

The chloride (Cl^-) and sodium (Na^+) ions remain in solution. They are the spectator ions.

CHAPTER SIX • *Acids, Alkalis and Chemical Calculations*

Insoluble Salts—Making Predictions

The name of the precipitate which is formed when two solutions are mixed can be predicted from a table of solubilities. For example, when calcium chloride solution is mixed with sodium carbonate solution, the possible precipitates are sodium chloride and calcium carbonate. Sodium chloride is 'very soluble' in water. Calcium carbonate is 'insoluble' in water, so the precipitate will be calcium carbonate.

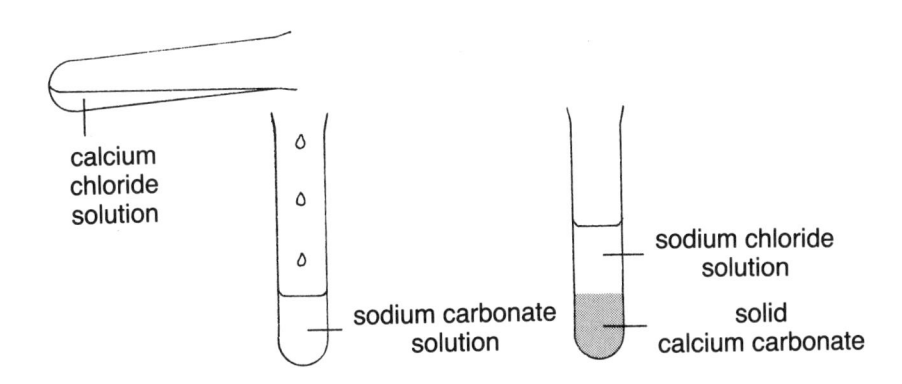

FORMULA MASS AND THE MOLE

The **formula mass** (or relative formula mass) of a substance is the total mass of all the atoms in its formula. The formula mass is given the units 'amu', 'atomic mass units'.

Carbon dioxide CO_2 contains 1 carbon atom and 2 oxygen atoms:
$$\text{carbon} \quad 1 \times 12 = 12$$
$$\text{oxygen} \quad 2 \times 16 = 32$$
$$\text{formula mass} = 44 \text{ amu}$$

The formula mass expressed in grams is known as 1 **mole**. 1 mole of carbon dioxide weighs 44 g.

Measuring the Concentration of a Solution

The concentration of a solution is given in **mol/*l***. This is the 'number of moles' dissolved in '1 litre of solution'. A litre is written as '*l*'. One litre is 1000 cm³.

$$\text{sodium carbonate } Na_2CO_3$$
$$\text{sodium} \quad 2 \times 23 = 46$$
$$\text{carbon} \quad 1 \times 12 = 12$$
$$\text{oxygen} \quad 3 \times 16 = 48$$
$$\text{formula mass} = 106 \text{ amu}$$
$$\text{mass of 1 mole} = 106 \text{ g}$$

A 1 mol/*l* solution of sodium carbonate contains 106 g/*l*.

The number of moles of a solute in a solution can be calculated if the concentration and volume of the solution are known:

$$\text{number of moles in solution} = \frac{\text{concentration} \times \text{volume (cm}^3\text{)}}{1000}$$

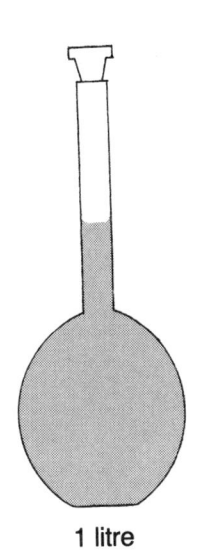

1 litre

CHAPTER SIX • *Acids, Alkalis and Chemical Calculations*

Example

500 cm³ of a 0.5 mol/l solution contain $\dfrac{0.5 \times 500}{1000}$ moles

= 0.25 mole

500 cm³ of *any* 0.5 mol/l solution will contain 0.25 mole of the solute in 1 litre of the solution.

If this is a solution of sodium hydroxide (NaOH), then
the mass of sodium hydroxide = 0.25 × mass of 1 mole of NaOH
= 0.25 × 40
= 10 g

Calculations

Finding the volume of an acid solution which can be neutralised by an antacid solution is called **titration**. You may have carried out a practical technique on titration.

When neutralisation occurs, the number of moles of H⁺ ions in the acid and the number of OH⁻ ions in the antacid are exactly balanced.

Here are three ways in which sodium hydroxide solution could be neutralised by an acid.

25 cm³ of 1 mol/l hydrochloric acid neutralises 25 cm³ of 1 mol/l of sodium hydroxide

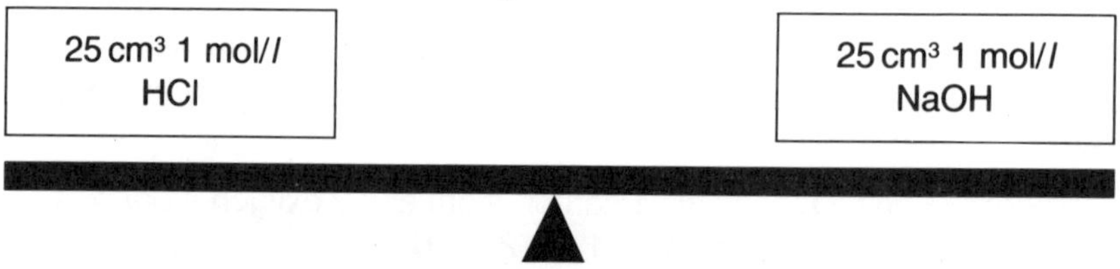

| 25 cm³ 1 mol/l HCl | | 25 cm³ 1 mol/l NaOH |

25 cm³ of 1 mol/l hydrochloric acid neutralises 50 cm³ of 0.5 mol/l of sodium hydroxide

| 25 cm³ 1 mol/l HCl | | 50 cm³ 0.5 mol/l NaOH |

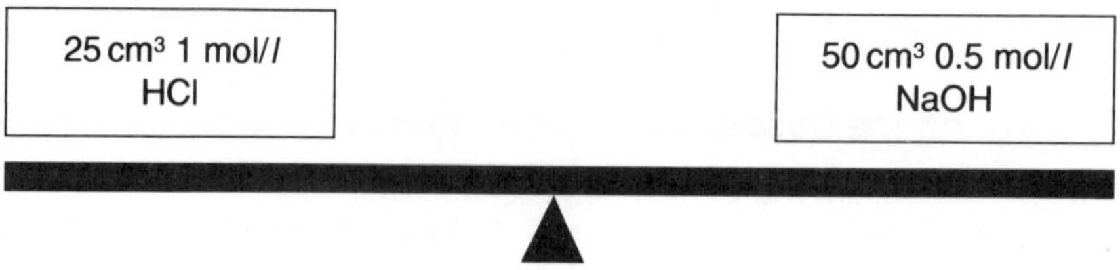

25 cm³ of 1 mol/l sulphuric acid neutralises 50 cm³ of 1 mol/l of sodium hydroxide

| 25 cm³ 1 mol/l H_2SO_4 | | 50 cm³ 1 mol/l NaOH |

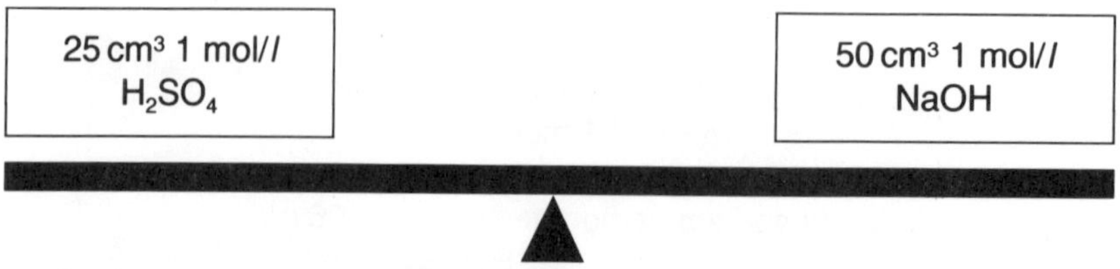

In the last example, sulphuric acid neutralised *more* of the 1 mol/l solution of sodium hydroxide than hydrochloric acid of the same concentration did. This is because sulphuric acid (H_2SO_4) contains two H⁺ ions. There is only one H⁺ ion in hydrochloric acid (HCl).

CHAPTER SIX • *Acids, Alkalis and Chemical Calculations*

In general:

[volume] × [concentration] × [number of H⁺ ions] = [volume] × [concentration] × [number of OH⁻ ions]

Here are some examples of calculations on titrations.

Example 1 What volume of 1 mol/l sulphuric acid will neutralise 100 cm³ of 4 mol/l of sodium hydroxide?

[volume] × [concentration] × [number of H⁺ ions] = [volume] × [concentration] × [number of OH⁻ ions]
volume × 1 × 2 = 100 × 4 × 1
volume = 200 cm³

Example 2 25 cm³ of hydrochloric acid is neutralised by 50 cm³ of 1 mol/l sodium hydroxide. What is the concentration of the hydrochloric acid?

[volume] × [concentration] × [number of H⁺ ions] = [volume] × [concentration] × [number of OH⁻ ions]
25 × concentration × 1 = 50 × 1 × 1
concentration = 2 mol/l

These calculations allow the concentration of a solution to be determined. In each case the formula of the acid and antacid (usually an alkali) must be known.

Reacting Masses

A balanced chemical equation indicates the numbers of moles of reactants and products. For example, this balanced equation for magnesium reacting with hydrochloric acid:

$$Mg + 2HCl \rightarrow H_2 + MgCl_2$$

states that:

'*1 mole of magnesium* reacts with *2 moles of hydrochloric acid* to form *1 mole of hydrogen* and *1 mole of magnesium chloride*'.

The numbers in front of formulae in the equation indicate the numbers of moles. If there is no number this is taken to mean 1 mole.

The mass of each substance which is reacting can be calculated from the balanced equation.

Mg	+	2HCl	→	H₂	+	MgCl₂
1 mole	+	2 moles	→	1 mole	+	1 mole
24 g	+	73 g	→	2 g	+	95 g

- *24 g of magnesium* will react with *73 g of hydrochloric acid* to give *2 g of hydrogen* and *95 g of magnesium chloride*.

24 g of magnesium is an enormous amount. Your chemistry class will not use that much magnesium in a year! It is, however, a simple matter to make calculations for other numbers of moles.

For example if only 2.4 g of magnesium was used:

- *2.4 g of magnesium* will react with *7.3 g of hydrochloric acid* to give *0.2 g of hydrogen* and *9.5 g of magnesium chloride*.

Or if 12 g of magnesium was used:

- *12 g of magnesium* will react with *36.5 g of hydrochloric acid* to give *1 g of hydrogen* and *47.5 g of magnesium chloride*.

Once a balanced equation is written, the quantities of any of the reactants or products can be calculated.

CHAPTER SIX • *Acids, Alkalis and Chemical Calculations*

Calculations with Moles

Here are some examples of calculations of reacting masses.

Example 1 What mass of lithium will react with 16 g of sulphur to form lithium sulphide?

Step 1 Write a balanced equation:

$$2Li + S \rightarrow Li_2S$$

Step 2 In the equation underline the substance whose mass is *given* and the substance whose mass you are asked to *find*.

$$\underline{2Li} + \underline{S} \rightarrow Li_2S$$

Step 3 Underneath the equation write down the numbers of reacting moles of these substances.

2 moles of lithium react with *1 mole of sulphur*.
(There is *no* need to mention lithium sulphide.)

Step 4 Now calculate the masses of the moles you have written down.

2 moles Li   1 mole S = 32 g
2 × 7 = 14 g

14 g of lithium react with 32 g of sulphur,
so 7 g of lithium react with 16 g of sulphur.
Answer: 7 g of lithium reacts.

Example 2 What mass of carbon dioxide forms when 5 g of calcium carbonate reacts with hydrochloric acid?

$$\underline{CaCO_3} + 2HCl \rightarrow \underline{CO_2} + H_2O + CaCl_2$$

1 mole of calcium carbonate gives *1 mole of carbon dioxide*.
1 mole $CaCO_3$ 1 mole CO_2
40 + 12 + (3 × 16) = 100 g   12 + (2 × 16) = 44 g
100 g of calcium carbonate gives 44 g of carbon dioxide.
5 g of calcium carbonate gives 2.2 g of carbon dioxide.
Answer: 2.2 g of carbon dioxide forms.

Example 3 What mass of nitric acid reacts with copper(II) oxide to form 18.8 g of copper(II) nitrate?

$$CuO + 2\underline{HNO_3} \rightarrow H_2O + \underline{Cu(NO_3)_2}$$

2 moles of nitric acid   give   *1 mole of copper(II) nitrate*.
2 moles HNO_3 1 mole $Cu(NO_3)_2$
2 × [1 + 14 + (3 × 16)] = 126 g   64 + (2 × 14) + (6 × 16) = 188 g
126 g of nitric acid gives 188 g of copper(II) nitrate.
12.6 g of nitric acid gives 18.8 g of copper(II) nitrate.
Answer: 12.6 g of nitric acid reacts.

CHAPTER SIX • *Acids, Alkalis and Chemical Calculations*

Calculating reacting masses is not always easy. You must be able to do all of these things.

- Write a balanced chemical equation from information given. (This will often be given.)
- Select the substance whose mass has to be found and the substance whose mass is given.
- Calculate the relative formula mass of the substances.
- Carry out the arithmetic required to get the answer.

A calculator will be required to work out the answer in some Credit questions.

Here is an example in which the arithmetic is more difficult.

Example 4 In an industrial process, ammonia (NH_3) is made by reacting together nitrogen and hydrogen. What mass of ammonia per hour is obtained if 8 kg per hour of nitrogen reacts completely with hydrogen?

$$N_2 + 3H_2 \rightarrow 2NH_3$$

1 mole of nitrogen gives 2 moles of ammonia.
1 mole N_2 2 moles NH_3
$2 \times 14 = 28\,g$ $2 \times [14 + (3 \times 1)] = 34\,g$
28 g of nitrogen gives 34 g of ammonia.

8 kg of nitrogen gives $\dfrac{34}{28} \times 8$ kg.

Answer: 9.71 kg/hour.

Practice Questions

S 1. Many acidic, alkaline and neutral substances are to be found about the house as can be seen in this passage.

> Vinegar and lemon juice are acids which will be found in the kitchen. Fizzy drinks such as lemonade are also acids.
> Baking soda is an example of an alkali. Many household cleaners are alkalis. Sodium carbonate is an alkali used for cleaning ovens and sodium hydroxide (a very strong alkali) is used to clear drains.
> Sulphuric acid, a strong acid, is found in a car battery.
> Tap water is neither acidic or alkaline, it is neutral. So too is a solution of salt in water.

Present the above information in the form of a table with **three** headings.

CHAPTER SIX • *Acids, Alkalis and Chemical Calculations*

2. There are many common acids used in chemistry laboratories.

   Which **one** of the following boxes contains a statement true **only** of hydrochloric acid?

A	It has a pH of less than 7.
B	It forms compounds called chlorides.
C	It contains hydrogen ions, H^+.
D	It gives hydrogen when electrolysed.

3. Potassium hydroxide solution is a common alkali with many uses.

   Which box (or boxes) contains a statement which is **true** about potassium hydroxide solution?

A	It contains more H^+ ions than water.
B	It produces 'acid' rain when dissolved in water.
C	It has a pH of more than 7.
D	It forms when potassium oxide dissolves in water.

4. Neutralisation is a common chemical reaction with many everyday applications.

   Which **two** of the following boxes contain statements referring to neutralisation?

A	Treatment of acid indigestion by antacid.
B	Formation of 'acid' rain in the atmosphere.
C	Treatment of acidic water in a lake by adding lime.
D	Dilution of acid solution by addition of water.

5. Gases form in many chemical reactions.

   Which **two** of the following boxes represent reactions in which a gas forms?

A	Reaction of zinc and hydrochloric acid.
B	Reaction of hydrochloric acid and sodium hydroxide solution.
C	Reaction of sodium sulphate solution and barium chloride solution.
D	Reaction of calcium carbonate and hydrochloric acid.

CHAPTER SIX • *Acids, Alkalis and Chemical Calculations*

6. Calculate the formula mass of the following.

   (a) NaF   (b) CaO   (c) $CaCO_3$
   (d) H_2SO_4 (e) nitric acid   (f) sodium hydroxide

7. Name the neutralisation product (salt) formed when each of the following substances react.

   (a) zinc and sulphuric acid
   (b) sodium hydroxide and hydrochloric acid
   (c) copper(II) carbonate and sulphuric acid
   (d) copper(II) oxide and hydrochloric acid
   (e) potassium hydroxide and nitric acid

8. (a) Write balanced state equations for each of the following reactions. **Do not show charges**.
      (i) magnesium and hydrochloric acid
      (ii) sulphuric acid and copper(II) oxide
      (iii) nitric acid and sodium hydroxide
      (iv) hydrochloric acid and calcium carbonate

   (b) Rewrite the above equations as ionic equations omitting the spectator ions.

9. Calculate the mass of each of the following.

   (a) 1 mole of water
   (b) 2 moles of calcium carbonate
   (c) 0.5 mole of sulphuric acid
   (d) 0.1 mole of nitric acid
   (e) 2 moles of sodium hydroxide

10. Calculate the number of moles in each of the following.

    (a) 10 g of calcium carbonate
    (b) 8 g of sulphur
    (c) 10.6 g of sodium carbonate
    (d) 100 cm³ of 1 mol/*l* of hydrochloric acid
    (e) 2 litres (2000 cm³) of 2 mol/*l* of sulphuric acid

11. Use the table of solubilities to state the name of any insoluble salts formed when the following solutions are mixed. (Not all of the mixtures of solutions give a precipitate.)

    (a) sodium sulphate and copper(II) chloride
    (b) barium nitrate and copper(II) sulphate
    (c) sodium hydroxide and ammonium nitrate
    (d) copper(II) chloride and sodium carbonate
    (e) potassium iodide and lead(II) nitrate

12. Lead(II) carbonate is an insoluble compound.

    (a) Use the table of solubilities to select **two** solutions which could be mixed to make lead(II) carbonate.
    (b) Write (i) the state equation for the reaction,
              (ii) the state equation omitting spectator ions (ionic equation).
    (c) What name is given to the above reaction?
    (d) Draw a diagram showing how you would separate the lead(II) carbonate from the solution in the above reaction. Label the 'lead(II) carbonate'.

CHAPTER SIX • Acids, Alkalis and Chemical Calculations

13. (a) What volume of 2 mol/l hydrochloric acid will neutralise 20 cm³ of 1 mol/l sodium hydroxide?
    (b) What volume of 1 mol/l sulphuric acid will neutralise 20 cm³ of 1 mol/l potassium hydroxide?
    (c) 25 cm³ of 1 mol/l sodium hydroxide neutralises 50 cm³ of nitric acid. What is the concentration of the nitric acid?
    (d) 50 cm³ of sulphuric acid neutralises 25 cm³ of 4 mol/l potassium hydroxide. What is the concentration of the sulphuric acid?

14. Sodium hydroxide can be neutralised by an acid.

    Which box (or boxes) contains an **incorrect** statement about the amount of acid required to neutralise 50 cm³ of 2 mol/l sodium hydroxide?

A	25 cm³ of 4 mol/l hydrochloric acid.
B	100 cm³ of 1 mol/l sulphuric acid.
C	100 cm³ of 1 mol/l nitric acid.
D	50 cm³ of 2 mol/l hydrochloric acid.

15. Sulphur combines directly with many elements when heated.

    (a) What mass of calcium reacts with 16 g of sulphur?
    (b) What mass of sulphur reacts with 23 g of sodium?
    (c) What mass of iron(II) sulphide forms when 5.6 g of iron are heated with sulphur?

16. Many elements burn in oxygen.

    (a) Calculate the mass of oxygen needed to burn each of the following.
       (i) 6 g of carbon (ii) 24 g of magnesium (iii) 2.3 g of sodium
    (b) Calculate the mass of the products when each of the following is burned.
       (i) 3 g of carbon (ii) 12 g of magnesium
       (iii) 16 g sulphur (which forms sulphur dioxide)

17. (a) What mass of hydrogen forms when 6 g of magnesium react with hydrochloric acid?
    (b) What mass of copper(II) carbonate precipitate forms when excess copper(II) sulphate solution is added to a solution containing 10.6 g of sodium carbonate?
    (c) What mass of carbon dioxide gas is formed when excess nitric acid is added to 10 g of calcium carbonate?
    (d) What mass of water forms when 4 g of methane (CH_4) is burned in oxygen?

18. Ethene reacts with bromine to form dibromoethane.

    Calculate the mass of dibromoethane which forms when 1 g of ethene reacts with bromine.

    $$\begin{array}{c} H \quad H \\ | \quad\quad | \\ C = C \\ | \quad\quad | \\ H \quad H \end{array} + Br-Br \rightarrow \begin{array}{c} H \quad H \\ | \quad\quad | \\ Br - C - C - Br \\ | \quad\quad | \\ H \quad H \end{array}$$

19. When chalk, calcium carbonate, is roasted it decomposes to form carbon dioxide and calcium oxide.

    Calculate the number of moles of chalk which should be roasted to form 0.1 g of carbon dioxide.

CHAPTER SEVEN

Making Electricity

ELECTRICITY

Energy changes occur in all chemical reactions.

When magnesium burns **light** is produced.
When an acid is neutralised **heat** is given out.

In certain chemical reactions it is possible for **electrical** energy to form. Electricity is produced by a chemical reaction in a **cell** or **battery**. The words 'cell' and 'battery' are often used as if they were the same thing. In fact a 'battery' is number of cells joined together.

There are two units used to describe electricity: amperes (A) and volts (V). Amperes, or amps, are a measure of the amount of current (electrons) flowing. Volts can be thought of as being the energy which these electrons have.

When a cell is 'done' the chemicals in it have been used up. In the same way a chemical reaction in a beaker or a test tube will come to a halt.

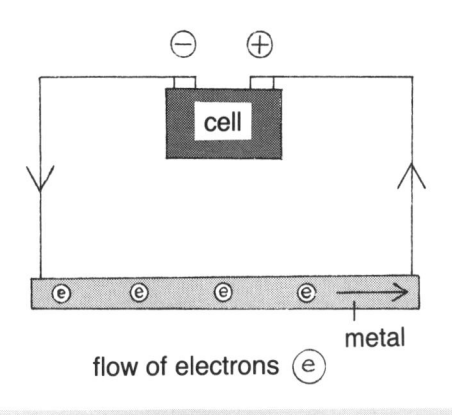

Analogue and digital ammeters

Rechargeable Cells

Cells in which the chemicals can be regenerated are called **rechargeable**. The most common of these are nickel-cadmium cells and lead-acid batteries used in cars. Here is a model of the lead-acid car battery.

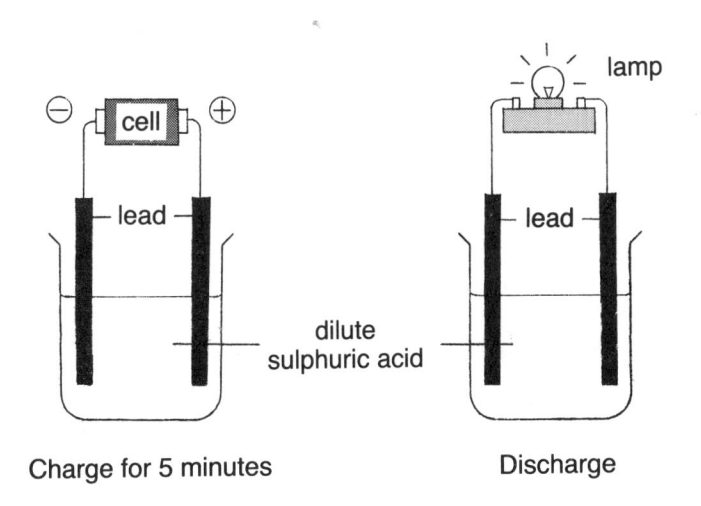

Charge for 5 minutes   Discharge

CHAPTER SEVEN • *Making Electricity*

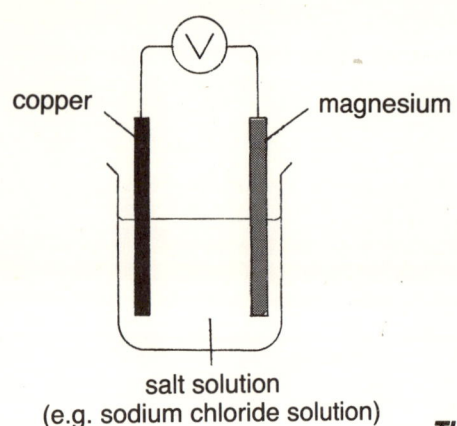

A Simple Cell

A simple cell can be made with two different metals connected by an electrolyte (ionic solution or paste). An electrolyte completes the electrical circuit. It is called a **salt bridge** or **ion bridge**.

Cells which are used for radios, toys, cameras, etc., contain no liquids. They are sometimes called 'dry' cells. The electrolytes in them, for example ammonium chloride, are in the form of pastes. Pastes are used because an entirely 'dry' cell would not conduct electricity.

THE ELECTROCHEMICAL SERIES

The **voltage** of a cell depends on the difference in the chemical reactivity of the two metals inside it. The diagram shows how the voltage between pairs of metals can be measured.

Metal 1 could be copper and a number of other metals can be used in turn as metal 2. This enables the voltages of a number of cells to be measured.

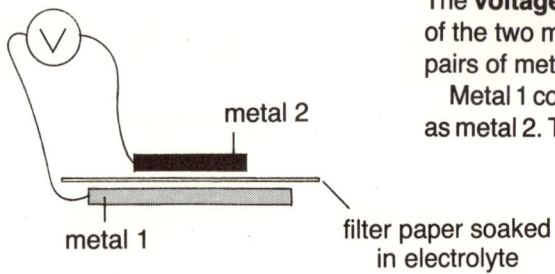

Metals are listed in order of these voltages in the **electrochemical series**. This series is given in full in the *Data Booklet*. Part of it is shown on the right.

$Na^+(aq)$	+	e	→	$Na(s)$
$Mg^{2+}(aq)$	+	2e	→	$Mg(s)$
$Al^{3+}(aq)$	+	3e	→	$Al(s)$
$Zn^{2+}(aq)$	+	2e	→	$Zn(s)$
$Fe^{2+}(aq)$	+	2e	→	$Fe(s)$
$Sn^{2+}(aq)$	+	2e	→	$Sn(s)$
$Pb^{2+}(aq)$	+	2e	→	$Pb(s)$
$2H^+(aq)$	+	**2e**	→	**$H_2(g)$**
$Cu^{2+}(aq)$	+	2e	→	$Cu(s)$
$Ag^+(aq)$	+	e	→	$Ag(s)$
$Au^+(aq)$	+	e	→	$Au(s)$

Reactivity of Metals

As well as being arranged in the electrochemical series, the metals can also be arranged in order of their chemical activity. The two orders are almost the same.

Sodium reacts violently with *water*.
Magnesium reacts slowly with *water*.
Copper does not react with *water*.

Magnesium reacts quickly with *dilute acids*.
Zinc reacts more slowly with *dilute acids*.
Copper does not react with *dilute acids*.

Displacement Reactions

The position of metals in the electrochemical series can be used to explain the results of **displacement reactions**.

As shown in the diagram, *zinc* metal reacts with *copper(II) sulphate* solution to form *copper* metal and *zinc sulphate* solution.

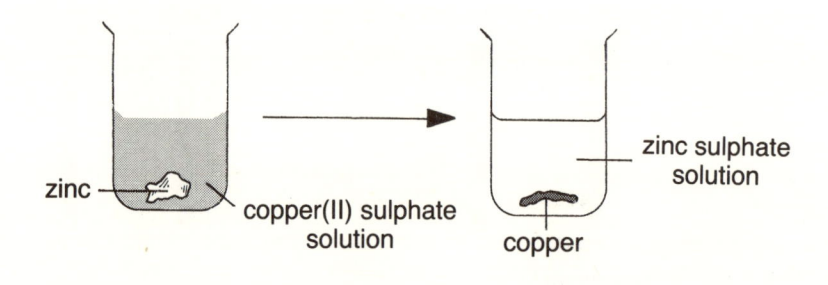

$$Zn(s) + CuSO_4(aq) \rightarrow Cu(s) + ZnSO_4(aq)$$
$$\text{or}\quad Zn(s) + Cu^{2+}(aq) \rightarrow Cu(s) + Zn^{2+}(aq)$$

CHAPTER SEVEN • *Making Electricity*

Zinc, being more reactive than copper, **displaces** the copper from copper (II) sulphate solution. Any metal in the electrochemical series will displace any other metal, which is less active, in the same way.

The Position of Hydrogen

Hydrogen can be given a place in the electrochemical series. This can be shown by using the reactions of copper and lead with acids.

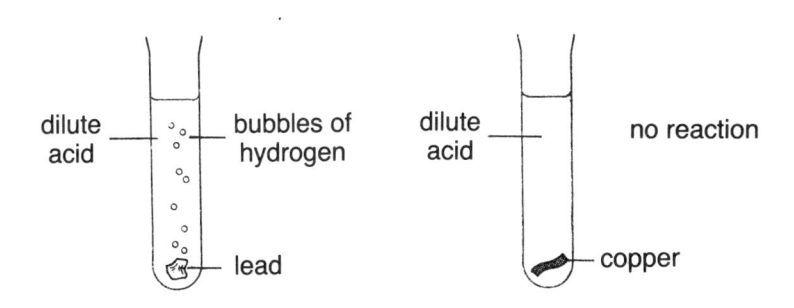

Metals which are more active than **copper** react with dilute acids to displace hydrogen. Metals which are less active than **lead** do *not* react with dilute acids to displace hydrogen.

Hydrogen can be seen to come between lead and copper in the electrochemical series.

CONSTRUCTING A CELL

In a **cell** two chemicals react to produce electricity. For example, zinc reacts with copper sulphate solution in a displacement reaction which can form a cell.

Zinc atoms, Zn(s), change from being neutral atoms to become positively charged ions, $Zn^{2+}(aq)$. Two electrons are lost:

$$Zn(s) \rightarrow Zn^{2+}(aq) + 2e$$

Copper ions, $Cu^{2+}(aq)$, gain two electrons to become neutral atoms, Cu(s):

$$Cu^{2+}(aq) + 2e \rightarrow Cu(s)$$

Electrons are transferred from zinc atoms to copper ions. An electric current is produced if the zinc and copper sulphate solution are separated as shown in the diagram.

A number of different substances could be used for solution X and metal Y. Solution X could be zinc sulphate solution and metal Y could be copper.

Paper soaked in an electrolyte will act as a **salt** or **ion bridge.** Ions move through the salt bridge to complete the circuit.

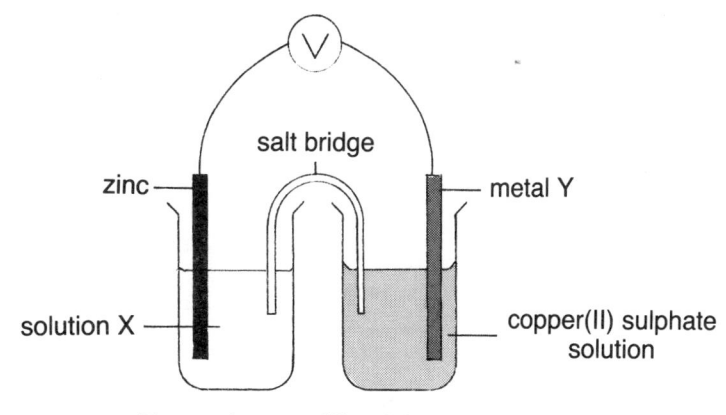

Zinc and copper(II) sulphate cell

CHAPTER SEVEN • *Making Electricity*

Designs for Cells

There are many possible designs for cells. What is required is:

- a substance which will *lose* electrons; and
- a substance which will *gain* electrons.

These reactants must be separated from each other and the circuit completed by suitable solutions, electrodes and a salt bridge.

Here are examples of cells.

Cell 1 Copper and silver nitrate solution cell

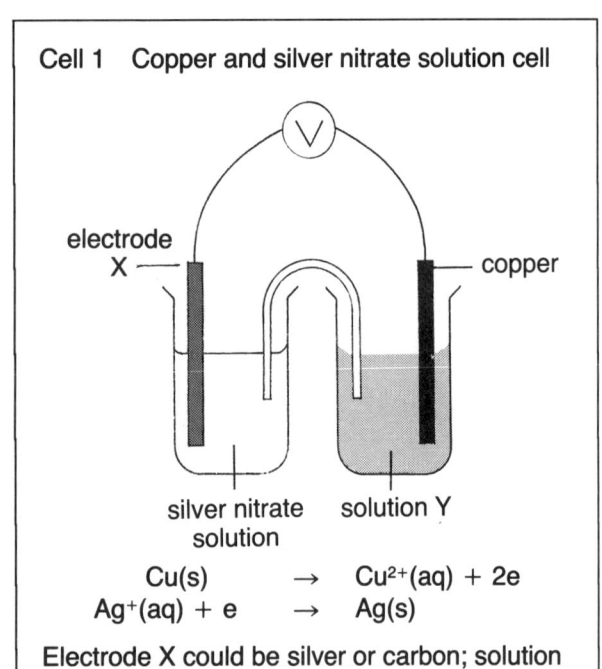

electrode X
copper
silver nitrate solution
solution Y

$Cu(s) \rightarrow Cu^{2+}(aq) + 2e$
$Ag^+(aq) + e \rightarrow Ag(s)$

Electrode X could be silver or carbon; solution Y could be copper(II) nitrate solution.

Cell 2 Iron(III) chloride solution and potassium iodide solution cell

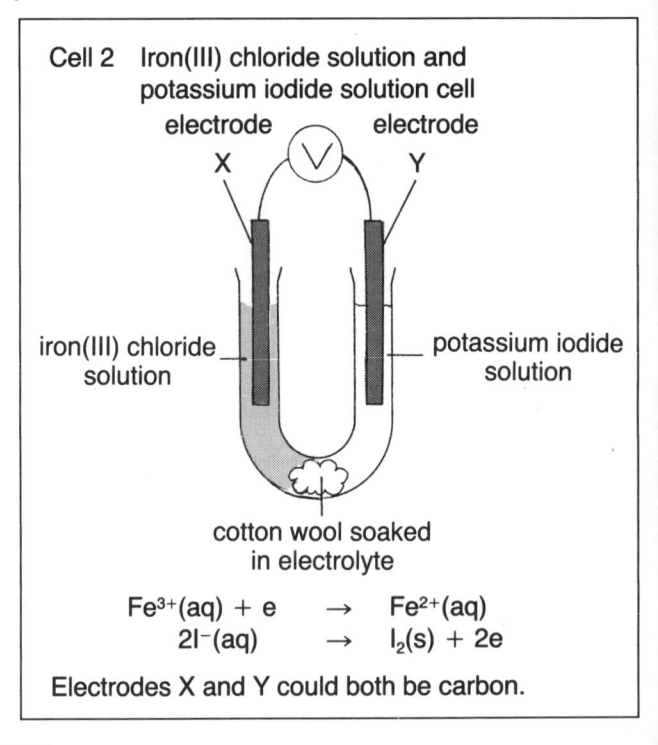

electrode X
electrode Y
iron(III) chloride solution
potassium iodide solution
cotton wool soaked in electrolyte

$Fe^{3+}(aq) + e \rightarrow Fe^{2+}(aq)$
$2I^-(aq) \rightarrow I_2(s) + 2e$

Electrodes X and Y could both be carbon.

Cell 3 Magnesium and copper(II) sulphate solution cell

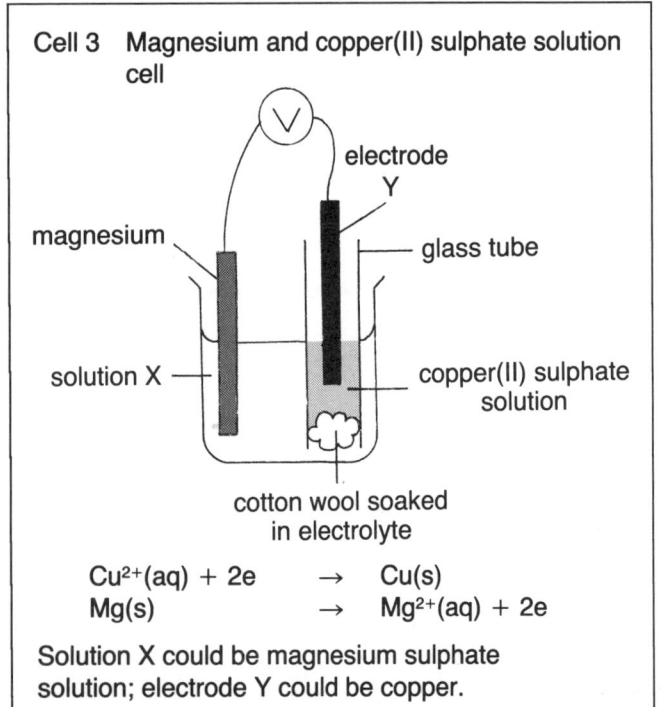

magnesium
electrode Y
glass tube
solution X
copper(II) sulphate solution
cotton wool soaked in electrolyte

$Cu^{2+}(aq) + 2e \rightarrow Cu(s)$
$Mg(s) \rightarrow Mg^{2+}(aq) + 2e$

Solution X could be magnesium sulphate solution; electrode Y could be copper.

The salt bridge should *not* react with the contents of either beaker. Filter paper or cotton wool soaked in potassium nitrate solution or sodium nitrate solution is always a convenient salt bridge.

Cells and batteries are both safer and more portable than mains electricity. However, they are more expensive, and can wear out at the wrong time!

OXIDATION AND REDUCTION (REDOX)

Chemical reactions which produce electricity are called **redox** (**red**uction and **ox**idation) reactions. One reactant will *lose* electrons and one will *gain*

CHAPTER SEVEN • *Making Electricity*

electrons. *Both* reduction *and* oxidation must take place for an electric current to be produced in a cell.

The process of losing electrons is called **oxidation** and that of gaining electrons is called **reduction**.

A way of remembering redox:

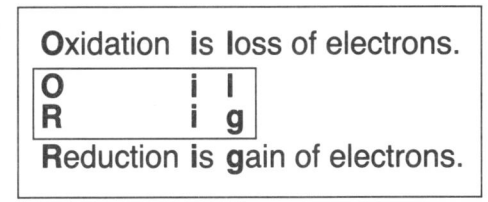

Oxidation **is l**oss of electrons.
O   i   l
R   i   g
Reduction **is g**ain of electrons.

Examples of Oxidation and Reduction

1. When a *metal forms from one of its compounds* the process is called *reduction*.

    Reduction $Fe^{3+}(aq) + 3e \rightarrow Fe(s)$
    Reduction $Cu^{2+}(aq) + 2e \rightarrow Cu(s)$

2. When a *metal forms a compound or corrodes* the process is called *oxidation*.

    Oxidation $Mg(s) \rightarrow Mg^{2+}(aq) + 2e$
    Oxidation $Na(s) \rightarrow Na^+(aq) + e$

3. Although you will nearly always encounter metal reactions in redox, it is possible for non-metals to be involved. For example, in Cell 2 iodide ions were oxidised.

    Oxidation $2I^-(aq) \rightarrow I_2(s) + 2e$

    Non-metals such as chlorine can be reduced.

    Reduction $Cl_2(g) + 2e \rightarrow 2Cl^-(aq)$

4. In some redox reactions it may be harder to spot what is gaining and what is losing electrons.

    Oxidation $SO_3^{2-}(aq) + H_2O(l) \rightarrow SO_4^{2-}(aq) + 2H^+(aq) + 2e$
    Reduction $2H^+(aq) + NO_3^-(aq) + e \rightarrow NO_2(aq) + H_2O(l)$

    These may seem to be very complicated equations. However, electrons are lost and gained in a similar way to the earlier examples.

Practice Questions

1. Which box represents a statement about a cell which is **untrue**?

A	A chemical reaction inside a cell produces electricity.
B	A cell goes done when the reactants inside are used up.
C	Electricity passing along wires from a cell is a flow of ions.
D	Lead-sulphuric acid batteries are rechargeable.

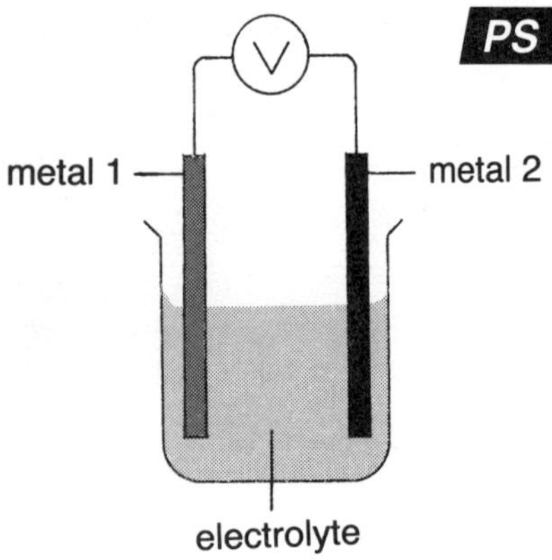

CHAPTER SEVEN • *Making Electricity*

PS 2. Which box represents the pair of metals which will give the **greatest** voltage when connected together in the cell illustrated?

	Metal 1	Metal 2
A	zinc	magnesium
B	zinc	copper
C	zinc	iron
D	magnesium	copper

PS 3. Which **one** box represents the most suitable electrolyte for the cell illustrated in question 2 above?

A	sodium nitrate solution
B	water
C	copper(II) sulphate solution
D	sulphuric acid

PS 4. In this question the element symbol 'X' does not refer to an actual symbol in the periodic table.
Here is some information about a metal 'X'.

> X reacts with a solution of copper(II) sulphate.
> X reacts with a solution of zinc sulphate.
> Aluminium reacts with a solution of X sulphate.
> Tin does *not* react with a solution of X sulphate.

From the information above which letter indicates the position of X in the reactivity series of metals?

sodium
magnesium
[A]
aluminium
[B]
zinc
iron
[C]
tin
lead
hydrogen
[D]
copper
silver

PS 5. Draw **labelled** diagrams of cells based on the following reactions.

(a) Magnesium reacting with copper(II) sulphate solution.
(b) Iron reacting with silver nitrate solution.
(c) Iron(III) chloride solution reacting with potassium iodide solution.
(d) Zinc reacting with copper(II) nitrate solution.

62

CHAPTER SEVEN • *Making Electricity*

6. In which of the following reactions is redox occurring?

A	$CH_4(g) + Br_2(g) \rightarrow CH_3Br\ (l) + HBr(g)$
B	$Ag^+(aq) + Cl^-(aq) \rightarrow Ag^+Cl^-(s)$
C	$Cu(s) + 2Ag^+(aq) \rightarrow Cu^{2+}(aq) + 2Ag(s)$
D	$Al^{3+}(l) + 3e \rightarrow Al(s)$

7. Which box (or boxes) could contain information which is **true** about the cell illustrated?

A	Electrons flow from zinc to copper through the meter.
B	Electrons flow through the salt bridge from X to Y.
C	Cu^{2+} ions gain electrons in beaker Y.
D	The blue colour in beaker Y will become more intense.
E	The salt bridge completes the circuit.

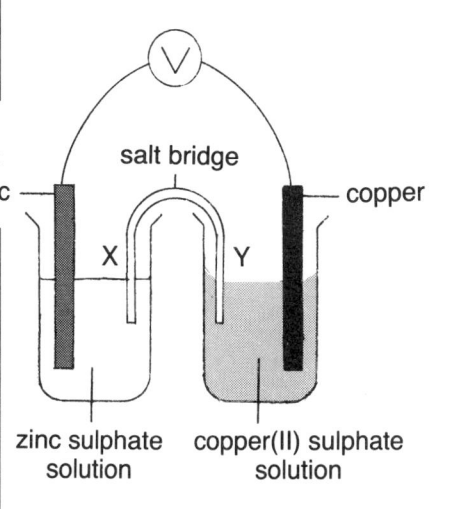

8. Here is the chemical equation showing how iron(III) chloride solution reacts with potassium iodide solution in a redox reaction.

$$2FeCl_3 + 2KI \rightarrow I_2 + 2KCl + 2FeCl_2$$

Which **one** of the following represents the reduction step?

A	$Fe^{3+}(aq) + e \rightarrow Fe^{2+}(aq)$
B	$I_2(aq) + 2e \rightarrow 2I^-(aq)$
C	$K^+(aq) + e \rightarrow K(s)$
D	$Cl_2(g) + 2e \rightarrow 2Cl^-(aq)$

9. In which box (or boxes) is a metal **atom** being oxidised?

A	$Fe^{3+}(aq) + e \rightarrow Fe^{2+}(aq)$
B	$2Cl^-(aq) \rightarrow Cl_2(g) + 2e$
C	$Mg(s) \rightarrow Mg^{2+}(aq) + 2e$
D	$Cu^+(aq) \rightarrow Cu^{2+}(aq) + e$
E	$Ag^+(aq) + e \rightarrow Ag(s)$
F	$Zn(s) \rightarrow Zn^{2+}(aq) + 2e$

10. Rewrite each of the following equations to show the reduction and oxidation steps.

    (a) $Mg + Cu^{2+}(Cl^-)_2 \rightarrow Mg^{2+}(Cl^-)_2 + Cu$
    (b) $Zn + 2H^+Cl^- \rightarrow Zn^{2+}(Cl^-)_2 + H_2$
    (c) $Zn + Cu^{2+}SO_4^{2-} \rightarrow Zn^{2+}SO_4^{2-} + Cu$
    (d) $2Fe^{3+}(Cl^-)_3 + 2K^+I^- \rightarrow I_2 + 2K^+Cl^- + 2Fe^{2+}(Cl^-)_2$
    (e) $Cl_2 + 2K^+Br^- \rightarrow 2K^+Cl^- + Br_2$

CHAPTER EIGHT

Metals

Metals are amongst the most versatile of materials. The choice of a metal for a particular purpose depends on its **properties**. The properties of metals can be altered by mixing them with other metals or non-metals. Such mixtures are called **alloys**.

Metals
- conduct electricity,
- conduct heat,
- can be hammered (malleable),
- can be twisted, bent, stretched (ductile),
- can be mixed to form alloys,
- are extracted from ores,
- may corrode.

SOME NOTES ON COMMON METALS

Copper   Good electrical and thermal conductivity. Because it is fairly unreactive it can be used for water pipes and tanks. Alloys include bronze (with tin) and brass (with zinc). Used for making coins.

Iron   Usually found in the form of alloys which are called 'steels'. Steels often contain carbon and small amounts of other metals to increase strength, hardness or rust resistance. Stainless steels contain chromium and are resistant to corrosion. Iron and steel are widely used for car and lorry bodies, ships, and girders for the construction industry.

Zinc   Protects steel (called galvanising) and is used as an electrode in cells and batteries.

Aluminium   One of the least dense ('lightest') metals. Does not require protection from corrosion. Used for light garden furniture and kitchen utensils. Overhead power lines are made from aluminium rather than copper. A major use is in making cooking foil and what is called 'silver paper'.

Tin   A soft metal. Expensive compared with others mentioned. Main use is in coating steel to form 'tin' cans. Tin cans are *not* made from pure tin but from steel coated with tin. Tin mixed with lead gives the low melting alloy called solder which is used for electrical connections.

Lead   Soft dense metal. Used in car batteries, in solder (see above) and as shielding in work involving X-rays and radioactive material.

Metal Ores

Reserves of metals are limited. Metals are **finite resources**. Apart from a few unreactive metals, such as gold and silver, metals occur combined with other elements in the earth's crust. These compounds are called **ores** and include oxides, sulphides and carbonates.

CHAPTER EIGHT • *Metals*

Geologists have their own names for metal ores, for example:

bauxite	aluminium ore
haematite	iron ore
cerussite	lead ore
pyrites	forms of iron sulphide, called 'fool's gold'.

Precious Metals

Precious metals occur uncombined in the earth. Although they do form compounds they are very resistant to corrosion. They are bought and sold for their own value or made into jewelry. They also have important uses in science and industry.

Silver   Extremely good electrical conductor. Main component of photographic films and papers. Also used in dentistry.

Gold   Mainly used for ornamental purposes. Rather soft on its own, it is alloyed with silver or copper to make it more wear resistant. Like silver it can be used in dentistry.

Platinum   Used for making jewelry, and in chemistry for special crucibles for use with very corrosive reactants. One of a group of transition metals which includes iridium and palladium which are catalysts. Used in catalytic convertors in car exhausts.

Mercury   The only liquid metal. Used in mercury vapour lamps, thermometers and in small batteries. Has the property of being a solvent for other metals, forming an alloy called an amalgam.

Because of the finite nature of metal resources it is becoming more and more important that methods of **recycling** be developed. Aluminium is an example of a metal which can be recycled.

REACTIONS OF METALS

Metals react with a whole variety of substances to form compounds. Some metals react more readily than others. The extent to which different metals react is given by their **reactivity**. The order of their reactivity is very similar to the electrochemical series which was described in Chapter Seven.

Reaction of Metals and Oxygen

Many metals, such as magnesium, burn in oxygen. Oxygen can be made by heating potassium permanganate. The reactivity of a series of metals with oxygen can be seen by burning the metals in gas jars of oxygen or as shown in the diagram. The most reactive metals burn most brightly.

Magnesium burns brightly $2Mg + O_2 \rightarrow 2MgO$
Copper burns feebly $2Cu + O_2 \rightarrow 2CuO$

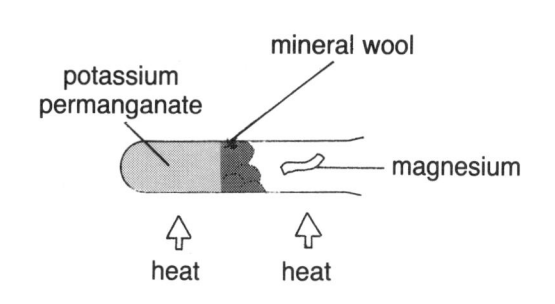

Reaction of Metals and Water

When iron becomes wet it rusts. Many other metals react with water. Some metals such as sodium and potassium react violently and must be stored under oil.

When metals react with water they form metal hydroxides (alkalis) and hydrogen.

Sodium reacts violently $2Na + 2H_2O \rightarrow 2NaOH + H_2$
Calcium reacts quickly $Ca + 2H_2O \rightarrow Ca(OH)_2 + H_2$

CHAPTER EIGHT • *Metals*

Reaction of Metals with Acids

Metals also react with acids. The most reactive metals, sodium and potassium, react with acids almost explosively. Magnesium, aluminium, zinc, iron and tin react increasingly slowly. Lead hardly reacts with acids, while the other metals, from copper to the least reactive, do not react at all.

In each case hydrogen forms. The other compound formed is a salt.

Magnesium $Mg + H_2SO_4 \rightarrow MgSO_4 + H_2$
Zinc $Zn + 2HCl \rightarrow ZnCl_2 + H_2$

Metals lose electrons in the reactions described above. The metal atoms are oxidised.

REDUCTION OF METAL ORES

The precious metals do not usually require a chemical process for their extraction. A gold mine, for example, produces gold which is uncombined with other elements.

Most metals, however, do require to be separated from the other elements with which they are combined in their ores. The process of making a metal from its ore is called **reduction**. A substance which removes the other elements from the ores is called a **reducing agent**.

A metal may be displaced from its ore by a more active metal. This, however, can be an expensive process. Carbon, carbon monoxide and hydrogen are much cheaper reducing agents.

Here are some examples of reducing agents in action:

carbon $2Pb^{2+}O^{2-} + C \rightarrow 2Pb + CO_2$
carbon monoxide $Fe^{2+}O^{2-} + CO \rightarrow Fe + CO_2$
hydrogen $Cu^{2+}O^{2-} + H_2 \rightarrow Cu + H_2O$

The reduction of metal ores can be demonstrated in the laboratory in two ways.

1. Carbon
   Powdered metal oxides are reduced to metal when roasted with carbon powder.

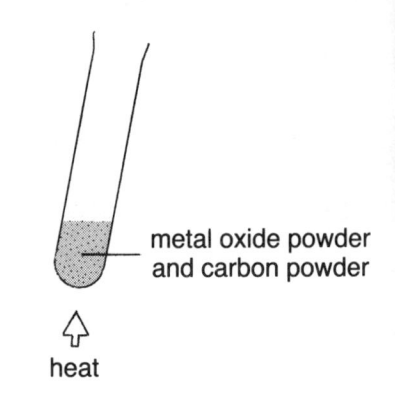

2. Hydrogen or carbon monoxide
   A method of reducing a metal oxide with a gas is as follows:

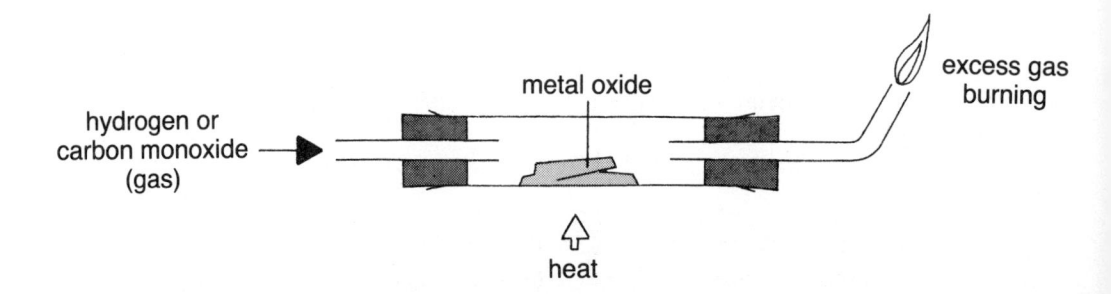

CHAPTER EIGHT • *Metals*

Discovery of Metals

As chemists have learned more about reduction, they have been able to make the more active metals such as sodium and potassium from their ores. The discovery of metals has occurred through the ages almost in the order of their chemical reactivity. Here are some examples.

Gold and silver	Occur naturally. No need for chemical reduction. Mentioned in the *Bible*.
Copper	Easily extracted from ore. *Bronze Age*.
Iron	Higher temperatures needed for reduction. *Iron Age*.
Zinc and nickel	Extracted from their ores for about *250 years*.
Aluminium, sodium and calcium	Have to be extracted by electricity. Made in *modern times*.

Iron

It is not easy to make iron from iron(III) oxide in a school chemistry laboratory. A much higher temperature is required to reduce iron ore than is required for lead or copper ores.

Iron is made in industry in a blast furnace. The 'blast' refers to blasts of air which, together with the reducing agent, enable the high temperature to be attained.

The blast furnace is loaded with *iron ore* (Fe_2O_3), *coke* (carbon, the reducing agent) and *limestone*. It is heated and air is blown into the hot mixture. Near the bottom of the furnace carbon burns, forming carbon dioxide. This further increases the temperature.

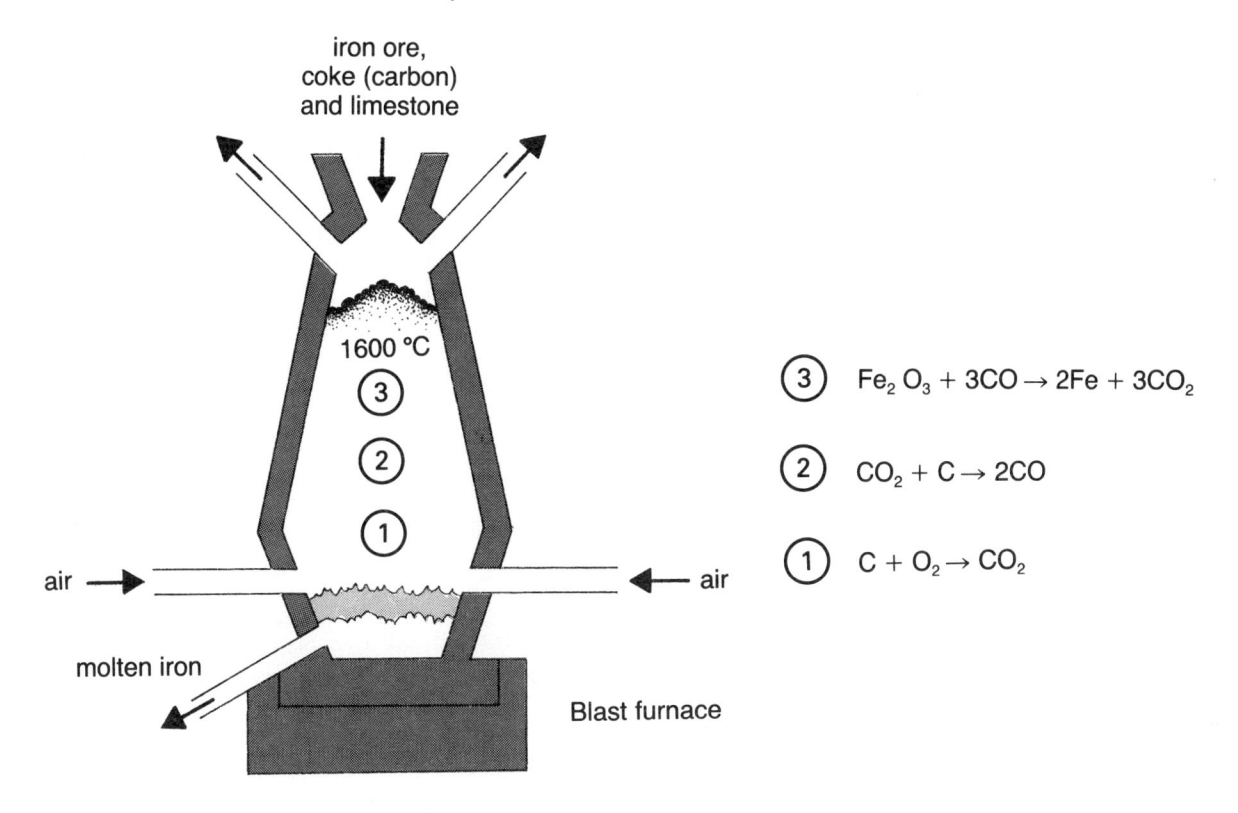

③ $Fe_2O_3 + 3CO \rightarrow 2Fe + 3CO_2$

② $CO_2 + C \rightarrow 2CO$

① $C + O_2 \rightarrow CO_2$

Blast furnace

CHAPTER EIGHT • *Metals*

Carbon burns: $C + O_2 \rightarrow CO_2$
The carbon dioxide rises and reacts with more carbon to form carbon monoxide.

Carbon monoxide forms: $CO_2 + C \rightarrow 2CO$
Carbon monoxide is the main reducing agent. Being a gas it reacts more effectively with the iron ore than lumps of carbon can.

Iron oxide is reduced: $Fe_2O_3 + 3CO \rightarrow 2Fe + 3CO_2$

In time all of the iron ore in the furnace is reduced to molten iron. Since it is molten it can be easily run off or 'tapped'.

Having been dug out of the earth, iron ore contains many impurities. These combine with limestone to form a 'slag' which floats on top of the molten iron. When this hot slag is tapped from a furnace it makes a dramatic sight in the sky at night.

Zinc, tin, lead and copper are other metals which can be made by reducing their oxides with carbon or carbon monoxide.

Other Methods of Reduction

Oxides of precious metals such as silver or mercury decompose when heated. The products are the metal and oxygen:

$$2Ag_2O \rightarrow 4Ag + O_2$$

Metals which are more active than zinc are made by electrolysis of their molten ores. This method is described later.

Metals can also be made by heating their oxides with a more active metal.

A Summary of the Properties of Common Metals

Potassium Sodium Lithium Calcium	React with cold water.	React violently with acid.	Made from ores by electrolysis
Magnesium Aluminium Zinc Iron Tin Lead	React slowly with water.	React with acids to give hydrogen.	Made from ores by heating with carbon.
(Hydrogen) Copper Mercury Platinum Silver Gold	Do not react with water.	Do not react with acids.	Oxides decompose on heating.

FORMULAE OF METAL OXIDES (EMPIRICAL FORMULAE)

The formulae of compounds can be written from the 'rules' for bonding. It is also possible to obtain the formula of a compound by experimental means. This can be conveniently done for metal oxides. The formula of a

CHAPTER EIGHT • *Metals*

compound obtained from experiments in this way is called the **empirical formula**.

The empirical formula of magnesium oxide can be found by burning magnesium, and that of copper oxide by reducing copper oxide.

Empirical Formula of Magnesium Oxide

Magnesium ribbon is weighed in a crucible with a loose-fitting lid. When the crucible is roasted for a time, the magnesium burns and forms magnesium oxide. The mass of the magnesium will increase.

Here is a set of results obtained in this experiment.

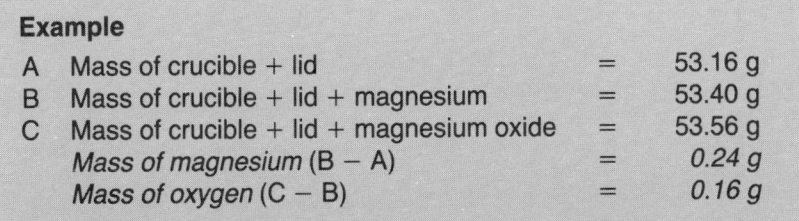

> **Example**
> A Mass of crucible + lid   = 53.16 g
> B Mass of crucible + lid + magnesium   = 53.40 g
> C Mass of crucible + lid + magnesium oxide = 53.56 g
> Mass of magnesium (B − A)   = 0.24 g
> Mass of oxygen (C − B)   = 0.16 g
>
> The formula of magnesium oxide is, however, *not* $Mg_{0.24}O_{0.16}$.
> The formula of a compound is the ratio of the *numbers* of atoms or ions and not of their *masses*.
> To calculate the numbers of ions their masses are divided by their relative atomic masses.
> Ratio of moles of magnesium : moles of oxygen
>
> $$= \frac{0.24}{24} : \frac{0.16}{16}$$
> $$= 0.01 : 0.01$$

magnesium + oxygen → magnesium oxide

Magnesium oxide can be seen from these results to contain equal numbers of moles of magnesium ions and oxide ions.

The empirical formula of magnesium oxide is MgO, the same as the formula obtained from the rules of bonding.

Empirical Formula of Copper Oxide

Copper oxide can be reduced to copper by using hydrogen or carbon monoxide. The mass of copper oxide becomes less in this experiment.

Here are sample results.

> **Example**
> A Mass of test tube   = 29.65 g
> B Mass of test tube + copper oxide = 30.37 g
> C Mass of test tube + copper   = 30.29 g
> Mass of copper (C − A)   = 0.64 g
> Mass of oxygen (B − C)   = 0.08 g
>
> Ratio of ions of copper : ions of oxygen in copper oxide
>
> $$\frac{0.64}{64} : \frac{0.08}{16}$$
> $$= 0.01 : 0.005$$
> $$= 2 : 1$$

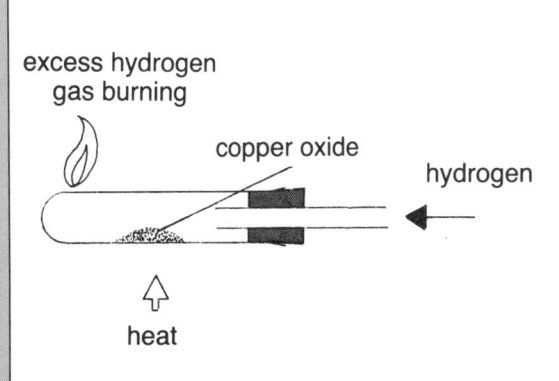

This shows that copper oxide contains two ions of copper to one ion of oxygen. The empirical formula of copper oxide is Cu_2O.

The name of this compound is copper(I) oxide. You have already met another oxide of copper, copper(II) oxide (CuO).

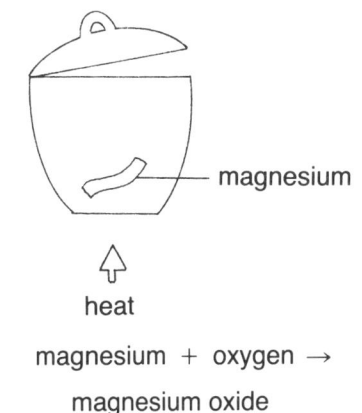

69

CHAPTER EIGHT • *Metals*

Empirical Formula from Percentage Composition

It is not necessary to know the masses of the elements making up a compound. The percentage composition will allow the empirical formula to be calculated.

> **Example** A compound has the composition by mass:
> 52% carbon
> 13% hydrogen
> 35% oxygen.
> What is the empirical formula of the compound?
>
> The masses of the elements in 100 g are:
> 52 g carbon; 13 g hydrogen; 35 g oxygen.
> Ratio of C : H : O = $\frac{52}{12} : \frac{13}{1} : \frac{35}{16}$
> = 4.33 : 13 : 2.19
> The simplest ratio is most easily found by *dividing by the smallest number.*
> = 2 : 6 : 1
> The empirical formula of the compound is C_2H_6O.

To find the empirical formula of a compound:
- the mass of all the elements in the compound must be known;
- the mass of each element is divided by its relative atomic mass;
- each of the numbers obtained is divided by the smallest number.

For ionic compounds the empirical formula and the formula obtained from the 'rules' are usually the same.

Practice Questions

PS 1. Use the information in the table below to draw a **bar chart** showing the price of some common metals.

Metal	Price per tonne (£) in 1990
Aluminium	1145
Copper	810
Lead	250
Nickel	5500
Tin	2950
Zinc	770

CHAPTER EIGHT • *Metals*

2. Metals are some of the most useful and versatile materials used today.

A brass	B copper	C mercury
D aluminium	E zinc	F tin
G gold	H magnesium	I sodium

Which metal:

(a) is used to galvanise steel?
(b) is a liquid at room temperature?
(c) occurs uncombined in the earth?
(d) is an alloy?
(e) is stored under oil?

3. Metals and their compounds react with a wide range of substances.

A zinc	B sodium	C potassium oxide
D hydrogen	E carbon monoxide	F carbon dioxide
G potassium hydroxide	H potassium carbonate	I oxygen

Which box refers to:

(a) a reducing agent which is used in the blast furnace?
(b) the compound formed when potassium reacts with water?
(c) the gas formed when magnesium reacts with dilute sulphuric acid?
(d) a metal which reacts with cold water?

CHAPTER EIGHT • *Metals*

4. Metals occur naturally as ores. Many of these ores are oxides.

A aluminium oxide	B iron(III) oxide
C potassium oxide	D mercury(II) oxide
E silver oxide	F copper(II) oxide

Which box (or boxes) could refer to metal oxides which are normally reduced to the metal by:

(a) electrolysis when molten?
(b) heat alone?
(c) heating with carbon?

5.
> **Aluminium**
>
> Aluminium is made by the electrolysis of molten aluminium oxide. This is an expensive process which uses a great deal of energy.
>
> Aluminium has many properties which make it suitable for a wide range of uses. It is an excellent conductor of both heat and electricity. It is light, strong and does not require protection against corrosion.

PS (a) Give the formula for aluminium oxide.
PS (b) Suggest **two** reasons why aluminium is used to make overhead electric power lines.
PS (c) From your knowledge of the activity of aluminium, explain why it is unusual that aluminium 'does not require protection against corrosion'.

PS 6. Use the information below to make a **table** with appropriate headings of the amounts of metals thought to be available in the earth's crust. Use the **names** of the elements in the table.

Percentage of metals available: Al 30, Fe 20, Ca 18, Mg 10, Na 8, K 5, Ti 2, Others 5

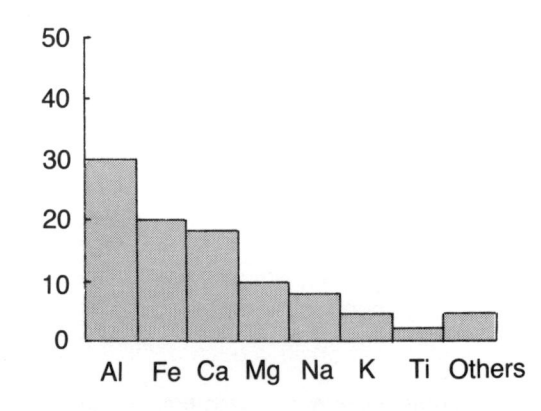

CHAPTER EIGHT • *Metals*

7. Use the *Data Booklet* to complete the table below.

Metal	Symbol	Melting point (°C)	Density (g/cm³)	Relative atomic mass
Aluminium	Al	660	2.7	27
Copper				
Iron				
	Pt			
		328	11.3	207

8.
> **Recycling Aluminium Cans**
>
> Aluminium is one of the easiest metals to recycle. Aluminium cans, not being magnetic, are quickly separated from 'tin' cans. They are also easy to crush which makes them convenient for storage in large quantities. It is even possible to get paid for handing in aluminium cans at some collection centres!
>
> Melting scrap aluminium needs only about half the energy required to make aluminium from its ore. However, although aluminium is a finite resource, only about 30% of the aluminium manufactured is recycled. As aluminium cans are made of unalloyed aluminium, little additional treatment is required to make new cans.

(a) Which property enables aluminium cans to be separated from 'tin' cans?
(b) What is meant by a 'finite' resource?
(c) (i) (Refer to the *Data Booklet*.) State the melting points of aluminium, copper and iron.
    (ii) Use your answer to (i) above to suggest a reason why 'aluminium is one of the easiest metals to recycle'.
(d) What is an alloy?

9. Metals can exist in many forms such as lumps, foils, powders or wires.

Explain how a fair test of three metals, magnesium, zinc and iron, could be carried out in order to arrange them in order of their activity.

10. Many chemical reactions produce gases. State the name of the **gas** produced in each of the following reactions.

(a) Heating potassium permanganate.
(b) Heating carbon with carbon dioxide.
(c) Zinc reacting with dilute hydrochloric acid.
(d) Burning carbon in a plentiful supply of oxygen.
(e) Heating copper(II) oxide with carbon.

11. Metal compounds can be reduced in a number of ways. State the names of the products in each of the following reactions.

(a) copper(II) oxide + hydrogen $\rightarrow$

CHAPTER EIGHT • *Metals*

    (b) lead(II) oxide + carbon   →
    (c) copper(II) chloride + zinc   →
    (d) iron(III) oxide + aluminium   →
    (e) iron(III) oxide + carbon monoxide →

12. A compound of calcium has the following composition:
    40% calcium; 48% oxygen; 12% carbon.

    Calculate its empirical formula. (Use the *Data Booklet* for atomic masses in this and the following questions.)

13. A compound of sodium has the following composition:
    57.5% sodium; 40% oxygen; 2.5% hydrogen.

    Calculate its empirical formula.

14. A compound has the following composition:
    40% carbon; 6.6% hydrogen; 53.4% oxygen.

    Calculate its empirical formula.

15. Silica is an oxide of silicon. It contains 46.6% silicon. What is its empirical formula?

CHAPTER NINE
More about Metals

Unprotected metals corrode when they react with oxygen and water in the atmosphere. The reaction is speeded up by the presence of polluted air or by sea water. The **corrosion** of a metal is an oxidation process.

metal → metal compound **oxidation**

Metals which are high in the activity or electrochemical series corrode most quickly.

Unprotected iron corrodes on the surface in a day or two. The product formed when iron corrodes is given a special name: **rust**.

Copper takes much longer to corrode than iron. When copper corrodes the corrosion product is green in colour. Lead pipes from Roman forts often show very little signs of corrosion even after nearly 2000 years, while objects made of gold are unlikely ever to corrode.

RUSTING OF IRON

Iron is one of the commonest metals and rusts quickly. The term 'rusting' is *not* applied to any other metals. For iron to rust *both water and oxygen (air)* are needed as the following experiments demonstrate.

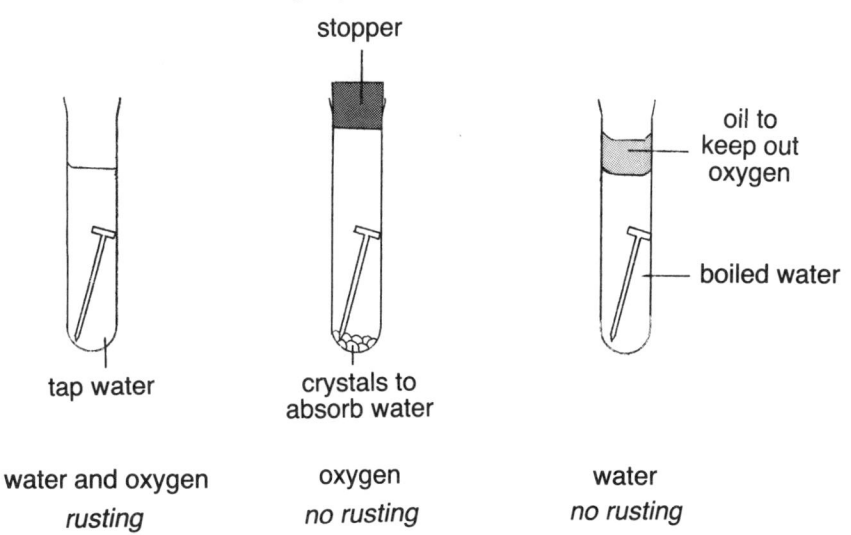

tap water	crystals to absorb water (stopper)	boiled water (oil to keep out oxygen)
water and oxygen	oxygen	water
rusting	*no rusting*	*no rusting*

Evidence of the corrosion of iron can be seen in a day or so with the formation of rust. However, an indicator (**ferroxyl indicator**) will show in only a few minutes if iron is rusting.

Ferroxyl indicator turns:
- *blue* when Fe^{2+} (aq) ions are forming;
- *red* when OH^- (aq) ions are forming.

The rusting of iron is a redox reaction. Fe^{2+} (aq) ions are the result of *oxidation* and OH^- (aq) ions are the result of *reduction*.

Iron oxidises in two stages:

Stage 1 $Fe(s) \rightarrow Fe^{2+}(aq) + 2e$
Stage 2 $Fe^{2+}(aq) \rightarrow Fe^{3+}(aq) + e$

The reduction step in the rusting of iron involves both water and oxygen.

$$2H_2O(l) + O_2(g) + 4e \rightarrow 4OH^-(aq)$$

CHAPTER NINE • *More about Metals*

Water contains very few ions and the presence of any extra ions in water will greatly accelerate corrosion. For example, dissolved carbon dioxide or sulphur dioxide produced when fuels burn will both increase the number of ions:

sulphur dioxide $SO_2(g) + H_2O(l) \rightarrow 2H^+(aq) + SO_3^{2-}(aq)$
cabon dioxide $CO_2(g) + H_2O(l) \rightarrow 2H^+(aq) + CO_3^{2-}(aq)$

These additional ions increase the rate of rusting.

In the same way, the presence of the ions in salt (sodium chloride) accelerates corrosion. Salt may come from sea spray in coastal areas or from grit for roads in winter.

Rusting of Iron: A Cell

The rusting of iron can be represented as a cell.

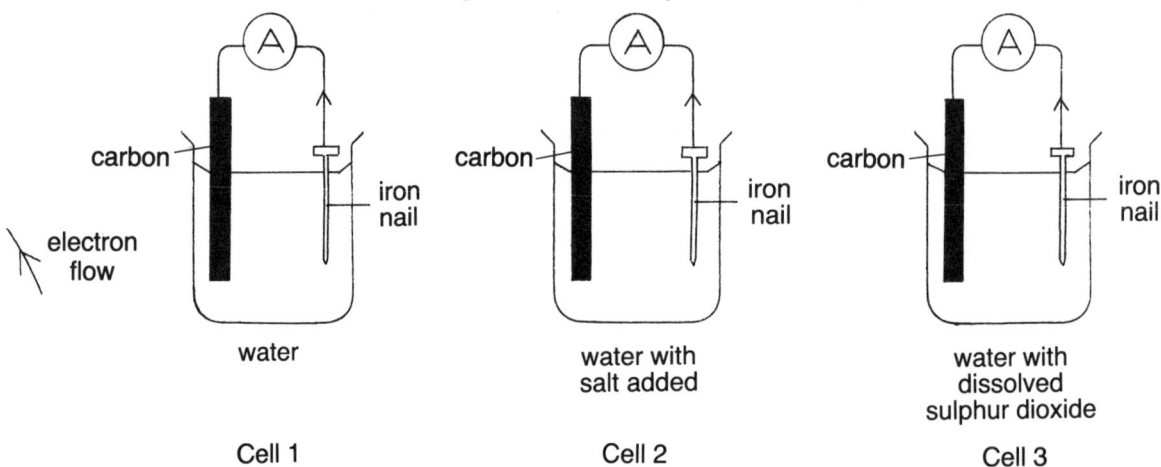

Cell 1 — water
Cell 2 — water with salt added
Cell 3 — water with dissolved sulphur dioxide

The direction of the electron flow indicates if rusting is taking place. If *electrons flow away from iron* then *rusting is occurring*. The current obtained in each of the cells 2 and 3 will be *greater* than the current in cell 1. This shows that iron rusts faster when there are more ions present in the water.

The iron in the nail in each of the above cells is *oxidised*:

$$Fe(s) \rightarrow Fe^{2+}(aq) + 2e$$

At the other electrode *reduction* is occurring:

$$2H_2O(l) + O_2(g) + 4e^- \rightarrow 4OH(aq)$$

Controlling Rusting

The cost of metal corrosion runs to billions of pounds to the nation every year. Often cars, whose engines are still operating, are scrapped because their body panels have rusted through.

Preventing rusting is not an easy or a permanent process. There are two kinds of methods for controlling rusting: surface coating and using electricity.

Surface Coating

Iron can be completely sealed off from air and water by a surface coating. Here are some examples:
- a plastic coating;
- a plating with another metal;
- painting;
- the coating of moving parts by grease or oil;
- galvanising.

Anodising is another method of providing a surface coating, but it is used only with aluminium.

CHAPTER NINE • *More about Metals*

Coating iron by dipping in molten zinc is called **galvanising**. Articles made of galvanised iron may not look very attractive but they do not need to be painted.

Tin-plated iron is used to make 'tin' cans. Tin does not taint food and it is not poisonous.

Iron can also be plated with precious metals such as gold and silver to make attractive and expensive looking trophies. The expensive metal is only a thin coating.

Most methods of protection which are based on coating will eventually fail when the coating barrier is broken.

Using Electricity

Using electricity offers another solution to the problem of rusting. Making an iron object negatively charged makes it more difficult for it to lose electrons and corrode.

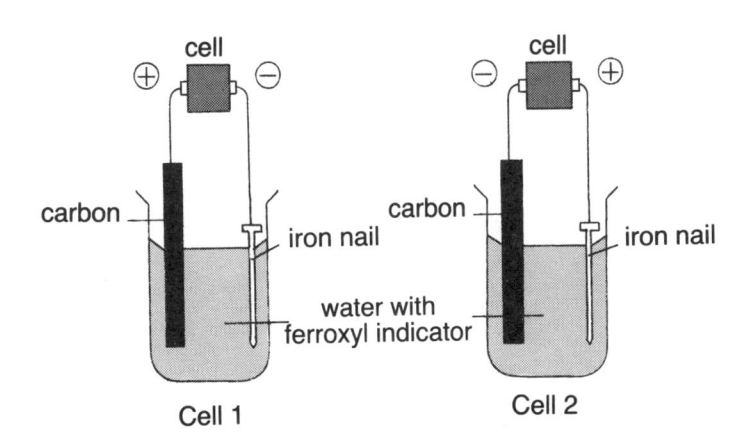

In cell 1 there will be no sign of iron rusting. In cell 2, however, a blue colour will quickly form around the iron, indicating that rusting is taking place. The positive terminal of the battery encourages the loss of electrons from iron. In a car, the negative terminal of the battery is connected to the body to help control rusting.

Instead of the negative terminal of a battery, a more active metal can be attached to iron. This also protects the iron.

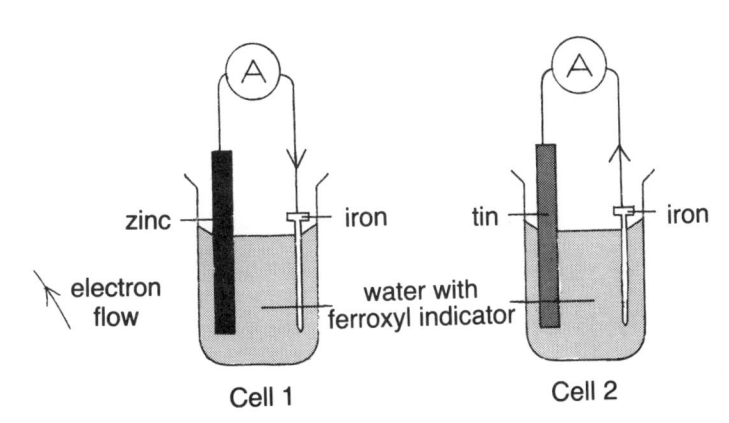

In cell 1 *no* rusting takes place. Electrons flow from the zinc to the iron, making it more difficult for the iron to lose electrons. Because zinc is above iron in the electrochemical series, it is zinc which corrodes rather than iron.

$$Zn(s) \rightarrow Zn^{2+}(aq) + 2e$$

Zinc is 'sacrificed' to protect the iron. This is called **sacrificial protection**. *Any* metal more active than iron will protect iron in the same way.

In cell 2 severe rusting takes place. Tin does *not* protect iron. The electrons flow from iron to tin. In this cell iron is rusting and the iron is protecting the tin.

The difference between zinc and tin coating can be seen from the two cells. An iron structure which is protected by zinc (galvanised) should not rust even if the zinc coating is damaged. However, a tin-coated object, such as a 'tin' can, will rust very quickly when the tin coating is broken.

There are other methods of sacrificial protection apart from galvanising. Iron or steel structures, pipelines or boats can be protected from rusting by being connected by a wire to scrap zinc or magnesium.

EXTRACTION OF METALS BY ELECTROLYSIS

Aluminium is one of the more active metals. It cannot be made from its ore by using reducing agents such as carbon. It has to be made by the **electrolysis** of molten aluminium oxide.

When a molten metal compound is electrolysed, the metal forms at the negative electrode. Aluminium, calcium, sodium and potassium are all extracted by electrolysis of molten compounds.

The ore of aluminium (bauxite) is composed mainly of aluminium oxide. The melting point of bauxite is very high, but it is lowered when bauxite is mixed with other aluminium compounds. Mixtures of substances melt at lower temperatures than pure substances.

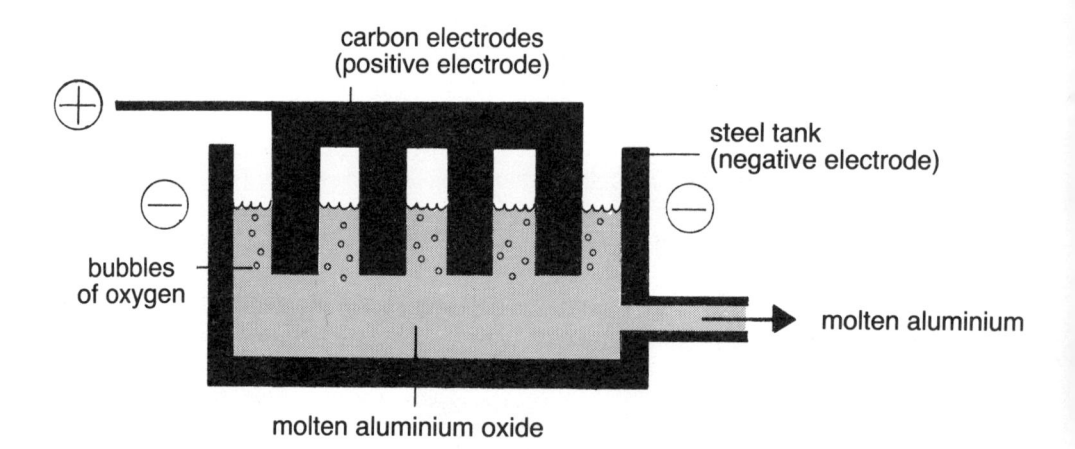

Reduction at negative electrode: $Al^{3+}(l) + 3e \rightarrow Al(s)$
Oxidation at positive electrode: $2O^{2-}(l) \rightarrow O_2(g) + 2e$

The extraction of aluminium requires large amounts of energy, both electricity and heat. For this reason aluminium extraction is carried out most economically where cheap electricity (usually hydroelectricity) is available.

Less active metals could also be extracted by electrolysis. In their cases, aqueous solutions can be used rather than molten compounds. Even so, this is an expensive process compared with using a reducing agent such as carbon, and is seldom used.

ANODISING ALUMINIUM

Aluminium is unusual in being an active metal which does not corrode.

CHAPTER NINE • More about Metals

Aluminium does not require protection against corrosion. There is a thin layer of oxide which adheres to the surface of the aluminium. This seals off the metal from the air and water.

The oxide layer on aluminium can be thickened in a process called **anodising**. *Aluminium* is made at the *positive electrode* (what used to be called the 'anode') in the electrolysis of dilute sulphuric acid.

Oxygen forms at the aluminium electrode and combines with the aluminium to form aluminium oxide.

$$4Al(s) + 3O_2(g) \rightarrow 2Al^{3+}{}_2O^{2-}{}_3(s)$$

Anodised aluminium is even more resistant to corrosion. When it is anodised it becomes dull rather than shiny. This is useful for fittings which could become disfigured by fingerprints. Anodised aluminium can also be dyed attractive colours.

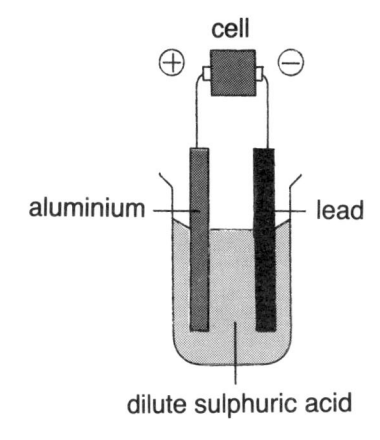

ELECTROPLATING

When one metal is coated with another metal in electrolysis the process is called **electroplating**. The diagram shows how a piece of copper can be electroplated with nickel.

Ni^{2+}(aq) ions gain electrons at the copper electrode and are reduced.

$$Ni^{2+}(aq) + 2e \rightarrow Ni(s)$$

Electroplating produces a thin film of one metal on top of the other. The plating metal is often a precious metal such as gold or silver. Chromium plating is also common.

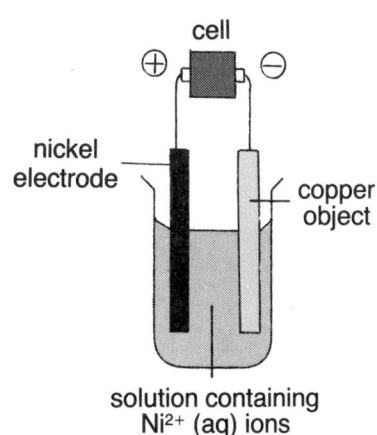

PURIFICATION OF METALS

Electrolysis can be used to purify metals. A piece of impure copper can be purified as shown in the diagram.

At the negative electrode Cu^{2+} (aq) ions (from the solution) are reduced and copper is deposited.

$$Cu^{2+}(aq) + 2e \rightarrow Cu(s)$$

At the positive electrode copper is oxidised and the impure copper goes into the solution.

$$Cu(s) \rightarrow Cu^{2+}(aq) + 2e$$

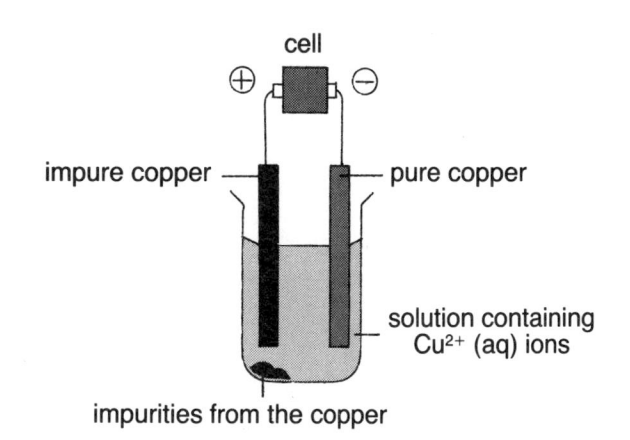

Eventually the positive electrode will disappear into solution and the copper from it will be redeposited on the negative electrode. The impurities from the positive electrode will lie at the bottom of the cell.

CHAPTER NINE • *More about Metals*
Practice Questions

1. The rusting of iron costs the nation dearly, and preventing rusting is an important process. In the following experiments the rate of rusting of an iron nail is being investigated.

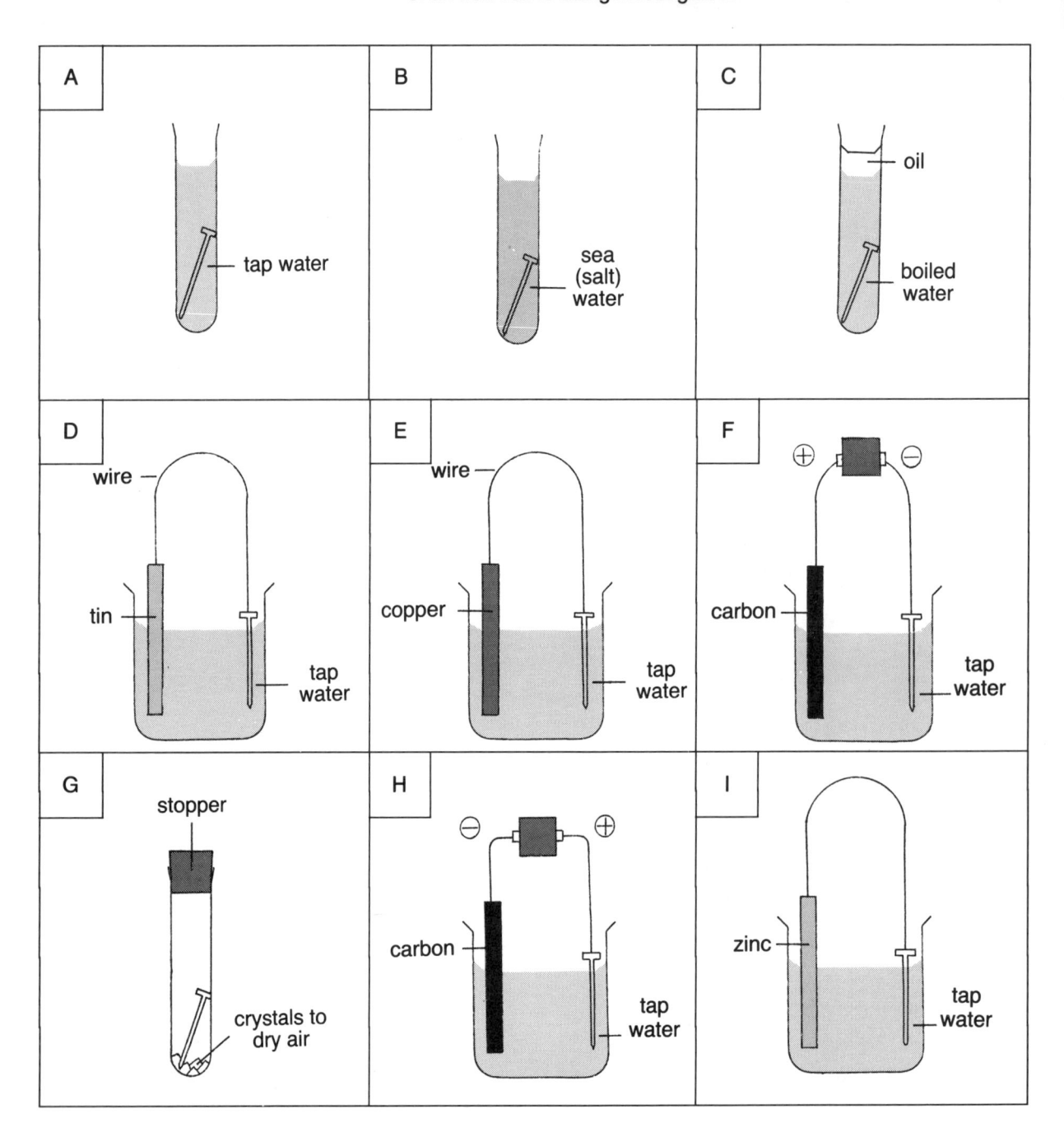

A	B	C
tap water	sea (salt) water	oil / boiled water

D	E	F
wire, tin, tap water	wire, copper, tap water	carbon, tap water (+/−)

G	H	I
stopper, crystals to dry air	carbon, tap water (−/+)	zinc, tap water

(a) In which box (or boxes) will there be **no** rusting of the iron nail?
(b) Which **three** boxes are needed to demonstrate that 'both water and oxygen are required for iron to rust'?
(c) Which box (or boxes) shows iron being protected by sacrificial protection?
(d) In which box (or boxes) will iron rust at a **greater** rate than A?

CHAPTER NINE • *More about Metals*

2. Prevention of the corrosion of metals is of the greatest importance.

A anodising	B tinplating
C connecting iron to scrap magnesium	D connecting to the positive terminal of a battery
E connecting to the negative terminal of a battery	F coating in plastic
G oiling or greasing	H galvanising iron

Which box (or boxes) above could refer to:

(a) sacrificial protection?
(b) a method of protecting aluminium only?
(c) protecting **without** a physical barrier?
(d) a method which fails if the physical barrier is broken?

3. The rusting of iron involves a redox reaction.

A	$Fe^{2+}(aq) + 2e \rightarrow Fe(s)$
B	$Fe(s) \rightarrow Fe^{2+}(aq) + 2e$
C	$Fe(s) \rightarrow Fe^{3+}(aq) + 3e$
D	$Fe^{2+}(aq) \rightarrow Fe^{3+}(aq) + e$
E	$2H_2O(l) + O_2(g) + 4e \rightarrow 4OH^-(aq)$

(a) Which **one** of the above half reactions forms ions which turn ferroxyl indicator blue?
(b) Which **one** of the above half equations forms ions which turn ferroxyl indicator red?
(c) In which box (or boxes) is reduction occurring?

4. Explain why iron coated with zinc does **not** rust even when the coating is damaged, whereas iron coated with tin rusts very badly when the tin coating is damaged.

CHAPTER NINE • *More about Metals*

5.

carbon — carbon

copper(II) chloride solution

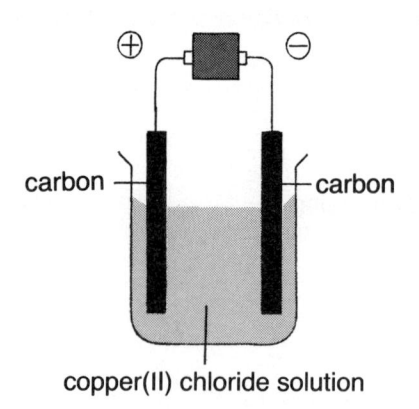

Copper(II) chloride solution contains ions and conducts electricity.

A		B	
	synthesis		decomposition
C		D	
	water		chlorine
E		F	
	copper		oxidation
G		H	
	electrolyte		reduction

(a) Which box refers to the copper(II) chloride solution?
(b) Which box refers to the substance forming at the **negative** electrode?
(c) Which box refers to the process occurring at the **negative** electrode?
(d) Which box refers to what is happening in a solution during electrolysis?

6. Write ion electron equations for each of the following.

(a) Molten aluminium being formed from molten aluminium oxide.
(b) Solid copper forming from copper(II) sulphate solution.
(c) Aluminium ions (solid) forming in anodising.
(d) Hydrogen gas forming in the electrolysis of an acid.
(e) Solid copper oxidising to form copper(II) ions in solution.

PS 7. Draw **labelled** diagrams to illustrate each of the following.

(a) A metal being electroplated with another metal.
(b) Aluminium being anodised.
(c) A method of testing to find if a solution conducts electricity.

82

CHAPTER NINE • *More about Metals*

8. It is very common for electricity to be used in chemistry.

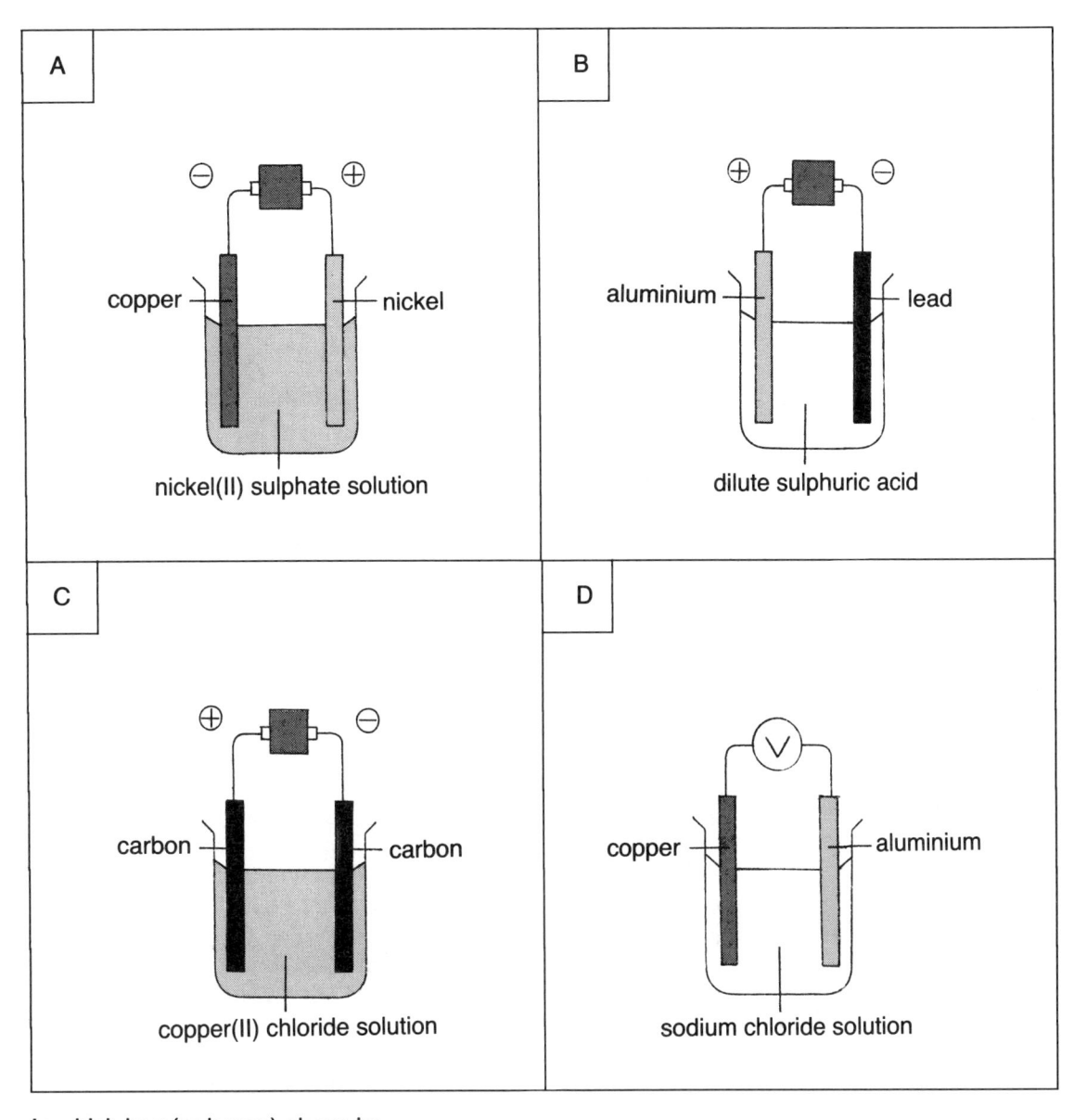

A — copper and nickel electrodes in nickel(II) sulphate solution (copper is negative, nickel is positive)

B — aluminium and lead electrodes in dilute sulphuric acid (aluminium is positive, lead is negative)

C — carbon electrodes in copper(II) chloride solution (left carbon is positive, right carbon is negative)

D — copper and aluminium electrodes in sodium chloride solution, connected to a voltmeter

In which box (or boxes) above is:

(a) a metal being electroplated?
(b) anodising taking place?
(c) the reduction of metal ions in solution taking place?

9. Write the ion electron equations for the reactions at the **negative** and **positive** electrodes in the electrolysis of each of the following.

(a) molten aluminium oxide
(b) molten lead(II) bromide
(c) copper(II) chloride solution
(d) hydrochloric acid
(e) nickel(II) chloride solution

CHAPTER TEN

Plastics and Synthetic Fibres

NATURAL AND SYNTHETIC MATERIALS

Materials can be grouped as natural and **synthetic**. Natural materials come from plants and animals, from farms, forests and quarries. Synthetic materials are made in factories.

Natural materials have been in use for thousands of years. Here are some examples:

- *wool* from sheep and goats;
- *leather* from animal skins;
- *wood* from trees;
- *silk* from silk worms;
- *stone* from rocks;
- *cotton* from plants.

Fabrics have always been made from natural fibres such as wool and cotton. Wool feels warm as it has good insulating properties. Cotton is still used for light summer wear. There are, however, drawbacks to all natural materials. Woolen garments are liable to shrink or stretch if not washed correctly; cotton is difficult to iron; wood requires protection against decay. All natural materials are liable to decompose in certain conditions and may be attacked by bacteria or eaten by certain types of insects. This means, however, that natural materials rot away when they are discarded. They are **biodegradable**.

It is impossible to satisfy the material demands of modern consumer society with natural materials alone. Over the last fifty years an increasing number of synthetic materials have been developed. Most of these are derived from raw materials made from oil. They include **plastics** and **synthetic fibres**.

Properties of Synthetic Materials

Synthetic fibres and plastics have many properties which enable them to take over from natural materials in many areas. They are light, are good thermal and electrical insulators and are not prone to deterioration from dampness.

Plastics are generally resistant to attack by common acids and alkalis as well as not being affected by water. Plastic (PVC) window frames do not require painting. Nylon shirts are 'non-iron'. Plastic kitchen utensils are lighter than their metal counterparts and do not need protection from corrosion. Plastics are ideal as electrical insulators, both as sheathing for wires and as casings for tools and switches.

There are drawbacks, however. This durability means that many plastics are to all extents and purposes indestructible. They are non-biodegradable. Plastic litter does not disintegrate when wet as paper and cardboard do. Plastic rubbish can only be buried out of sight.

CHAPTER TEN • *Plastics and Synthetic Fibres*

There are other problems. For example, like all chemicals derived from oil, they burn. This limits their use in the kitchen— no plastic frying pans or plastic oven-ware are possible.

Some plastics contain elements other than carbon and hydrogen. When these burn, they give off a cocktail of poisonous gases such as carbon monoxide, hydrogen cyanide and hydrogen chloride. Most people who die in house fires nowadays die from poisoning rather than from burns.

POLYMERS

'Plastic' is the word by which the new synthetic materials have come to be known. They are referred to as **polymers** by chemists.

Types of Polymers

There are two types of polymers: **thermoplastic** and **thermosetting**.

Thermoplastic polymers soften and melt when heated. They can be moulded into a variety of shapes and can be spun into fibres. Most polymers are thermoplastic. Polythene and nylon are common examples.

Thermosetting polymers do not melt when heated. They may be made from liquids which harden when heated. Many glues are in this category, and the casings for electrical fittings are made from thermosetting polymers.

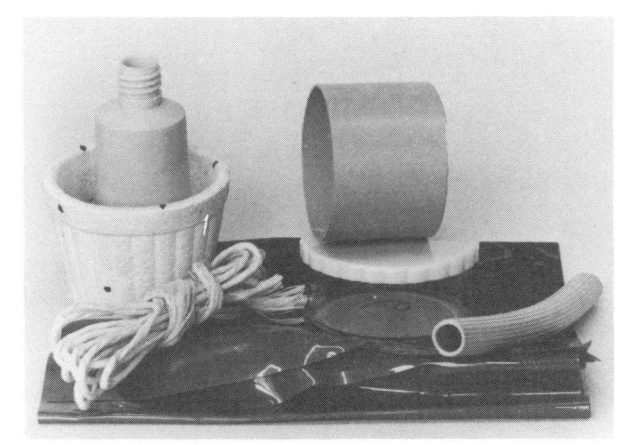

Thermoplastic polymers

Monomers and Polymerisation

Polymers are long chain molecules which are made by the joining together or **polymerisation** of small molecules called **monomers**. The simplest model of polymerisation is a chain of paper clips. Each paper clip is a 'monomer' and the chain is a 'polymer'.

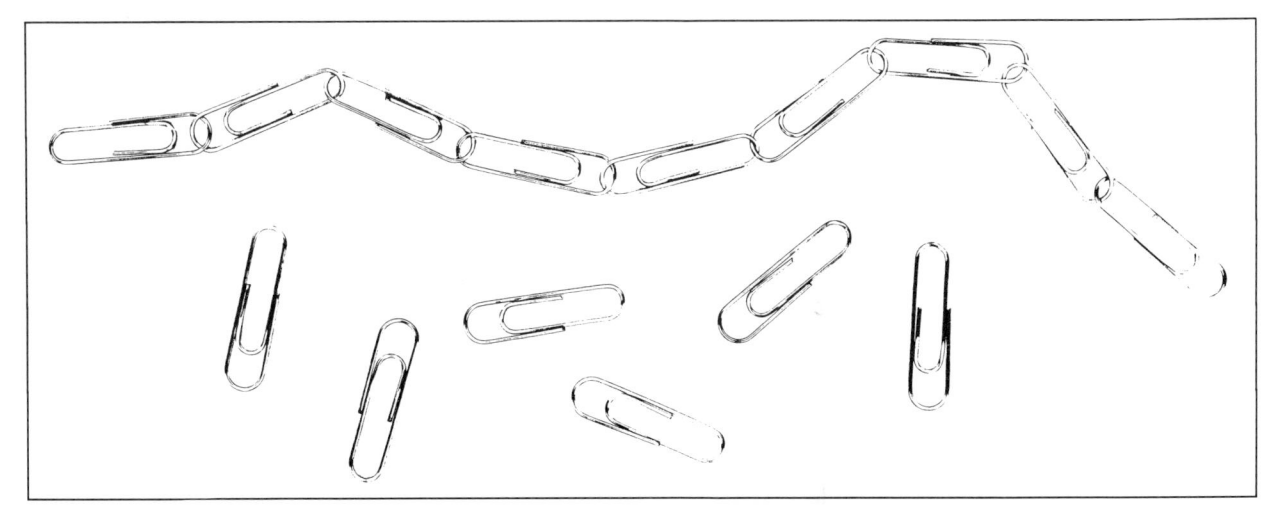

Polymerisation model

CHAPTER TEN • *Plastics and Synthetic Fibres*

One of the first polymers was made by joining together ethene molecules to form poly(ethene), commonly known as polythene. Here is how ethene molecules polymerise:

```
  H   H     H   H     H   H
  |   |     |   |     |   |
  C = C     C = C     C = C
  |   |     |   |     |   |
  H   H     H   H     H   H
```

high pressure and catalyst | polymerises ↓

```
  H   H   H   H   H   H
  |   |   |   |   |   |
- C - C - C - C - C - C -
  |   |   |   |   |   |
  H   H   H   H   H   H
```

Writing out polymer structures in this way takes a long time! Structures of polymers are usually written showing only the **repeating unit**. For poly(ethene) this is:

```
  H   H
  |   |
- C - C -
  |   |
  H   H
```

The structural formula of poly(ethene) is written in the following shortened way.

$$\left(\begin{array}{c} \text{H} \quad \text{H} \\ | \quad | \\ -\text{C} - \text{C}- \\ | \quad | \\ \text{H} \quad \text{H} \end{array} \right)_n$$

In this structural formula 'n' is a very large number. It can be many thousands of units.

This process continues as many thousands of ethene molecules join together and the *polymer* called *poly(ethene)* results. In the same way other types of alkene monomers can join together to form other types of polymers.

A polymer which is formed from alkene monomers is called a **polyalkene**. Each alkene molecule contains a double bond. Alkenes are unsaturated hydrocarbons. The polymers formed are saturated hydrocarbons. This type of polmerisation is called **addition polymerisation**.

Here is a small part of the polymerisation of *monochloroethene* (vinyl chloride) monomers to form *poly(monochloroethene)* or PVC.

```
  H   H     H   H     H   H
  |   |     |   |     |   |
  C = C     C = C     C = C
  |   |     |   |     |   |
  H   Cl    H   Cl    H   Cl
```

high pressure and catalyst | polymerisation ↓

```
  H   H   H   H   H   H
  |   |   |   |   |   |
- C - C - C - C - C - C -
  |   |   |   |   |   |
  H   Cl  H   Cl  H   Cl
```

CHAPTER TEN • *Plastics and Synthetic Fibres*

The repeating unit of PVC is:

```
    H   H
    |   |
  — C — C —
    |   |
    H   Cl
```

The usual way of representing PVC is to write the structural formula as:

$$\left(\begin{array}{c} \text{H} \quad \text{H} \\ | \quad | \\ -\text{C}-\text{C}- \\ | \quad | \\ \text{H} \quad \text{Cl} \end{array} \right)_n$$

Many other polyalkenes are known. Most are known by their trade names rather than their chemical names. Here are some examples.

Monomer	Polymer	Other names	Uses
ethene	poly(ethene)	polythene	packaging
monochloroethene	poly(monochloroethene)	PVC	gutters, rainware
propene	poly(propene)	polypropylene	buckets, kitchenware
styrene	poly(styrene)		packing
tetrafluoroethene	poly(tetrafluoroethene)	PTFE, Teflon, Fluon	non-stick linings
methylmethacrylate	poly(methylmethacrylate)	Perspex	glass substitute

Polyalkenes are thermoplastic. The monomers, alkenes, are made from the products of cracking oil. There are a few naturally occuring polyalkenes, the best known of which is rubber.

Fibres

Polyalkenes are not ideal for spinning into fibres for making fabrics. Other polymers can be more easily spun, the most successful of these is nylon. Nylon is a polymer which bears a resemblance to natural fibres such as wool.

Here is how nylon can be made from the molecules of its monomer.

```
 H           O      H           O      H           O
 |          //      |          //      |          //
 N — □ — C         N — □ — C         N — □ — C
 |           \      |           \      |           \
 H           OH    H           OH    H           OH
```

↓ polymerisation

```
 H           O      H      O      H           O
 |           ||     |      ||     |          //
 N — □ — C — N — □ — C — N — □ C          + 2H₂O
 |                                  \
 H                                  OH
```

The repeating unit in this form of nylon is:

```
    H       O
    |       ||
  — N — □ — C —
```

CHAPTER TEN • *Plastics and Synthetic Fibres*

A reaction in which small molecules join together to form one long molecule with the elimination of water is called **condensation polymerisation**. Nylon is a condensation polymer. It is also a thermoplastic polymer. In the monomer structure above a box was used. The structural formula for the monomer could be as follows:

$$\underset{\text{structural formula}}{\text{H-N-C-C-C-C-C-C}\begin{smallmatrix}\text{O}\\\\\text{OH}\end{smallmatrix}} \quad \text{or} \quad \underset{\text{shortened version}}{\text{H-N-(CH}_2)_5\text{-C}\begin{smallmatrix}\text{O}\\\\\text{OH}\end{smallmatrix}}$$

Other forms of nylon can be made, for example from *two* monomers instead of one:

$$\text{H-N-}\square\text{-N-H} \qquad \text{HO-C-}\square\text{-C-OH}$$

If these monomers are used in the form of two imiscible solutions, then nylon 'fibre' can be made in a beaker.

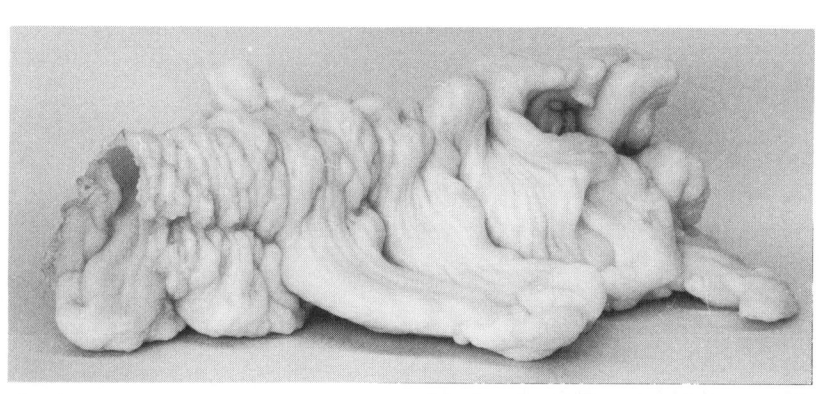

Crude nylon

Most natural fibres such as wool, cotton and silk are condensation polymers.

Repolymerisation

It is possible to 'undo' or depolymerise natural condensation polymers. When this is done the resulting monomers can then be repolymerised. An example of this is regenerating cellulose to form rayon. A polymer such as *rayon* is a *condensation polymer*.

Even a polymer such as casein, a protein in milk (not a fibre), can be regenerated. The resulting polymer can be used for making buttons, pot handles, fibres and adhesives.

Practice Questions

1. Name the polymers made from the following monomers.
    - (*a*) ethene
    - (*b*) propene
    - (*c*) tetrafluoroethene
    - (*d*) styrene
    - (*e*) monochloroethene

CHAPTER TEN • *Plastics and Synthetic Fibres*

2. Polymers occur in many forms and have a wide variety of everyday uses. The grid below includes some common polymers.

A	B	C
oil	ethane	wool
D	E	F
silk	nylon	cotton
G	H	I
poly(ethene)	rocks	PVC

(a) Which box contains the source of most synthetic addition polymers?
(b) Which **three** boxes contain natural polymers?
(c) Which **two** boxes contain polymers made from alkenes?

3. Polymers are compounds which are made from monomers. The grid below includes some examples of monomers.

A	B	C
H H | | C = C | | H H ethene	H H | | H – C – C – H | | H H ethane	O = C = O carbon dioxide
D	E	F
H H | | C = C | | H Cl monochloroethene (vinyl chloride)	H – Cl hydrogen chloride	H | H – C – H | H methane

(a) Which box (or boxes) contains compounds which will polymerise?
(b) Which **two** boxes contain compounds which are produced when PVC, poly(monochloroethene), burns?
(c) Which box (or boxes) could contain **hydrocarbons** which do **not** polymerise?

4. (a) State if you would use a **thermoplastic** polymer or a **thermosetting** polymer to manufacture each of the following.
   (i) ashtray (ii) washing-up basin (iii) electric switch casing
   (iv) drinking cup (v) handle of a frying pan (vi) drain pipe
(b) Explain you answer to (v) above.

CHAPTER TEN • *Plastics and Synthetic Fibres*

5. The chemical name of the polymer Perspex is poly(methyl methacrylate). It is a thermoplastic polymer made from the monomer with the structure:

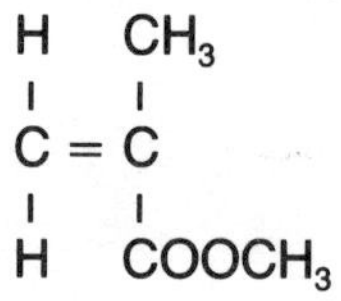

$$\begin{array}{cc} H & CH_3 \\ | & | \\ C = C \\ | & | \\ H & COOCH_3 \end{array} \quad \text{methyl methacrylate}$$

(a) Explain what 'thermoplastic' means.
(b) To which series of compounds does the monomer shown above belong?
(c) What is the formula mass of methyl methacrylate?
(d) Draw the polymer Perspex showing **three** monomers polymerised.

6. Nylon is a polymer which begins to form in the following way:

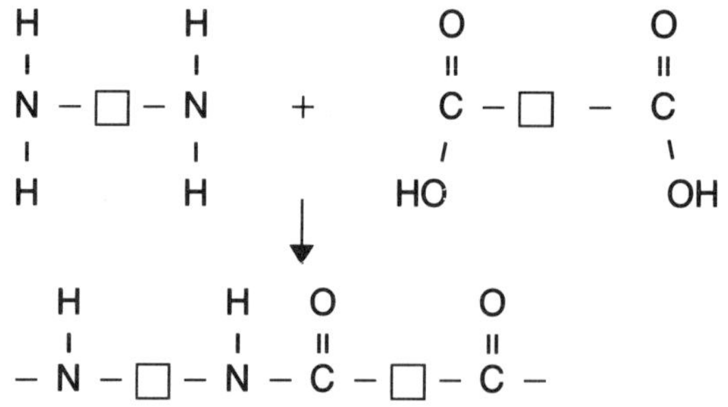

$$\begin{array}{cccc} H & H & O & O \\ | & | & \| & \| \\ N-\square-N & + & C-\square-C \\ | & | & / & \backslash \\ H & H & HO & OH \end{array}$$

↓

$$\begin{array}{cccc} H & H & O & O \\ | & | & \| & \| \\ -N-\square-N-C-\square-C- \end{array}$$

(a) What name is given to the kind of polymerisation shown above?
(b) As well as nylon which **other** substance forms in the above polymerisation?
(c) Copy the above equation, adding another molecule at each end.

7.
> ### Plastics
> Many fractions obtained from crude oil can be used as fuels. Some fractions, however, are turned into compounds which are then used to make plastics.
> These plastics are buried in rubbish tips when they are discarded. However, they *could* be effectively used as fuels. Most plastics give out a great deal of heat when they burn, Poly(ethene), for example, gives out more than twice as much energy in burning as wood does!
> Burning plastics requires great care for not all plastics are simple hydrocarbons.

(a) Name **three** fractions obtained from the fractional distillation of crude oil.
(b) Name the series of monomers used to make plastics which are called addition polymers.
(c) Name the process used to make the monomers for addition polymerisation.
(d) Why do plastics not rot away in rubbish tips?
(e) Why is it said that the use of plastics as fuels requires 'great care for not all plastics are simple hydrocarbons'?

CHAPTER TEN • *Plastics and Synthetic Fibres*

8. Parts of the structural formulae of a number of important polymers are shown below.

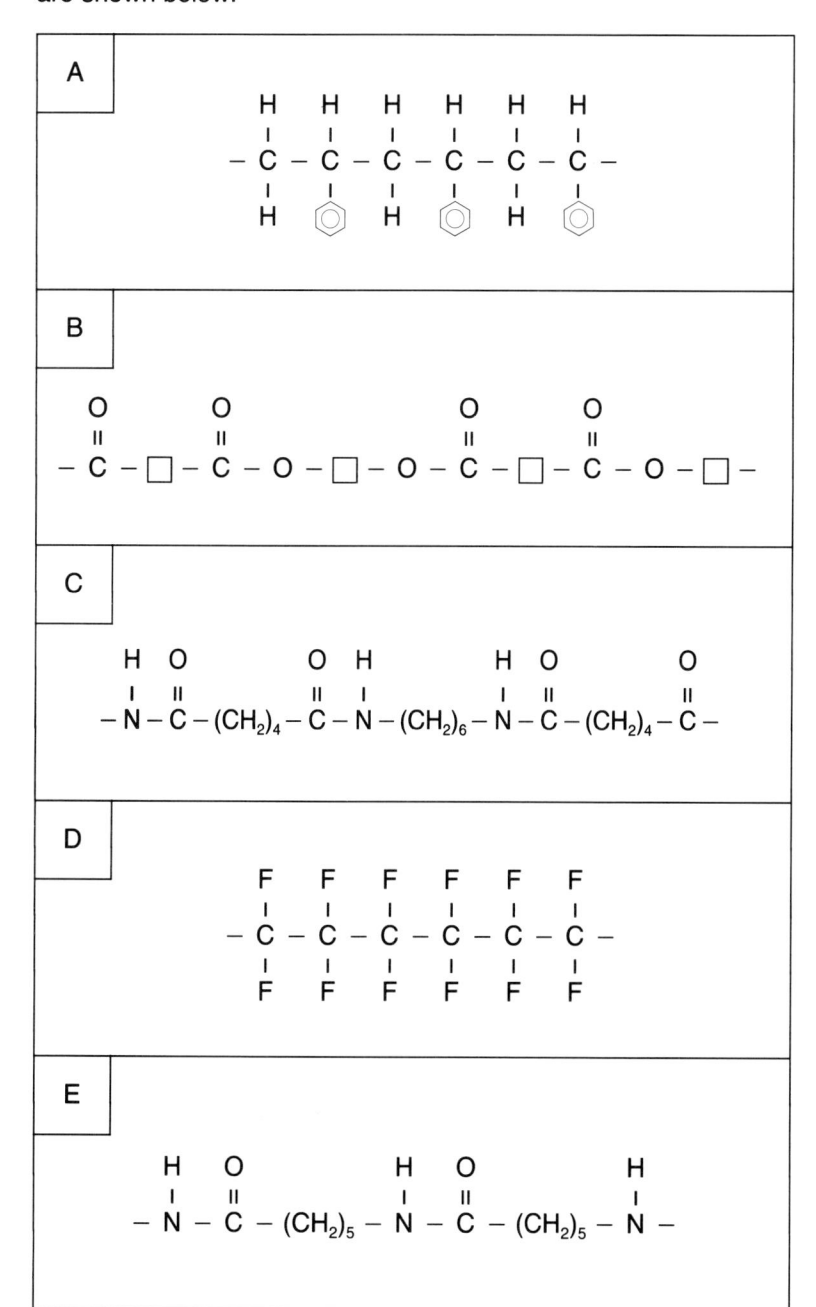

A

$$-\underset{\underset{H}{|}}{\overset{\overset{H}{|}}{C}}-\underset{\underset{\bigcirc}{|}}{\overset{\overset{H}{|}}{C}}-\underset{\underset{H}{|}}{\overset{\overset{H}{|}}{C}}-\underset{\underset{\bigcirc}{|}}{\overset{\overset{H}{|}}{C}}-\underset{\underset{H}{|}}{\overset{\overset{H}{|}}{C}}-\underset{\underset{\bigcirc}{|}}{\overset{\overset{H}{|}}{C}}-$$

B

$$-\overset{O}{\overset{\|}{C}}-\square-\overset{O}{\overset{\|}{C}}-O-\square-O-\overset{O}{\overset{\|}{C}}-\square-\overset{O}{\overset{\|}{C}}-O-\square-$$

C

$$-\underset{}{\overset{H}{\overset{|}{N}}}-\overset{O}{\overset{\|}{C}}-(CH_2)_4-\overset{O}{\overset{\|}{C}}-\overset{H}{\overset{|}{N}}-(CH_2)_6-\overset{H}{\overset{|}{N}}-\overset{O}{\overset{\|}{C}}-(CH_2)_4-\overset{O}{\overset{\|}{C}}-$$

D

$$-\underset{\underset{F}{|}}{\overset{\overset{F}{|}}{C}}-\underset{\underset{F}{|}}{\overset{\overset{F}{|}}{C}}-\underset{\underset{F}{|}}{\overset{\overset{F}{|}}{C}}-\underset{\underset{F}{|}}{\overset{\overset{F}{|}}{C}}-\underset{\underset{F}{|}}{\overset{\overset{F}{|}}{C}}-\underset{\underset{F}{|}}{\overset{\overset{F}{|}}{C}}-$$

E

$$-\overset{H}{\overset{|}{N}}-\overset{O}{\overset{\|}{C}}-(CH_2)_5-\overset{H}{\overset{|}{N}}-\overset{O}{\overset{\|}{C}}-(CH_2)_5-\overset{H}{\overset{|}{N}}-$$

(a) State which of the above represent parts of addition polymers.
(b) Draw the monomer from which polymer **D** is made.
(c) Draw the structural formulae of the **two** monomers from which polymer **C** is made.
(d) Draw the repeating units in polymer **A**.

CHAPTER ELEVEN

Fertilisers

Growing plants require food in the same way that animals do. The 'food' needed for their growth must contain a number of essential elements, of which the most important are *nitrogen*, *phosphorus* and *potassium*. The exact proportions of the three elements depend on the plants and the stages of their growth.

TYPES OF FERTILISERS

Fertilisers contain compounds which are necessary for the growth of plants. These compounds are often salts containing nitrogen, phosphorus and potassium. Examples of fertilisers are:
- potassium sulphate;
- ammonium sulphate;
- calcium phosphate;
- ammonium nitrate;
- urea.

The effectiveness of fertilisers can be estimated from the percentage composition of the essential elements.

The example gives a comparison of two fertilisers.

Example

Which contains more nitrogen, ammonium phosphate or ammonium sulphate?

$(NH_4)_3PO_4$

nitrogen	$3 \times 14 = 42$
hydrogen	$12 \times 1 = 12$
phosphorus	$1 \times 31 = 31$
oxygen	$4 \times 16 = 64$
relative formula mass	$= 149$

percentage nitrogen $= \dfrac{42}{149} \times 100$

$= 28\%$

$(NH_4)_2SO_4$

nitrogen	$2 \times 14 = 28$
hydrogen	$8 \times 1 = 8$
sulphur	$1 \times 32 = 32$
oxygen	$4 \times 16 = 64$
relative formula mass	$= 132$

percentage nitrogen $= \dfrac{28}{132} \times 100$

$= 21\%$

Ammonium phosphate contains more nitrogen than ammonium sulphate.

Solubility of Fertilisers

The mass of essential elements is not the only factor that makes a fertiliser an effective one. After being added to the soil, the fertiliser must then dissolve in water before it can be taken up by the roots of the plant. The compound magnesium phosphate may contain the essential element phosphorus, but the table of solubilities shows that magnesium phosphate is insoluble in water. This means that it is less effective as a fertiliser than soluble compounds of phosphorus.

There is a danger that, in areas of high rainfall or flooding, highly soluble ionic compounds will simply be washed out of the soil. For this reason less soluble fertilisers such as urea (CH_4N_2O), which is not ionic, are often used. Urea dissolves in water more slowly than other fertilisers.

CHAPTER ELEVEN • *Fertilisers*

Natural Fertilisers

Plants grew successfully long before artificial fertilisers were developed. Essential elements are taken into plants *naturally* in different ways.

After death an animal or plant decays and the compounds within it break down into simpler compounds which contain the essential elements. Today this process only occurs in primitive forests or in wilderness areas. In our gardens and public parks dead animals, fallen leaves and rotting plants are quickly removed long before they have a chance to decay!

Plant remains which are used as fertilisers are called *compost*. Animal remains include bone meal, dried blood, manure and processed sewage.

There is a move today to make more use of natural fertiliser and compost in gardening. For example, rather than putting leaves into a dustbin they can be allowed to rot down in a container and then be dug back into the soil.

Natural fertilisers are sometimes used in preference to artificial fertilisers and may be cheaper. In this case the essential elements such as nitrogen are being recycled. Natural fertilisers avoid problems caused when very soluble fertilisers such as nitrates are washed into rivers and reservoirs. The presence of nitrates in rivers and reservoirs is harmful to both animals and humans.

However, it is now impossible to rely on natural fertilisers alone to substain the increasing world population. Artificial fertilisers are needed and their use in agriculture has to be controlled.

Fixing Nitrogen

Nitrogen is essential for the synthesis of **proteins**, chemicals which are present in all living things. However, most living things are unable to absorb this nitrogen from the air. The process of turning 'free' nitrogen in air into nitrogen compounds is called **fixation**.

Some plants such as peas, beans, lupins and clover contain bacteria called **nitrifying bacteria** in their root nodules which can fix nitrogen. These plants increase the fertility of the soil in which they are growing. This was known for a long time before the chemistry of the process was understood. Farmers often allowed a field to remain uncultivated for a year in a rotation of crops. In that year the clover which grew restored nitrogen to the soil. Plants like peas and beans which can fix atmospheric nitrogen are in the *leguminosae* family.

MAKING FERTILISERS

The fixation of atmospheric nitrogen is the first and most important step in the manufacture of artificial fertilisers. **Ammonia** (NH_3) which is formed in fixation is then oxidised to make oxides of nitrogen and finally **nitric acid** (HNO_3). From these two compounds, ammonia and nitric acid, a whole range of fertilisers can be manufactured.

The fixation of nitrogen and hydrogen to form ammonia is called the **Haber process**. Nitric acid is produced from the **Ostwald process**.

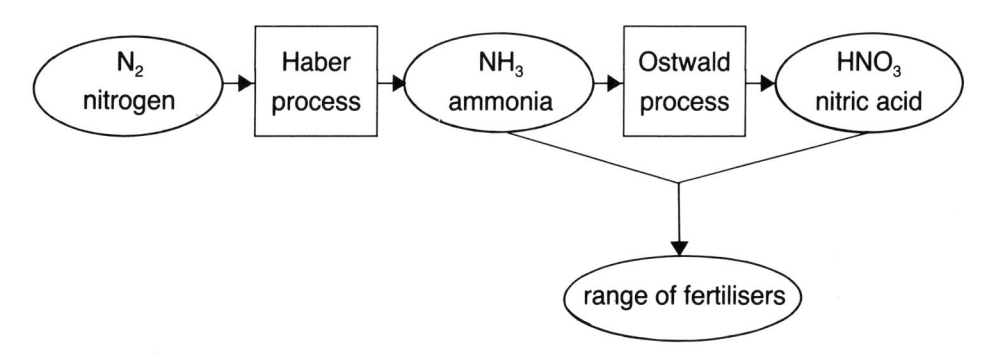

N_2 nitrogen → Haber process → NH_3 ammonia → Ostwald process → HNO_3 nitric acid → range of fertilisers

CHAPTER ELEVEN • *Fertilisers*

The Haber Process (Forming Ammonia)

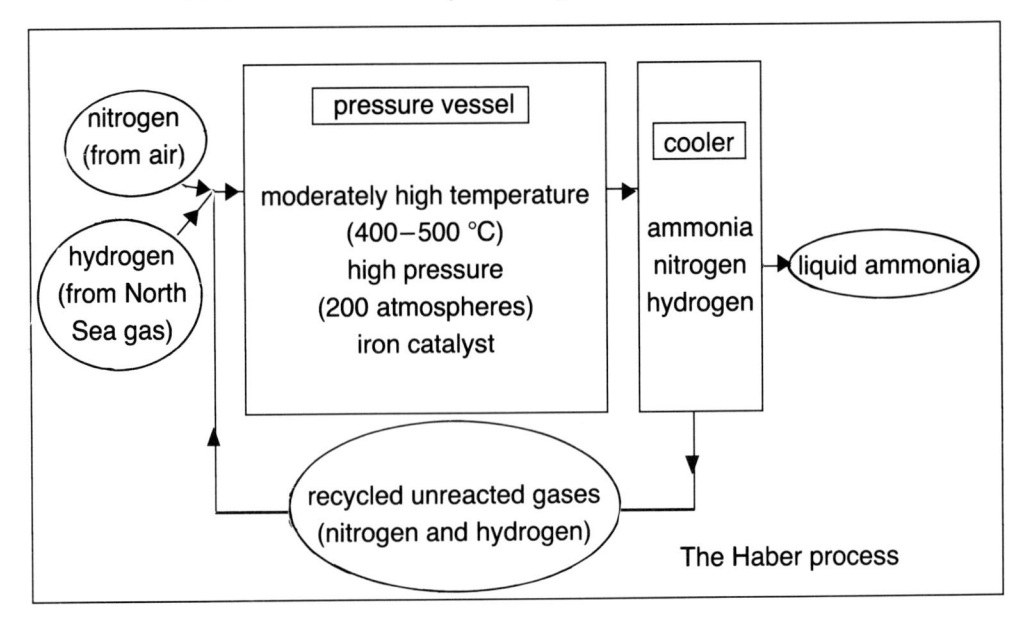

The Haber process

Nitrogen (from air) and hydrogen (from North Sea gas) are fed into a pressure vessel operating at moderately high temperature (400–500 °C), high pressure (200 atmospheres), with an iron catalyst. The output goes to a cooler, where ammonia, nitrogen and hydrogen emerge; ammonia is drawn off as liquid ammonia, and the unreacted gases (nitrogen and hydrogen) are recycled.

The pressure referred to in the diagram, '200 atmospheres', means 200 times normal air pressure. The higher the pressure, the more ammonia forms.

The reaction of nitrogen and hydrogen is a reversible reaction in which the sign ⇌ is used instead of the normal → sign:

$$N_2(g) + 3H_2(g) \rightleftharpoons 2NH_3(g)$$

The rate of the *reverse* reaction increases at high temperatures (compounds normally decompose at high temperatures). In spite of this, the reaction is carried out at a 'moderately high temperature'.

The following table indicates how the choice of temperature used in the Haber process is made.

Low temperature	High temperature
slow reaction	fast reaction
high percentage of ammonia	low percentage of ammonia

(or)

A moderately high temperature is a compromise condition which produces a reasonable yield of ammonia at a moderate rate.

Not all of the hydrogen and nitrogen used in the Haber process is converted into ammonia. This does not matter as ammonia gas liquefies in the cooler and separates as a liquid from the nitrogen and hydrogen gases. The nitrogen and hydrogen can then be recycled.

Making Ammonia in the Laboratory

Ammonia can also be made in the laboratory from ammonium compounds. Ammonia gas is produced when *any ammonium compound* is heated with *any alkali*.

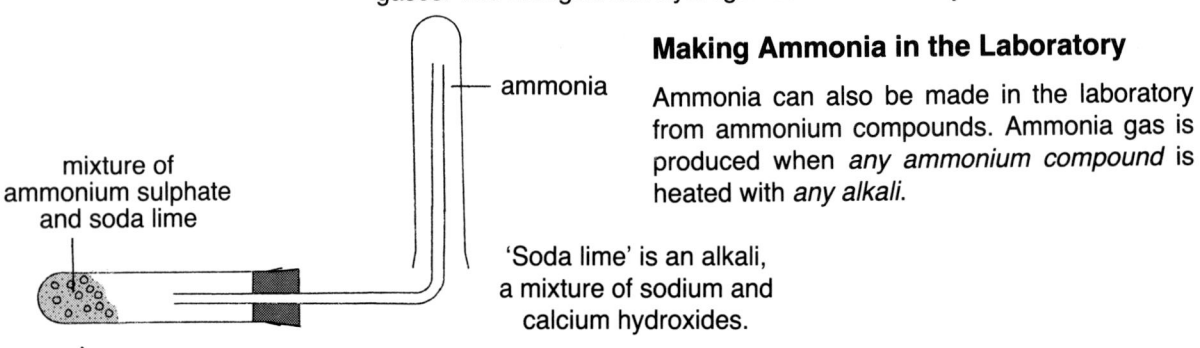

'Soda lime' is an alkali, a mixture of sodium and calcium hydroxides.

$$(NH_4)_2SO_4(s) + 2NaOH(s) \rightarrow Na_2SO_4(s) + 2H_2O(l) + 2NH_3(g)$$

(mixture of ammonium sulphate and soda lime, heated, gives off ammonia)

CHAPTER ELEVEN • *Fertilisers*

Ammonium Compounds

Ammonia is a poisonous gas with a strong unpleasant smell. It can easily be converted into ammonium compounds. These ammonium compounds are especially important as fertilisers.

When ammonia dissolves in water it forms an alkaline solution. The pH of a 1 mol/l solution of ammonia is about 12.

$$\text{ammonia} + \text{water} \rightarrow \text{ammonium hydroxide}$$
$$NH_3(g) + H_2O(l) \rightarrow NH_4^+(aq) + OH^-(aq)$$

The experiment shown demonstrates how soluble ammonia is in water.

A solution of ammonia in water, ammonium hydroxide, neutralises acids to form ammonium salts. Here is an example of ammonium hydroxide neutralising an acid.

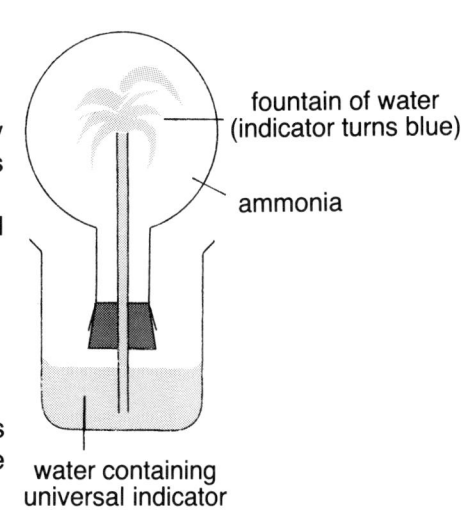

ammonium hydroxide + hydrochloric acid → ammonium chloride + water
    (alkali)   (acid)   (salt)
$$NH_4OH(aq) + HCl(aq) \rightarrow NH_4Cl(aq) + H_2O(l)$$

Nitric Acid

Nitric acid forms when nitrogen dioxide is dissolved in water. Nitrogen dioxide *cannot* be made by burning either nitrogen or ammonia.

Nitrogen dioxide forms when a spark is passed through air. This happens during thunderstorms and in the sparking plugs in car engines. The small amounts of nitrogen dioxide produced find their way into the soil as nitrates.

Sparking air provides the enormous amount of energy required to break the strong bonds in the nitrogen molecule and enables nitrogen to combine with oxygen.

Nitrogen dioxide can be made by sparking air in a laboratory. It is a dangerous and an expensive method, and is not economical for the manufacture of nitrogen dioxide on a large scale.

The Ostwald Process (Manufacture of Nitric Acid)

Nitrogen dioxide is made industrially by the catalytic oxidation of ammonia in the **Ostwald** process.

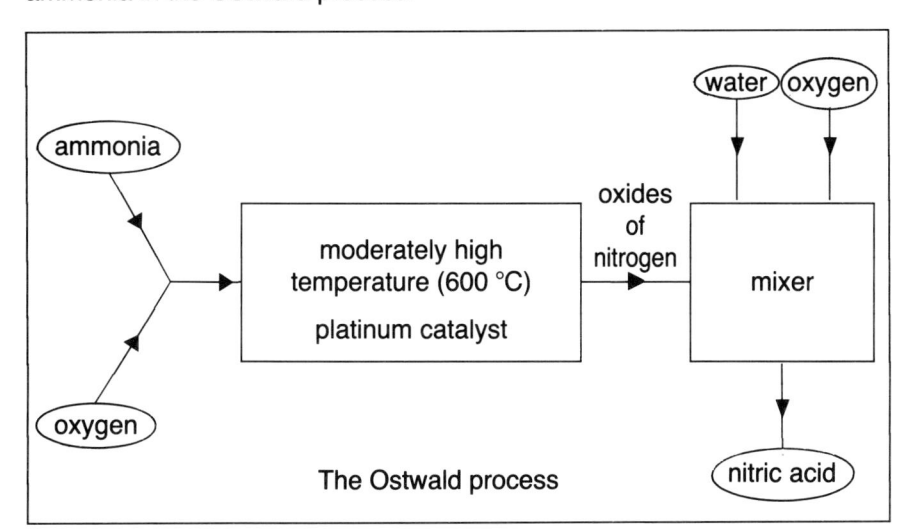

The Ostwald process

$$\text{ammonia} + \text{oxygen} \rightarrow \text{nitrogen dioxide} + \text{water}$$
$$NH_3 + O_2 \rightarrow NO_2 + H_2O \quad \text{(unbalanced)}$$

$$\text{oxygen} + \text{nitrogen dioxide} + \text{water} \rightarrow \text{nitric acid}$$
$$O_2 + NO_2 + H_2O \rightarrow HNO_3 \quad \text{(unbalanced)}$$

CHAPTER ELEVEN • *Fertilisers*

This process can be carried out in a laboratory as shown in the diagram.

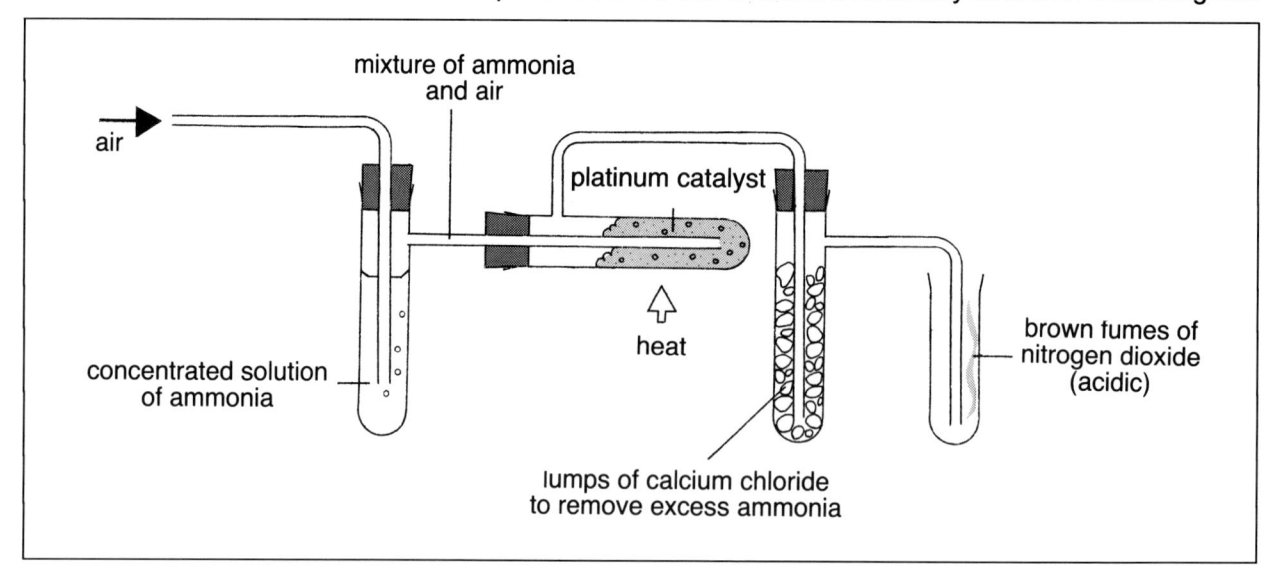

The reaction of ammonia and oxygen (or air) is exothermic. After a time the platinum catalyst can be seen to glow red hot. Even when the source of heat is removed the catalyst will continue to glow.

Nitrates

Nitric acid reacts to form nitrate salts with hydroxides, oxides and carbonates. All nitrate salts are soluble in water and any of the methods described in Chapter Six for making soluble salts can be used.

Some Chemical Tests

The presence of potassium ions, ammonium ions and other ions in fertilisers can be shown by different chemical tests.

Flame Tests

You may have learned to carry out flame tests as a practical technique. Some metal ions will colour a Bunsen flame. These ions are listed in the *Data Booklet*.

Here are some of the metal ions which are found in fertilisers.

Element	Ion	Flame colour
sodium	Na^+	yellow
potassium	K^+	lilac
calcium	Ca^{2+}	orange-red

Flame testing

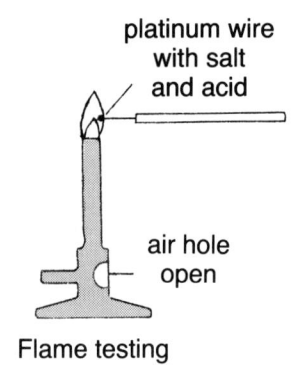

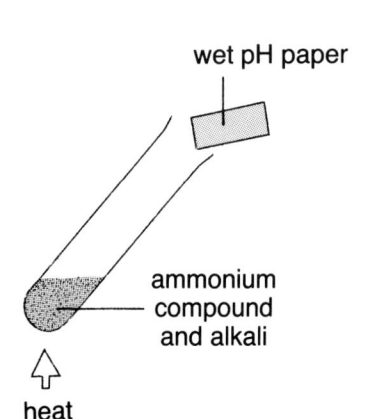

Test for Ammonium Ion

The presence of the ammonium ion can be detected by warming the ammonium compound with an alkali. Ammonia is given off. This turns wet pH paper a blue colour.

Ammonia is the only common gas which forms an alkaline solution.

CHAPTER ELEVEN • *Fertilisers*

THE NITROGEN CYCLE

Nitrogen makes up the greater part of air. It can be fixed in the root nodules of plants of the *leguminosae* family or, industrially, by the Haber process. Finding its way into animals which feed on plants, it will eventually return to the atmosphere in some form when the animals die or the plants decay. This interchange of nitrogen between living things and the air is called the **nitrogen cycle**.

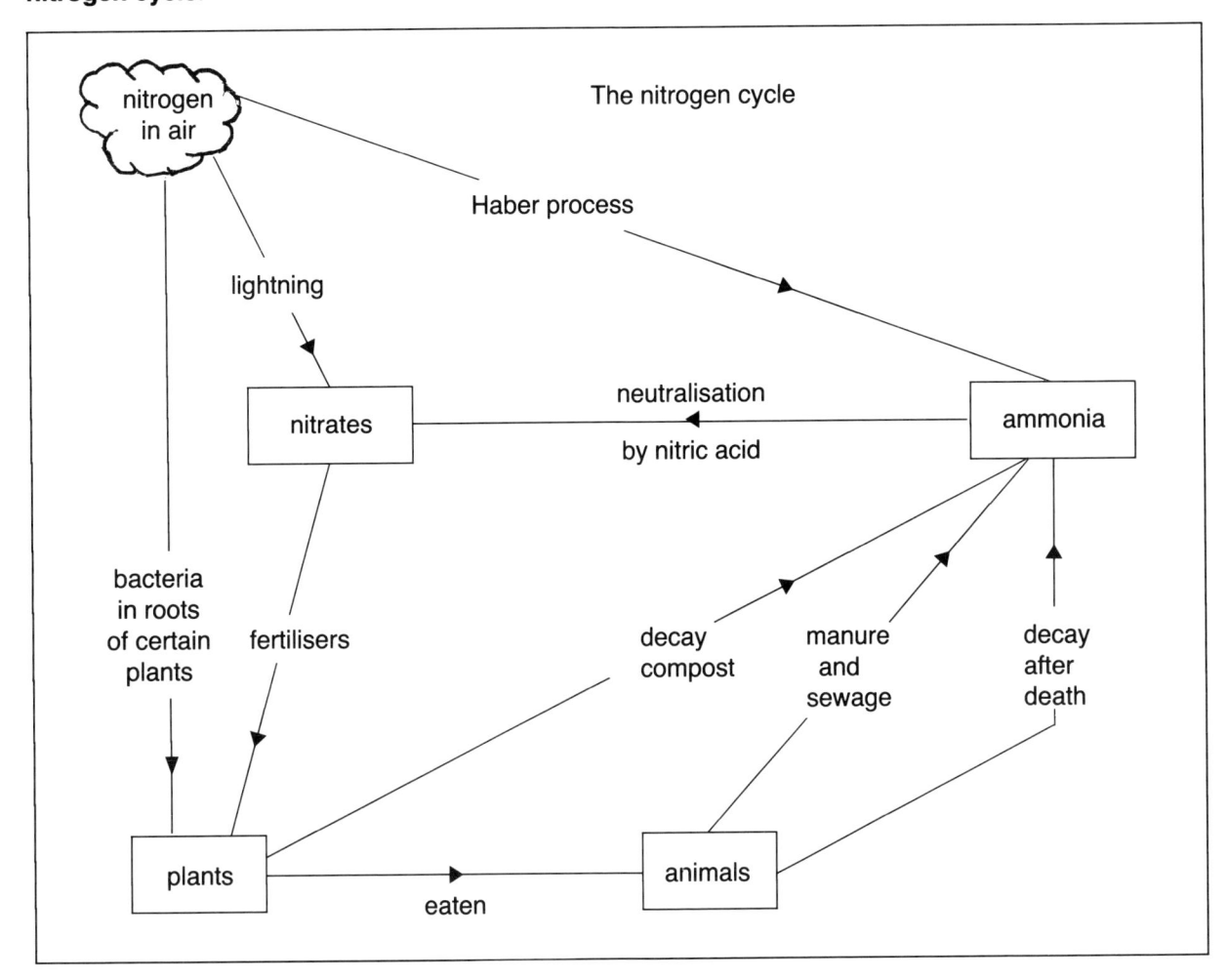

The nitrogen cycle — a diagram showing: nitrogen in air → Haber process → ammonia; nitrogen in air → lightning → nitrates; nitrates ← neutralisation by nitric acid ← ammonia; bacteria in roots of certain plants → plants; fertilisers (from nitrates) → plants; plants → animals (eaten); plants → decay/compost → ammonia; animals → manure and sewage → ammonia; animals → decay after death → ammonia.

Practice Questions

1. Name **three** 'essential' elements for plant growth.

2. Calculate the percentage mass of:
   (a) potassium in potassium sulphate.
   (b) nitrogen in ammonium nitrate.
   (c) phosphorus in calcium phosphate.

3. Explain how nitrogen from the atmosphere can be taken into certain plants.

4. The solubility of a fertiliser in water is important.
   Explain why this is so.

CHAPTER ELEVEN • *Fertilisers*

5. The flow diagram represents the Haber process.

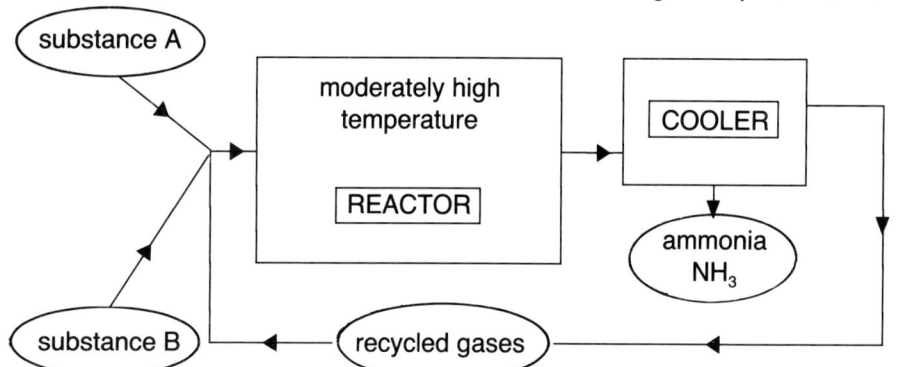

   (a) Name substances A and B.
   (b) Name the catalyst used in the reactor.
   (c) Name the 'recycled gases'.
   (d) Why is the reaction carried out at a 'moderately high temperature'?

6. Copy and complete the table below using the following entries: slow reaction rate; fast reaction rate; low percentage of ammonia; high percentage of ammonia.

Low temperature	High temperature

7. **PS** Ammonia gas can be made in the laboratory by heating together powdered ammonium sulphate and powdered soda lime. Ammonia is soluble in water and is collected in a dry test tube.

   Draw a **labelled** diagram showing this method of preparing ammonia.

8. **Name** the main substance formed when:

   (a) ammonia dissolves in water
   (b) nitrogen reacts with hydrogen in the Haber process
   (c) potassium hydroxide reacts with nitric acid
   (d) ammonium sulphate is heated with sodium hydroxide
   (e) ammonium hydroxide neutralises nitric acid.

9. Write the formulae for each of the following.

   (a) ammonia   (b) nitrogen
   (c) ammonium hydroxide (d) ammonium chloride
   (e) ammonium nitrate   (f) ammonium sulphate
   (g) nitric acid   (h) calcium nitrate

10. **PS** Describe how you could demonstrate that ammonia gas was soluble in water.

11. The flow diagram illustrates the process used to make nitric acid.

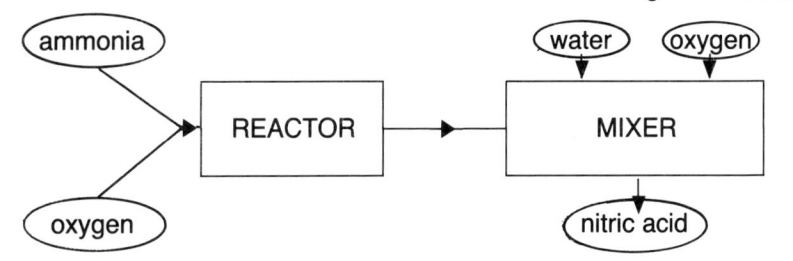

    (a) What is the name of the process illustrated?
    (b) What is the source of ammonia for this process?
    (c) Why is oxygen not directly combined with nitrogen?
    (d) Heat is given out in the reaction. What is such a reaction called?

12. Write **balanced** chemical equations for the reactions of:

    (a) potassium hydroxide and nitric acid

CHAPTER ELEVEN • *Fertilisers*

(b) magnesium carbonate and nitric acid
(c) copper(II) oxide and nitric acid
(d) ammonium hydroxide and nitric acid.

13. Describe how to make a pure dry sample of calcium nitrate starting from calcium carbonate and dilute nitric acid.

14.

A Na^+	B H_2	C K^+
D N_2	E NO_2	F NH_3
G O_2	H Ca^{2+}	I H_2O

Which box (or boxes) contains a substance which:
(a) is taken in by nitrifying bacteria?
(b) forms an acid solution?
(c) gives a lilac flame colour?
(d) forms an alkaline solution?
(e) is formed in the Haber process?
(f) is a reactant in the Ostwald process?

15. Use the table of solubilities to answer this question.
    (a) Make a table with the headings '**soluble**' and '**insoluble**' and enter in it the following compounds:
    ammonium nitrate; calcium carbonate; calcium phosphate; ammonium sulphate; magnesium phosphate; ammonium phosphate; potassium nitrate.
    (b) What do you notice, in general, about the solubility of nitrogen compounds?

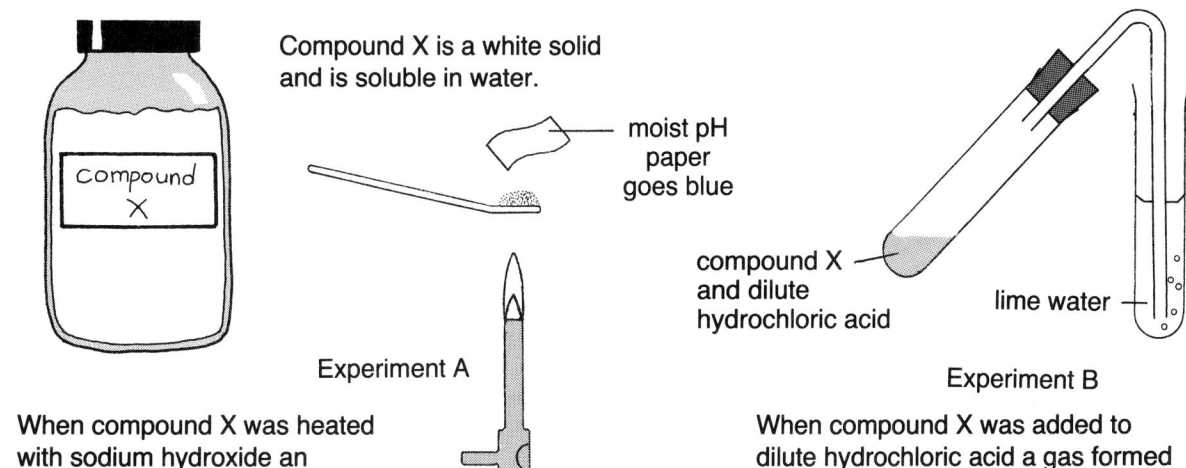

16. Compound X is a white solid and is soluble in water.

    moist pH paper goes blue

    compound X and dilute hydrochloric acid

    lime water

    Experiment A

    Experiment B

    When compound X was heated with sodium hydroxide an alkaline gas formed.

    When compound X was added to dilute hydrochloric acid a gas formed which turned lime water chalky.

    (a) What does experiment **A** tell you about compound X?
    (b) What does experiment **B** tell you about compound X?
    (c) Suggest a name for compound X.
    (d) Write the formula for compound X.
    (e) Find compound X in the table of solubilities. Does the entry agree that it is 'soluble in water'?

99

CHAPTER TWELVE

Carbohydrates and Related Substances

CARBOHYDRATES

Carbohydrates are naturally occuring compounds which contain carbon, hydrogen and oxygen.

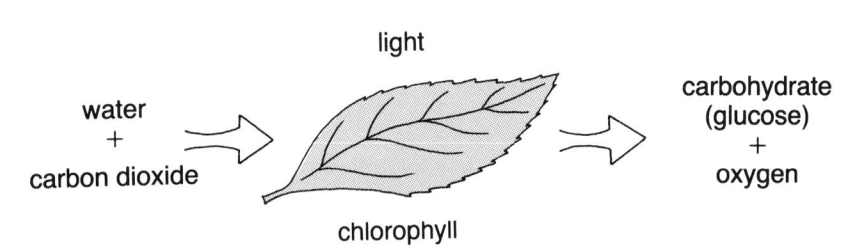

Photosynthesis

Carbohydrates are formed when carbon dioxide and water react in the leaves of plants in a process called **photosynthesis**. Oxygen is also produced in the reaction. Photosynthesis is activated by the sun's light energy which is absorbed by chlorophyll, a green substance present in the leaves of plants.

water + carbon dioxide → (light, chlorophyll) → carbohydrate (glucose) + oxygen

Respiration

Carbohydrates can be thought of as having 'trapped' energy from the sun. This energy can be used again by plants and also by animals which have eaten the plants. When plants and animals utilise carbohydrates to produce energy the process is called **respiration**. Respiration is the opposite of photosynthesis.

In photosynthesis energy is absorbed whereas in respiration energy is released.

$$\text{carbohydrate} + \text{oxygen} \rightarrow \text{carbon dioxide} + \text{water} + (\text{energy})$$

Carbohydrates ('food') are to animals and plants what oil products ('fuel') are to machines.

The formation of carbon dioxide and water in respiration shows that carbohydrates contain carbon and hydrogen.

food → oxygen → CO_2 (lime water turns chalky) and H_2O (mirror steams up) → energy

The products of respiration

CHAPTER TWELVE • *Carbohydrates and Related Substances*

Although we usually think of our body's 'energy' in terms of movement, this is only one form of energy which is produced. Heat energy is also produced, as is sound, and even, in some living creatures, light. Energy is also needed in living organisms for growth.

The Carbon Cycle

Photosynthesis uses up carbon dioxide from the air and produces oxygen. Respiration does the opposite. As the level of these gases remains fairly constant in the atmosphere, there is clearly a balance between the two processes.

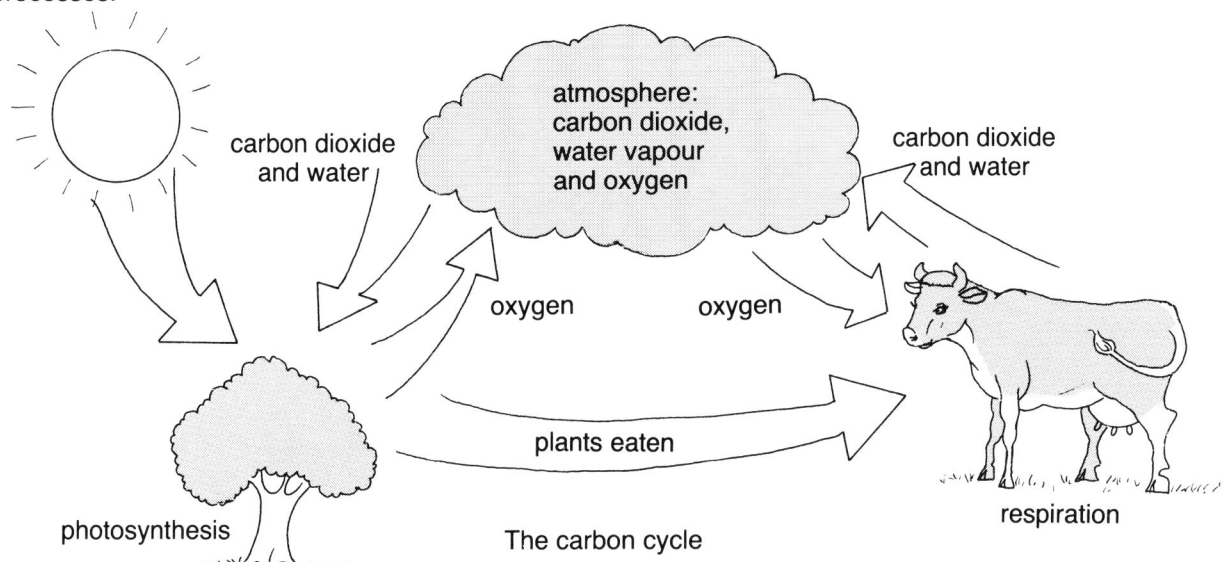

The carbon cycle

Recently concern has been expressed at activities which threaten to upset the balance of this cycle. Extra amounts of carbon dioxide have been produced by the burning of hydrocarbon fuels in the last hundred years. The growth in the world's population has also contributed to this increase. At the same time, extensive clearing of forests has taken place.

The effect of these activities over a long period of time will be to increase the proportion of carbon dioxide in the atmosphere. Most scientists agree that this will cause the temperatures on earth to rise. This will result in what has been called the 'greenhouse effect'.

Common Carbohydrates

The carbohydrate which is formed in plants in photosynthesis is **glucose**. However, glucose is only one of a number of carbohydrates.

Fructose is an isomer of glucose. Carbohydrates such as glucose and fructose have the same molecular formulae but different structural formulae.

Here are some common carbohydrates.

Carbohydrate	Molecular formula
glucose	$C_6H_{12}O_6$
fructose	$C_6H_{12}O_6$
maltose	$C_{12}H_{22}O_{11}$
sucrose	$C_{12}H_{22}O_{11}$
starch	polymer
cellulose	polymer

Carbohydrates contain chains or rings of carbon atoms with the general

CHAPTER TWELVE • *Carbohydrates and Related Substances*

formula $(CH_2O)_n$. Carbohydrates such as glucose and fructose with six carbon atoms in their molecules are called **monosaccharides**. Maltose and sucrose molecules with twelve carbon atoms are double the length of those of glucose and fructose and are called **disaccharides**. Starch is a **polysaccharide**. Starch molecules contain hundreds of carbon atoms.

Disaccharides and polysaccharides form when the simpler monosaccharides join together with the loss of water.

$$2C_6H_{12}O_6 \rightarrow C_{12}H_{22}O_{11} + H_2O$$
monosaccharide   disaccharide

$$nC_6H_{12}O_6 \rightarrow \text{polysaccharide} + nH_2O$$
monosaccharide

In the second example 'n' is a large number.

The formation of a polysaccharide such as starch from a monosaccharide such as glucose is another example of condensation polymerisation. Plants contain starch which forms when glucose molecules polymerise.

Mono, di, and polysaccharides differ in their chain length and also in some of their chemical properties. The short chain molecules are soluble in water. The longer chained molecules are less soluble. Some carbohydrates such as glucose and sucrose have a sweet taste.

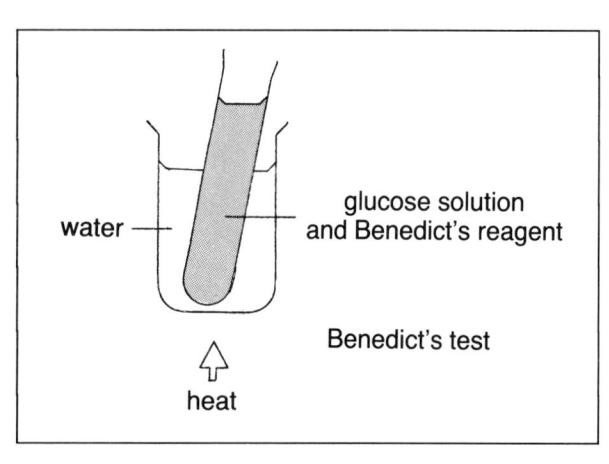

Two Chemical Tests

1. A blue solution called **Benedict's reagent** turns a *red colour* when heated with glucose, fructose or maltose. Carbohydrates which give a positive test with Benedict's reagent are called **reducing sugars**.

   Sucrose and the polysaccharides such as starch do not affect Benedict's reagent.

2. When yellow iodine solution is added to starch solution a black colour is formed. The other carbohydrates do not affect iodine solution.

Benedict's test (diagram: water bath heated, with test tube containing glucose solution and Benedict's reagent)

A summary of the properties of some common carbohydrates is given in the table.

Carbohydrate	Type	Formula	Notes
glucose	monosaccharide	$C_6H_{12}O_6$	soluble, sweet, turns Benedict's reagent red
fructose	monosaccharide	$C_6H_{12}O_6$	soluble, sweet, turns Benedict's reagent red
maltose	disaccharide	$C_{12}H_{22}O_{11}$	soluble, turns Benedict's reagent red
sucrose	disaccharide	$C_{12}H_{22}O_{11}$	soluble, sweet
starch	polysaccharide	polymer	slightly 'soluble', turns iodine solution black

Tyndall Beam

There is another way of distinguishing between the monosaccharides and the polysaccharide starch. If a beam of light is shone through water containing starch, it will show an intense beam. A glucose solution will have no such beam.

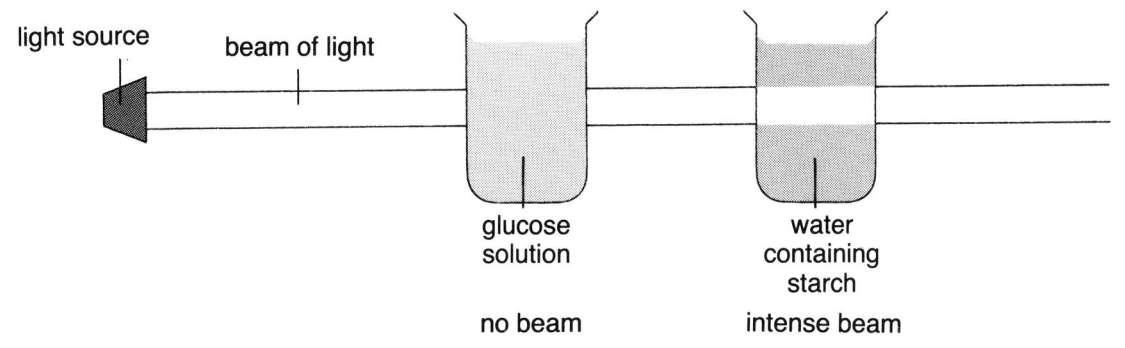

CHAPTER TWELVE • *Carbohydrates and Related Substances*

The effect in the starch is called the **Tyndall beam**. The intense beam is caused by the reflection of the light by large groups of starch molecules. Starch does not really dissolve in water. This is why it is described as 'water containing starch' rather than a solution of starch. Starch forms a suspension of large particles in water which is known as a **colloid**.

Digestion

Carbohydrates and other foods are carried round the body in the bloodstream. To pass into the bloodstream molecules of carbohydrates have to pass through the wall of the gut. In the digestive system large starch molecules are broken down into smaller glucose molecules which are soluble in water. This process is called **digestion**.

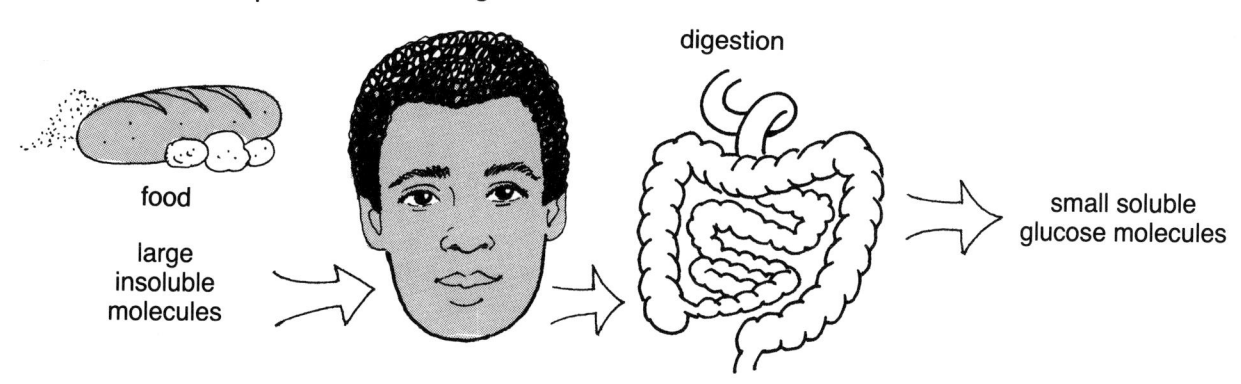

Starch molecules are broken down in the digestive system by the addition of water and the effect of both acid and biological catalysts called **enzymes**.

$$\text{starch} + \text{water} \rightarrow \text{glucose}$$

The breaking down of long chain molecules by the addition of water is called **hydrolysis**. Hydrolysis is the opposite of condensation, in which water is eliminated.

Glucose is carried around the body in the bloodstream. It reacts with oxygen in the cells of the body in the process of respiration.

Oxygen and the products of respiration, carbon dioxide and water, are also carried in the bloodstream. Oxygen, carbon dioxide and water vapour all enter and leave the body through the lungs.

FERMENTATION

Fruits and vegetables which contain starch or glucose are the source of alcoholic drinks. The type of drink varies with the plant source as shown in the table.

What is described as 'alcohol' is called **ethanol** and is one of the members of a series of compounds called **alkanols**.

Drink	Source
wine	grapes
beer	hops
cider	apples
whisky	barley
vodka	potatoes
brandy	grapes

CHAPTER TWELVE • *Carbohydrates and Related Substances*

```
    H   H
    |   |
H - C - C - OH
    |   |
    H   H
   ethanol
```

Ethanol forms from carbohydrates in a process called **fermentation**. An enzyme present in yeast, a living organism, acts as a catalyst for this reaction.

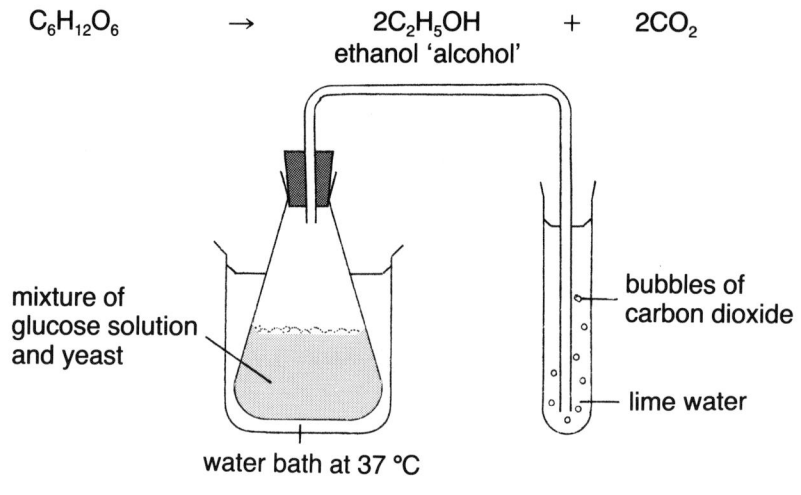

$$C_6H_{12}O_6 \rightarrow 2C_2H_5OH + 2CO_2$$
$$\text{ethanol 'alcohol'}$$

Fermentation

Carbon dioxide is a byproduct of this reaction. Fermentation is an important source of carbon dioxide.

Conditions must be controlled in the large scale production of alcoholic drinks. The enzymes in yeast are complex compounds which are sensitive to changes in both temperature and pH. They cannot tolerate high concentrations of alcohol and are killed off when the concentration of alcohol exceeds a certain point.

Strength of Alcoholic Drinks

After a few days of fermentation the rate will slow down and carbon dioxide will stop bubbling. There may still be glucose left in the solution but as the concentration of alcohol increases, the effectiveness of the enzyme is reduced. The alcohol 'poisons' the yeast cells.

Drinks made by fermentation alone include beer, cider and wine. The concentration of alcohol in wines is around 10%.

Drinks which contain larger amounts of alcohol, for example whisky or brandy, are made by distillation. They have alcohol concentrations of over 40%.

Distillation

Distillation increases the alcohol concentration of the fermentation products.

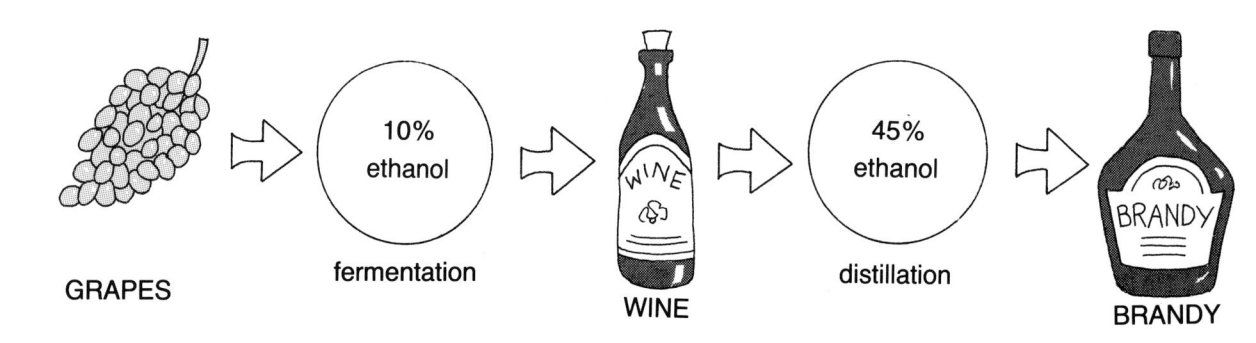

Making brandy

CHAPTER TWELVE • *Carbohydrates and Related Substances*

When a mixture of liquids is heated, the one with the lowest boiling point boils off first. The liquid which boils first in the distillation illustrated is ethanol. The temperature when this happens will be about 78 °C. Ethanol can be separated from water by using distillation.

Liquid	Boiling point (°C)
water	100
ethanol	78

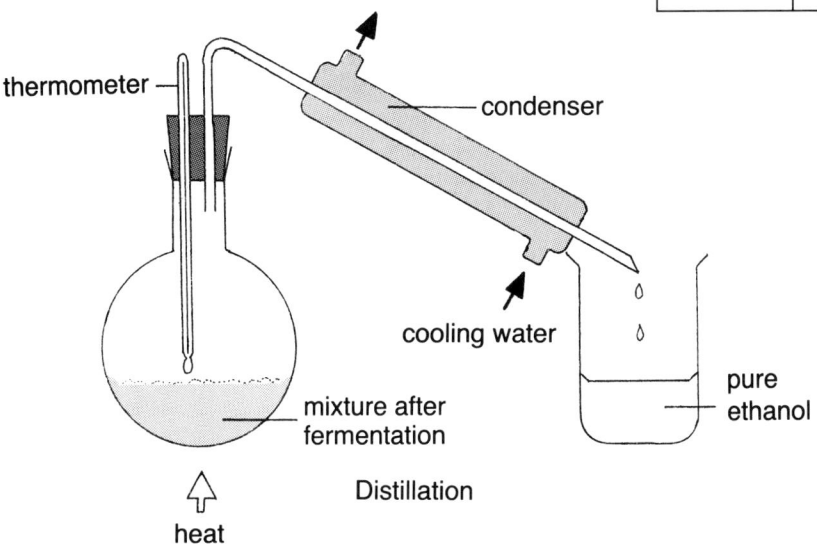

Distillation

Effects of Alcohol

All the alkanols are poisonous. Only ethanol is present in alcoholic drinks in any quantities. The body can tolerate small amounts of ethanol and it has become known as a 'socially acceptable drug'.

Alchoholic drinks have, however, unpredictable effects and even small amounts impair the working of the mind and body. Tasks requiring care become difficult and manipulation clumsy; speech becomes slurred and movements unsteady; some people become aggressive. Reaction times are slowed down and people become more accident prone. The risk of having a car accident is greatly increased, which is why it is illegal for car drivers to have over the legal limit of alcohol in the blood. The rule is 'Do not drink and drive'.

In the long term, alcohol consumption can lead to liver damage and can increase the chances of heart, liver and other diseases. The disease called alcoholism can develop in heavy drinkers who are addicted to alcohol.

What should you call people who slaughter 1,100 a year?

IF YOU DRINK AND DRIVE YOU'RE A MENACE TO SOCIETY.

Practice Questions

1. Give the formulae of substances W, X, Y and Z in the following equations of reactions involving carbohydrates.

    (a) $C_{12}H_{22}O_{11} + W \rightarrow 2C_6H_{12}O_6$
    (b) $6CO_2 + 6H_2O \rightarrow C_6H_{12}O_6 + 6X$
    (c) $C_6H_{12}O_6 \rightarrow 2C_2H_5OH + 2Y$
    (d) $2C_6H_{12}O_6 \rightarrow Z + H_2O$

2. Describe how to distinguish between glucose and starch using:

    (a) Benedict's reagent
    (b) iodine solution
    (c) a Tyndall beam.

CHAPTER TWELVE • *Carbohydrates and Related Substances*

3. Photosynthesis is a process which takes place in plants. Respiration takes place in both plants and animals and is the opposite process to photosynthesis.
   The grid shows some of the substances which are involved in these processes.

A water	B oxygen
C carbon dioxide	D light
E glucose	F chlorophyll
G heat	H starch

   (a) Which **two** boxes contain the products of photosynthesis?
   (b) Which box contains a chemical which traps light energy?
   (c) Which box contains a polymer?
   (d) Which **two** boxes contain the products of respiration?

4. Give **two** reasons why the level of carbon dioxide in the atmosphere has risen in recent years.

5. Carbohydrates are transported through the bloodstream.

   Give **two** reasons why starch must be hydrolysed to glucose before this can happen.

6. Ethanol (alcohol) and carbon dioxide form when glucose solution is fermented.

   $$C_6H_{12}O_6 \rightarrow 2C_2H_5OH \rightarrow 2CO_2$$

   (a) State **two** conditions which must be controlled in the fermentation of glucose.
   (b) What is the mass of
      (i) 1 mole of glucose?
      (ii) 2 moles of carbon dioxide?
   (c) What mass of gas forms in the above reaction when 9 g of glucose is used, and fermentation stops when 40% of the glucose has reacted?
   (d) Give the test for carbon dioxide.

7. Consult the *Data Booklet* for this question.

   (a) What are the boiling points of (i) octane, (ii) cyclohexane?
   (b) Explain why a mixture of these two liquids can be separated by distillation.

CHAPTER TWELVE • *Carbohydrates and Related Substances*

8. Carbohydrates are naturally occurring compounds which are also called saccharides.

A glucose	B chlorophyll
C maltose	D sucrose
E starch	F fructose
G iodine	H water

   (a) Which box (or boxes) could refer to monosaccharides?
   (b) Which **two** boxes refer to substances which form when glucose polymerises?
   (c) Which **two** substances react to give a black colour?
   (d) Which substance always forms in a condensation reaction?
   (e) Which substance has a sweet taste but does **not** react with Benedict's reagent?

9. Here is the structural formula of the compound known as 'alcohol' which is found in alcholic drinks.

$$\begin{array}{c} \text{H} \quad \text{H} \\ | \quad \; | \\ \text{H} - \text{C} - \text{C} - \text{OH} \\ | \quad \; | \\ \text{H} \quad \text{H} \end{array}$$

   'alcohol'

   (a) Copy and complete these sentences:
       'Alcohol' is a member of the alkanol family and is called _____. It is made by the _____ of glucose by _____.
   (b) Calculate the relative formula mass of 'alcohol'.
   (c) Some alcoholic drinks have alcohol concentrations of about 10%. In others the concentration is about 40%.
       Explain how 40% concentration is achieved.

10. Describe the effects of alcohol on the body and mind.

CHAPTER THIRTEEN

Problem Solving

Half of the questions in the written exams in Standard Grade Chemistry are tests of 'problem solving'. You may think it strange that only one chapter of this book is devoted to problem solving. Many problem solving questions are, however, applications of knowledge and understanding. There are many questions on problem solving in earlier chapters. Many of these questions are about applications of knowledge as well as, for example, selecting and presenting information.

Here are the areas of problem solving which you should practise.

- Selecting information
- Presenting information
- Selecting procedures
- Concluding and explaining
- Predicting and generalising

You may find selecting and presenting information to be the most straightforward areas to master. Success in other areas may depend on your knowledge and understanding. Many of the problem solving questions in exams will be about concluding, explaining and predicting.

Several experiments and substances mentioned in the questions which follow will be unfamiliar to you. If the chemistry is not contained in the earlier chapters, then it is *not* part of the learning outcomes for Standard Grade Chemistry and you do not need to know them.

Parts of some of the questions which follow also test knowledge and understanding. You must expect to cope with both areas within one question.

The questions have been arranged under each of the five areas listed above. However, usually only one part of each question is about the area described in the title of the section. A question about selecting information may also contain parts about several other problem solving areas. This is what you must expect in a Standard Grade Chemistry exam.

Practice Questions

SELECTING INFORMATION

Questions in which you are asked to select information are usually straightforward. You may be asked to select information from sources such as the *Data Booklet*, line and bar graphs, picture keys, flowcharts, pie charts, diagrams, passages of writing, word or chemical equations.

1. Use the *Data Booklet* to find the following:

    (*a*) the melting point of sodium;

    (*b*) the boiling point of cyclohexane;

    (*c*) the date of the discovery of phosphorus;

CHAPTER THIRTEEN • *Problem Solving*

(d) the flame colour of the barium ion;
(e) the density of silicon;
(f) the solubility of magnesium phosphate;
(g) the electron arrangement of sulphur;
(h) the formula of the nitrate ion.

2. The graph shows the rate of a chemical reaction at different temperatures.

   (a) Normally the rate of a chemical reaction increases with temperature.
   What is unusual about the rate of this reaction?
   (b) At what temperature is the reaction rate **greatest**?

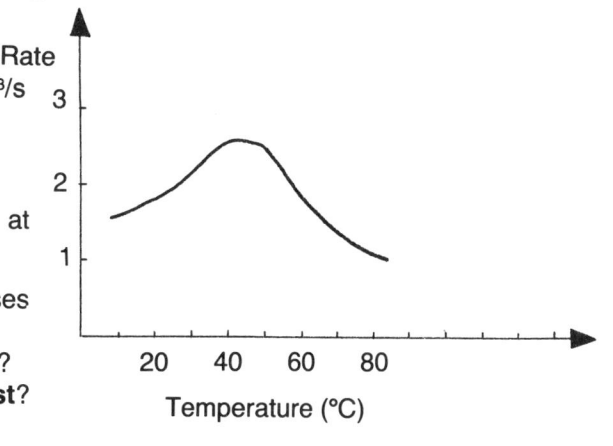

3. Here is a diagram of the apparatus used to make carbon monoxide gas. The carbon monoxide produced in the flask may be contaminated with carbon dioxide.

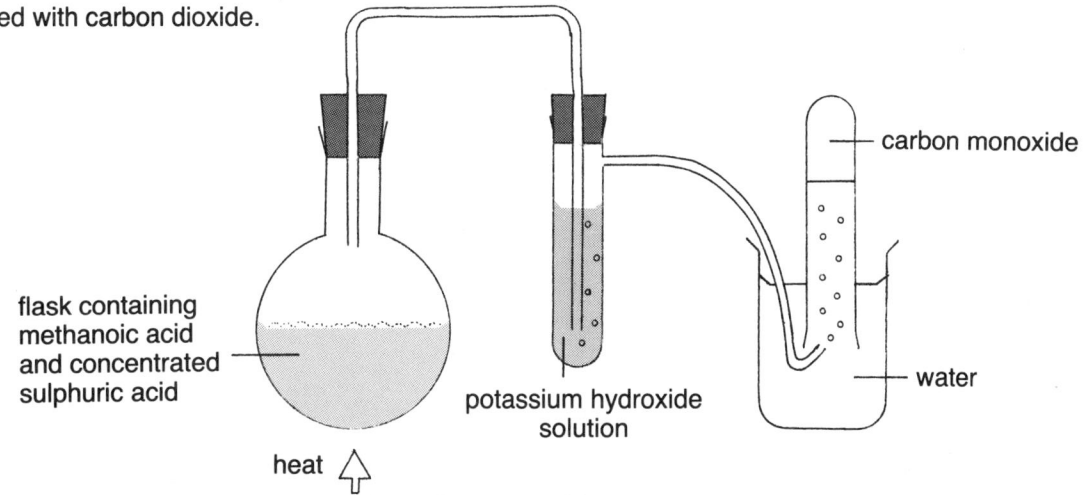

   (a) Name the reactants used to make carbon monoxide.
   (b) A solution of carbon dioxide is acidic. Carbon monoxide does not form an acidic solution. Explain how this enables the two gases to be separated in the experiment above.
   (c) Here is the chemical equation for the reaction.

   $$2H_2CO_2 \rightarrow 2CO + 2X$$

   State the formula of compound X.

4. Nickel forms many alloys. The following pie charts show the composition of some of the common alloys.

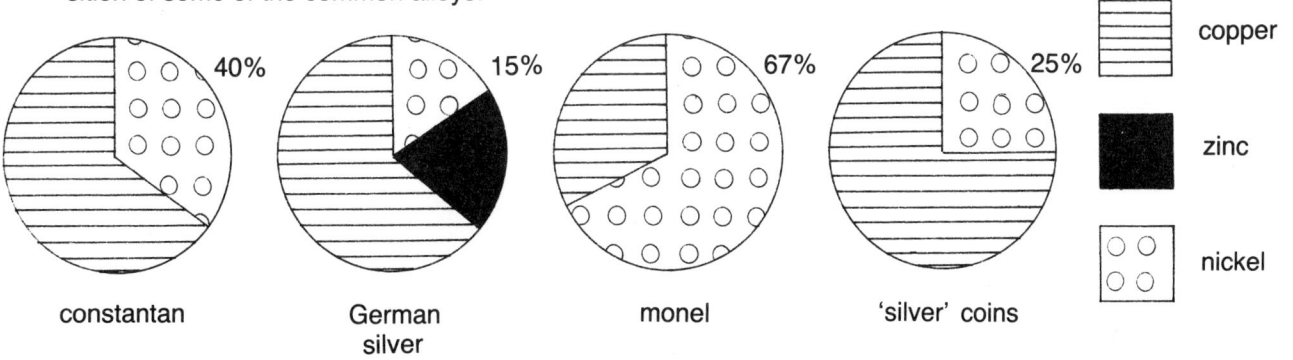

   constantan — 40%
   German silver — 15%
   monel — 67%
   'silver' coins — 25%

   (a) What is an alloy?
   (b) Draw a **table** with appropriate headings to show the amount of nickel in each of the four alloys.
   (c) Name the metals which are present in monel.

109

CHAPTER THIRTEEN • Problem Solving

5. The flowchart shows the manufacture of sulphuric acid.

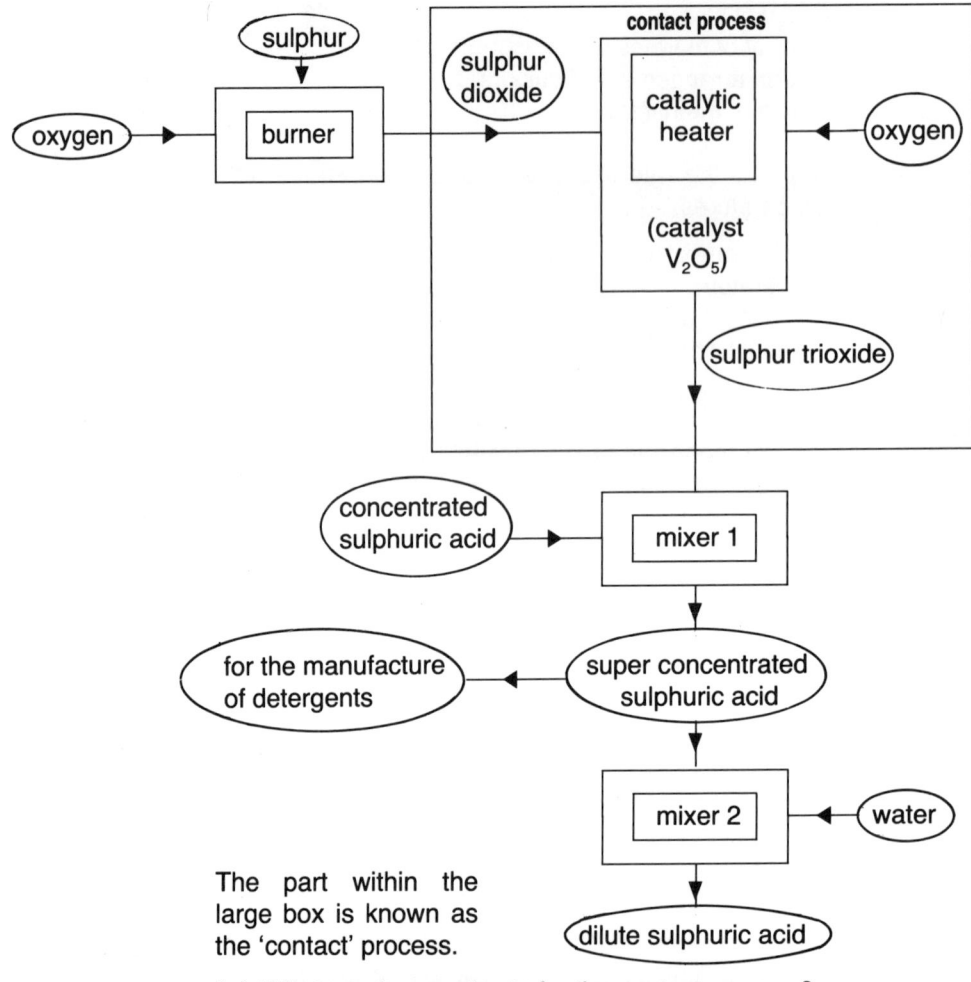

The part within the large box is known as the 'contact' process.

(a) What are the **reactants** for the contact process?
(b) What is the **product** of the contact process?
(c) What are **two** uses of super concentrated sulphuric acid?
(d) How is super concentrated sulphuric acid made?
(e) Write the formula for sulphur trioxide.

PRESENTING INFORMATION

You may be asked to present information as tables, bar and line graphs. You may also be asked to select your own method of presenting information. Whichever method you choose must be easy to understand and accurate. In the Credit paper the data which you have to handle will be more complex than in the General paper.

1. The table gives the boiling points of **four** members of the cycloalkane series.

Cycloalkane	Number of carbon atoms	Boiling point (°C)
cyclopentane	5	49
cyclohexane	6	81
cycloheptane	7	119
cyclooctane	8	151
cyclononane	9	not available

CHAPTER THIRTEEN • *Problem Solving*

(a) Draw a **bar chart** showing the information about the first **four** compounds above.

(b) Estimate the boiling point of cyclononane.

2. (a) Construct a table showing the boiling points of the following compounds: **ethane, butane, propane, pentane** and **methane**. The information will be found in the *Data Booklet*.

(b) Draw a **bar chart** of the boiling point against the number of carbon atoms in each compound.

(c) State which of the compounds is/are liquid at 10 °C.

3. A glaze for pottery consists of 40% lead oxide, 30% fine sand, 25% soda and 5% cobalt salt.

Present this information in a suitable way.

4. Sulphur dioxide can be made by adding concentrated sulphuric acid to copper turnings. Water and copper(II) sulphate solution also form.

Choose a suitable format and present this information.

5. Substances can be classified as compounds or elements. Elements can be further divided into metals and non-metals.
Here are some examples of such substances: **ethane, aluminium, silicon, sulphur, water, ammonia, zinc**.

Present the information above in a suitable way.

6.
> Aluminium compounds have many everyday uses.
> Aluminium oxide is an abrasive used in sandpaper, and aluminium sulphate is used to settle solids in water treatment. Aluminium hydroxide is an effective antacid for treating indigestion. Both aluminium sodium silicate and sodium aluminium phosphate have uses as food additives.

Present this information as a **table** with suitable headings.

7. Lorna added 5 g of powdered iron to 100 cm^3 of copper(II) sulphate solution. She measured the temperature every minute and recorded the results.

Temperature (°C)	Time (minutes)
22	0
24	2
28	4
32	6
31	8
29	10
28	12

Draw a **line graph** of the temperature against time for her results.

SELECTING PROCEDURES

You may be asked to select a method of carrying out an experiment, or to

CHAPTER THIRTEEN • *Problem Solving*

put a jumbled set of instructions into order. You may be asked, more simply, how you would carry out a procedure. A labelled diagram will often be your best method of explanation.

In addition you are expected you have some idea of what is termed *fairness*. When an investigation is carried out the result must be conclusive. There are several comparisons in the questions that are clearly 'unfair'.

1. Making and using electricity are important processes in chemistry.

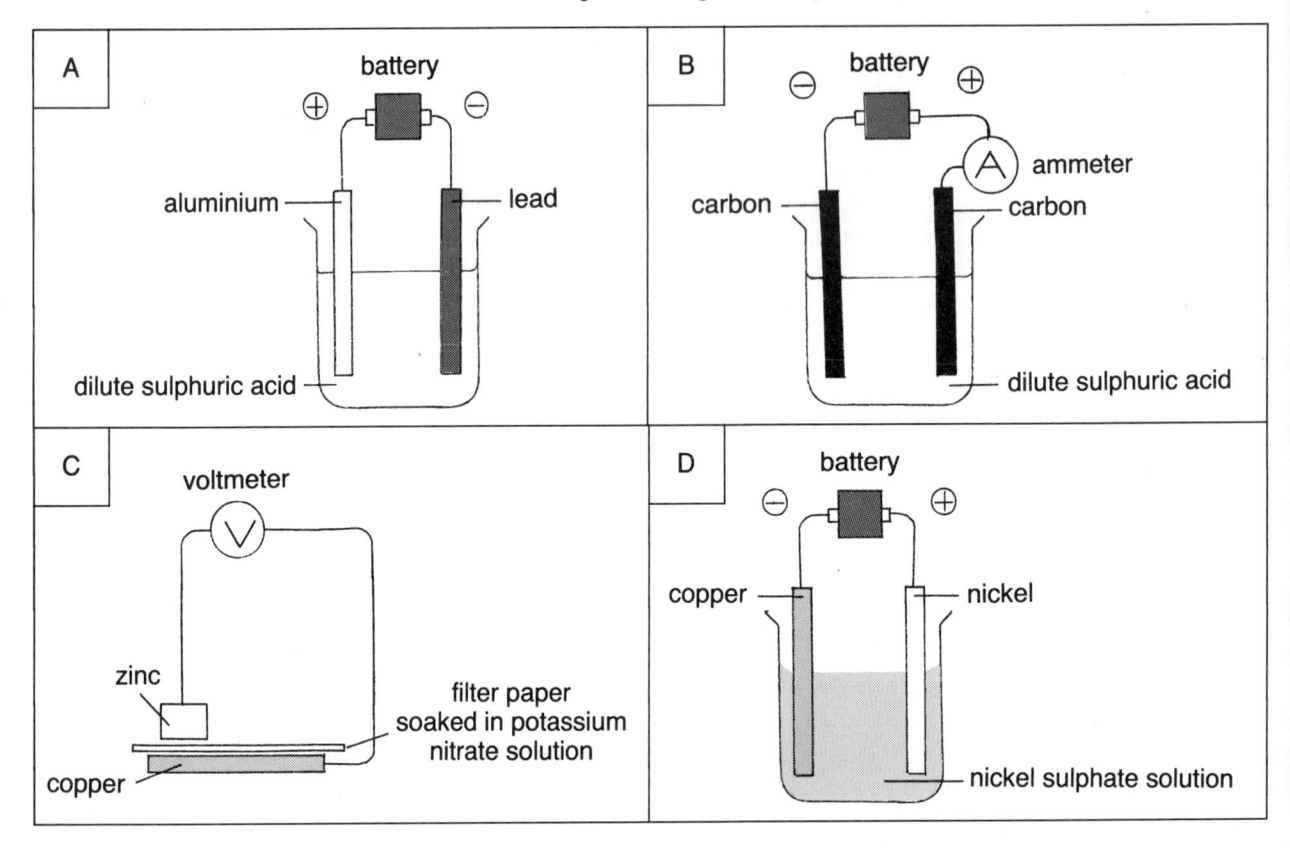

A — battery, aluminium and lead electrodes in dilute sulphuric acid.

B — battery, ammeter, two carbon electrodes in dilute sulphuric acid.

C — voltmeter, zinc and copper with filter paper soaked in potassium nitrate solution.

D — battery, copper and nickel electrodes in nickel sulphate solution.

Which box (or boxes) could be used to measure:

(a) the position of a metal in the electrochemical series?
(b) the conductivity of a solution?

2. Copper(II) sulphate crystals can be made by the reaction of copper(II) carbonate powder and dilute sulphuric acid.

Write down **all** the letters from the grid below to show the order you would use to make copper(II) sulphate crystals.

A	Continue to add copper(II) carbonate until no more reacts.
B	Allow the solution to evaporate to dryness.
C	Measure 100 cm³ of dilute sulphuric acid into a beaker.
D	Filter the solution to remove excess copper(II) carbonate.
E	Add copper(II) carbonate powder to the sulphuric acid.

CHAPTER THIRTEEN • *Problem Solving*

3. Carbon monoxide can be made by passing carbon dioxide over red hot carbon.
   Unreacted carbon dioxide can be removed by passing the gas formed through potassium hydroxide solution.
   Carbon monoxide is insoluble in water.

   Write down **all** of the letters from the grid below in the correct order to prepare carbon monoxide.

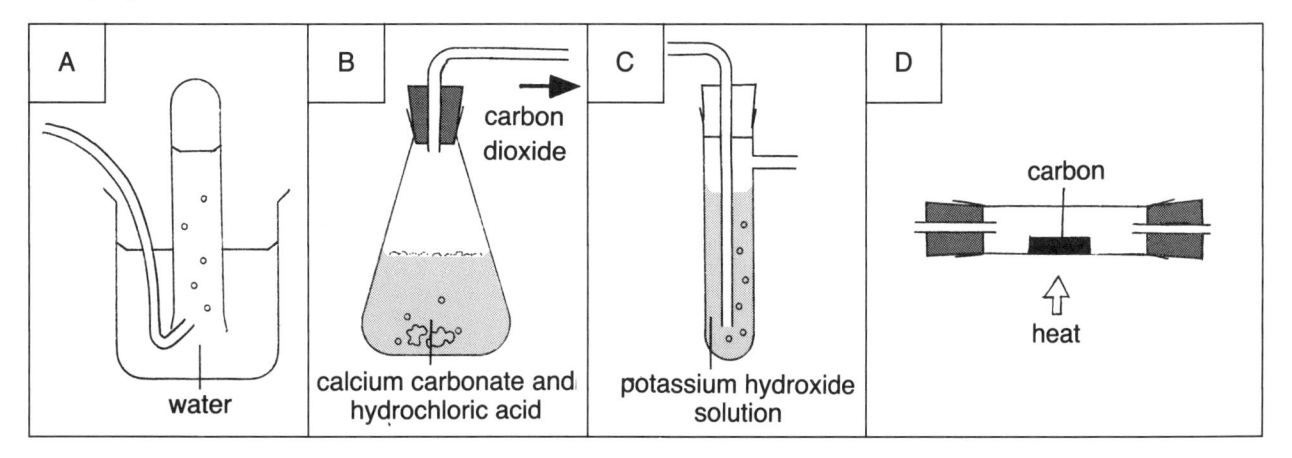

A	B	C	D
water	calcium carbonate and hydrochloric acid	potassium hydroxide solution	carbon / heat

4. Ammonia is less dense than air and is soluble in water but insoluble in paraffin.

   Which box (or boxes) in the grid could be used to enable a **full** test tube of ammonia to be collected?

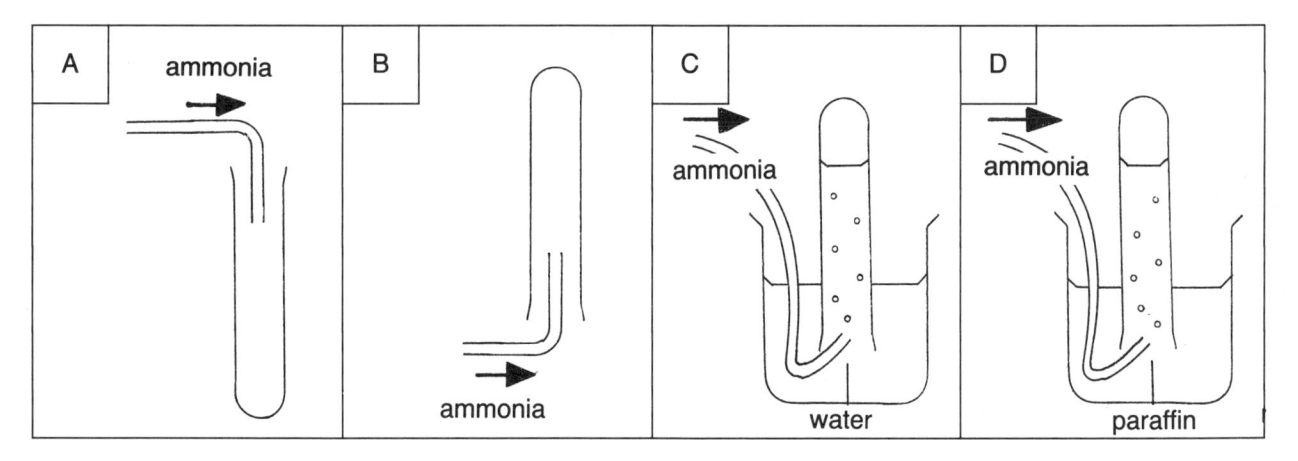

A	B	C	D
ammonia (downward into tube)	ammonia (upward into inverted tube)	ammonia over water	ammonia over paraffin

5. (a) Describe how you would show that carbon dioxide gas formed when zinc carbonate powder was added to dilute hydrochloric acid.
   (b) Describe how you would test a toffee to show that it contained glucose.

6.
   Manganese dioxide — a catalyst

   A catalyst speeds up a chemical reaction but is not used up. When lumps of manganese dioxide, a catalyst, were added to hydrogen peroxide solution, oxygen gas formed. There appeared to be as much manganese dioxide at the end of the reaction as there was at the start.

   Describe how you would show that the manganese dioxide was **not** 'used up'.

CHAPTER THIRTEEN • *Problem Solving*

7. Colin requires dry alcohol to carry out a practical investigation. He knows that calcium reacts with water but not with alcohol.
   His teacher supplies him with three bottles of alcohol and asks him to find out which one contains **dry** alcohol.
   Describe how he determines which bottle to use.

8. Naeem has recorded in his chemistry notebook the approximate pH of some 1 mol/*l* solutions.

Solution (1 mol/*l*)	pH
sodium chloride	7
sulphuric acid	0.5
ammonium hydroxide	12
potassium hydroxide	14
potassium nitrate	7
ammonium sulphate	4
hydrochloric acid	1

   (a) In what way has it been made certain that this is a fair comparison?
   (b) When Naeem was revising his chemistry notes he told his dad 'All salts have a pH of 7.'
       Which **one** of the solutions above is **an exception** to this statement?
   (c) 25 cm^3 of 1 mol/*l* hydrochloric acid (HCl) was added to 30 cm^3 of 1 mol/*l* potassium hydroxide.
       Which **one** of the following will be the pH of the resulting solution?

       A more than 7   B exactly 7   C less than 7

9. The rate of rusting of an iron nail can be slowed down by connecting the iron nail by a wire to a more active metal. Here are some experiments concerned with this process.

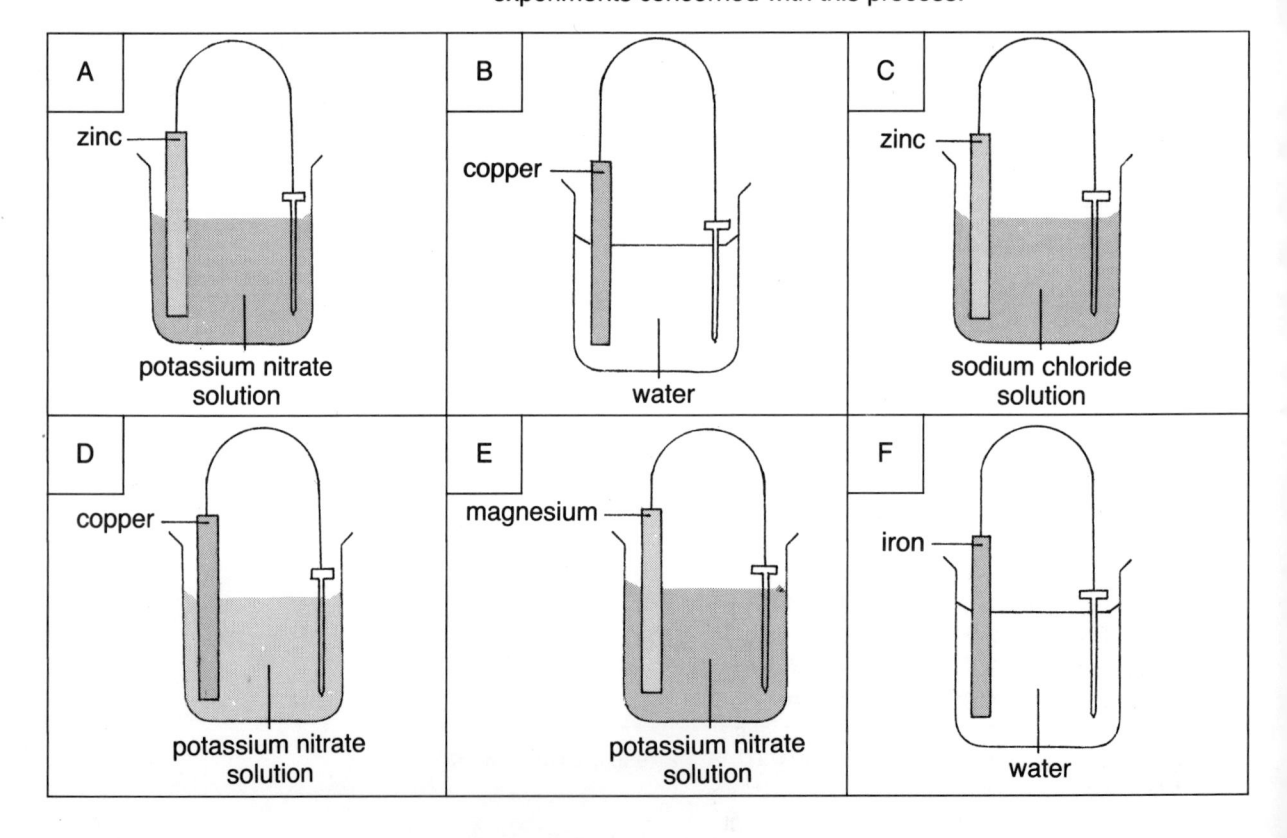

| A: zinc in potassium nitrate solution | B: copper in water | C: zinc in sodium chloride solution |
| D: copper in potassium nitrate solution | E: magnesium in potassium nitrate solution | F: iron in water |

CHAPTER THIRTEEN • *Problem Solving*

(a) Select the **three** experiments which show **fairly** that the rusting of iron 'can be slowed down by connecting the iron nail to a more active metal'.

(b) Which **two** experiments show **fairly** that the presence of an ionic solution affects the rate of rusting of an iron nail?

10. Kim and Ali were asked to carry out a practical investigation to compare two types of yeast.
The effectiveness of the yeast was measured by the rate of production of carbon dioxide gas in fermentation.
The apparatus is shown in the diagram.

State **four** things that Kim and Ali could control in order to make the comparison a **fair** one.

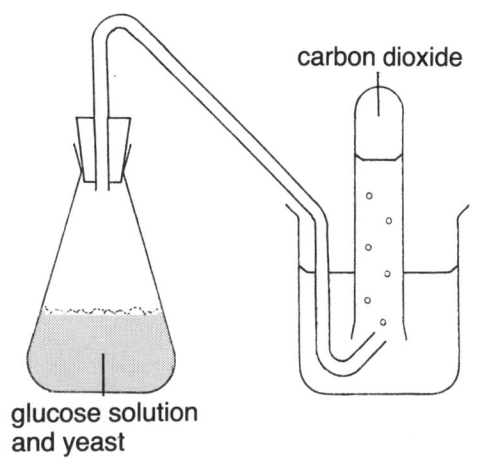

CONCLUDING AND EXPLAINING

These are the commonest types of questions that you will be asked. They are the kind of questions that your teacher probably asks you every day of your chemistry course:

'This substance turns pH paper a blue colour. What does this mean?'
'Why did this metal react with this solution?'

Most of the questions are applications of your knowledge. You may sometimes find that calculations are needed to draw conclusions.

1. A substance reacts with water forming **only** calcium hydroxide, $Ca(OH)_2$, and ethyne, C_2H_2.

   Name the **two** elements which must be present in the substance.

2. A white powder dissolved in water to form a solution which conducted electricity. When dilute sulphuric acid was added to the solution which had formed, carbon dioxide was given off. When a flame test was carried out a yellow colour was seen.

   (a) What does the evidence above tell you about the kind of bonding in the compound?
   (b) Which types of compounds give off carbon dioxide when an acid is added?
   (c) Use information in the *Data Booklet* to help you deduce the name of the compound.

3. Lynsey was carrying out a practical investigation with a black powder. She was told that it was a **mixture** of **two** substances, one an element and the other a compound.
She found that **neither** substance dissolved in water.
When she heated them both with dilute sulphuric acid, **one** of the substances produced a blue solution. The other did not react with the acid.
When she heated the mixture of the two substances she noticed that carbon dioxide and a brown metal formed.
Lynsey suggested that the black powder was a mixture of **copper(II) oxide** and **carbon**. Her teacher agreed.

   Explain how she had arrived at her conclusion.

115

CHAPTER THIRTEEN • *Problem Solving*

4. The table lists the boiling points of a number of liquids.

Liquid	Boiling point (°C)
ethanol	78
propanone	56
hexane	69
heptane	98
octane	—

(a) Use the *Data Booklet* to find the boiling point of octane.
(b) Which of the three hydrocarbons shown will boil first when heated?
(c) Name the method used to separate a mixture of liquids.
(d) Explain why the boiling point of heptane is between those of hexane and octane.

5. The table gives the formulae of some compounds of metals.

Compound	Formula
cadmium oxide	CdO
mercury chloride	HgCl
thorium chloride	$ThCl_2$
chromium oxide	Cr_2O_3
manganese sulphate	$MnSO_4$
iron nitrate	$Fe(NO_3)_3$

Write the name of each compound, indicating the **valency** of the metal. For example, cadmium oxide is written **cadmium(II) oxide**.

6. Some substances are made by dehydration. Dehydration means the removal of water. For example, carbon monoxide can be made by dehydrating oxalic acid.

$$H_2C_2O_4 \rightarrow CO + CO_2 + H_2O$$

State the formulae of **X, Y** and **Z** in each of the following dehydration reactions.
(a) **X** $\rightarrow H_2O + CO$
(b) $C_3H_6O_3 \rightarrow 3$**Y** $+ 3H_2O$
(c) $C_2H_6O \rightarrow$ **Z** $+ H_2O$

7. The presence of mercury in mercury chloride solution can be detected by adding copper foil.

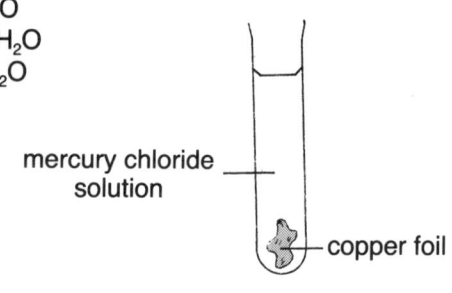

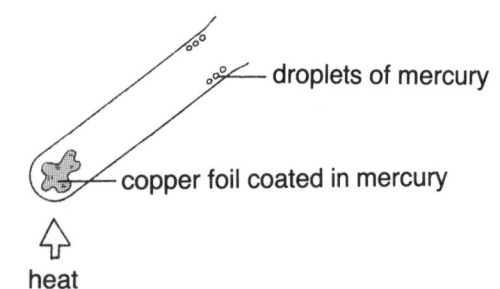

Mercury will be deposited as a grey layer on the copper. The grey coated copper is then removed from the test tube, put into a second dry test tube and warmed.
The mercury will vaporise and be seen to condense in droplets at the mouth of the test tube.

(a) Why does copper react with a compound of mercury?
(b) What would be the result of adding copper foil to a solution of zinc chloride?
(c) Soluble silver compounds react with copper in exactly the same ways as soluble mercury compounds.

CHAPTER THIRTEEN • *Problem Solving*

Use the table of melting and boiling points in the *Data Booklet* to explain how the **second** part of the experiment could be used to distinguish them.

PREDICTING AND GENERALISING

Predicting is not the same as guessing! Once you have a certain amount of knowledge, it is possible to predict what may happen in a situation which is unfamiliar to you. You may deduce from a graph, for instance, what will happen between the points which are drawn. Or you may spot a trend in results and be able to predict what will happen next.

Although you may meet someone who claims that it once snowed in June you would know yourself that that was very unusual weather! *In general* the weather is very pleasant in June. When you look at the results of a series of experiments you may be able to make a 'generalisation'. You are stating what *usually* happens in a given situation.

1. Here is a summary of the results of a number of experiments in which solutions were electrolysed.
    The products at the electrodes are given.

Solution	Product at the negative electrode	Product at the positive electrode
sodium chloride	hydrogen	chlorine
potassium chloride	hydrogen	chlorine
zinc chloride	hydrogen	chlorine
copper(II) chloride	copper	chlorine
sodium fluoride	hydrogen	oxygen
silver nitrate	silver	oxygen
copper(II) sulphate	copper	oxygen

    Give the correct words for (*a*) to (*d*) in the following statement.
    'When a solution is electrolysed ___(*a*)___ always forms at the negative electrode unless a very ___(*b*)___ metal is present. When a solution of calcium nitrate is electrolysed ___(*c*)___ will form at the negative electrode and ___(*d*)___ will form at the positive electrode.'

2. Use information in the *Data Booklet* to answer this question.

    (*a*) Construct a table with suitable headings showing the solubility of the following compounds: ammonium carbonate; ammonium sulphate; calcium carbonate; aluminium carbonate; ammonium chloride; calcium phosphate.
    (*b*) What do you notice, in general, about the solubility in water of the ammonium compounds?

3. The graph shows the solubility of two compounds in water at different temperatures.

    (*a*) Give a general rule about the solubility of the compounds in water at different temperatures.
    (*b*) What is the solubility of compound **A** in water at 60 °C?
    (*c*) At what temperature are both compounds equally soluble?
    (*d*) 1 litre of a solution of compound **A** is cooled down from 60 °C to 40 °C. What mass of compound **A** will crystallise?

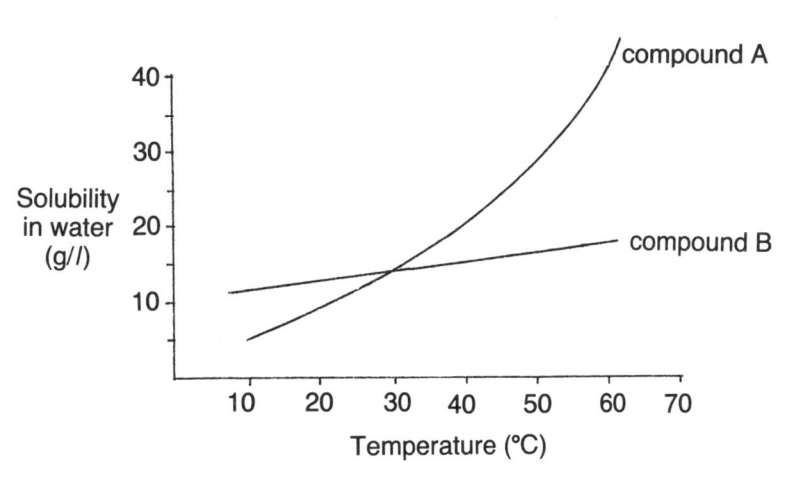

117

CHAPTER THIRTEEN • Problem Solving

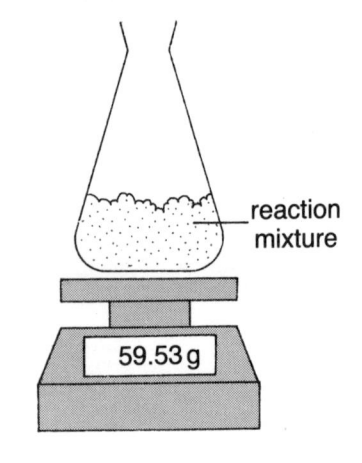

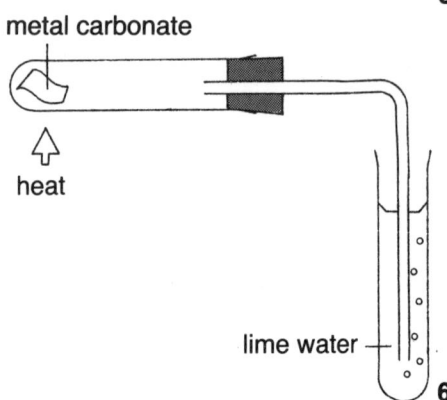

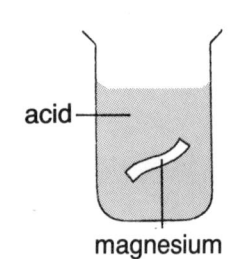

4. The change in mass which may take place during a chemical reaction can be measured by putting the reaction flask on a balance as shown.

   State whether the reading of mass on the balance will **increase**, **decrease** or **remain the same** during the reactions described by the following chemical equations.

   (a) $Mg(s) + 2HCl(aq) \rightarrow MgCl_2(aq) + H_2(g)$
   (b) $CaCO_3(s) + 2HCl(aq) \rightarrow CaCl_2(aq) + CO_2(g) + H_2O(l)$
   (c) $Zn(s) + CuCl_2(aq) \rightarrow ZnCl_2(aq) + Cu(s)$
   (d) $2Fe(s) + O_2(g) + 2H_2O(l) \rightarrow 2Fe(OH)_3(s)$

5. When metal carbonates are heated, they often decompose forming the metal oxide and carbon dioxide gas.
   The carbonates of the **least active metals** decompose **most easily**. The carbonates of the **most active metals** such as sodium and potassium **do not decompose** on heating.

   (a) Describe how the above procedure could be used to place **sodium**, **copper** and **zinc** in the order of their reactivity.
   (b) From the information above, write a **word** equation showing the effect of heat on zinc carbonate.
   (c) Suggest what you would observe if you compared the rate of decomposition of copper and zinc carbonates.

6. Here are the results of an experiment in which equal volumes of different concentrations of an acid were added to magnesium.

Experiment	Concentration of acid (mol/l)	Time for magnesium to react (minutes)
1	1.00	2
2	0.10	14
3	0.01	79
4	0.001	192

   (a) In which experiment was the **most** concentrated acid used?
   (b) In which experiment was the rate **greatest**?
   (c) Predict what the time would be for the magnesium to react if acid of concentration 2 mol/l was used.
   (d) Suggest **two** ways in which the rate of reaction in experiment 4 could be increased **without** altering the concentration.
   (e) Why were equal volumes of the acid used in each experiment?

7. Inflated balloons go down after a time, even though they do not leak. Balloons containing hydrogen go down more quickly than balloons filled with oxygen. It is thought that the different sizes of the gas molecules can explain this observation.

   (a) Suggest a reason why balloons go down after a time.
   (b) Use your answer to (a) to explain why balloons filled with hydrogen go down more quickly than balloons filled with oxygen.
   (c) Predict the rate at which a balloon filled with xenon gas would go down. Give a reason for your answer.

Answers to Practice Questions

CHAPTER ONE

1. (a) A, D, F, H *In each case a new substance forms.*
   (b) B, E
   (c) F *Water is a compound of hydrogen and oxygen.*
   (b) G

2. (a) C   (b) Ne   (c) Fe   (d) Cl
   (e) Na (f) Cr   (g) Cu   (h) W   (i) He
   Consult the periodic table.
   The first letter of a symbol is always a capital letter, the second one a small letter.

3. (a) phosphorus (b) nitrogen   (c) argon
   (d) potassium   (e) platinum   (f) bromine
   (g) calcium   (h) gold   (i) boron

4. (a) magnesium and oxygen
   (b) zinc and chlorine
   (c) potassium, hydrogen and oxygen
   (d) copper, carbon and oxygen
   (e) barium and iodine
   (f) potassium, sulphur and oxygen
   (g) calcium, hydrogen and oxygen
   (h) sodium, carbon and nitrogen

5. (a) zinc chloride   (b) iron oxide
   (c) sodium fluoride   (d) copper sulphate
   (e) hydrogen oxide   (f) magnesium nitride

6. The mixture of iron and sulphur can be separated into iron and sulphur. For example, iron could be removed with a magnet. Iron sulphide, on the other hand, is a compound in which the atoms of the elements iron and sulphur are joined together. Iron sulphide cannot be separated by a magnet.

7. The mixture of sand and salt should be added to water in a beaker, then stirred until all the salt has dissolved. The sand can be separated from the salt solution by filtration. The sand left behind in the filter paper should then be dried. The salt can be obtained by boiling the salt solution dry in an evaporating dish.

8. (a) Solute: copper sulphate; solvent: water.
   (b) Label: copper sulphate solution.

9. (a) A *D would also work but would require heating.*
   (b) B *(salt in water)* and E *(gas, etc., in water)*

   H is not a solution, oil does not dissolve in water.
   (c) C
   (d) D *Water boils off and salt remains.*

10.

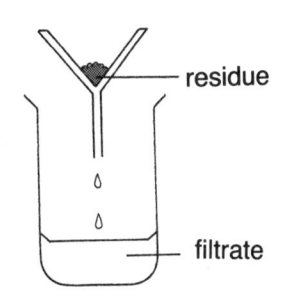

    Ruler or stencil. Accurate labels. No 'art' work required. Items like 'bench' or 'stand' are not required.

11. (a) H *Concentrated, high temperature and powder.*
    (b) A *Dilute, low temperature and lump.*
    (c) A and G or B and D or C and E or F and H *Only one variable, the concentration of acid, changes.*

12. Adding ice cools the acid and slows the rate of the reaction. Ice will also melt and dilute the acid which will also slow down the reaction rate.

13. (a) Two beakers are required with equal volumes of water at the same temperature in each. Add the same mass of sugar to each, one in lump form, the other ground. Stir each in the same way. Make a note of the times required for the sugar to dissolve in each.
    (b) The variables are: volume of water, temperature of water, rate or method of stirring.

14. (a) A   (b) F   (c) D

15. (a) The formation of a new substance, a gas, is evidence of a chemical reaction.
    (b) It slowed down when hydrogen peroxide was being used up, and so its concentration was reducing.
    (c) Manganese dioxide
    A catalyst is unchanged in a reaction.
    (d) 2.00 g of manganese dioxide. As the catalyst is unchanged, the mass at the end will be the same as at the start.

CHAPTER TWO

1. (a) C   Group 0
   (b) A and F   Group I
   (c) B and H
   (d) D and E   Group VII
   (e) E, F and G
   (f) C, D, E and G

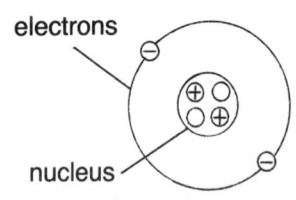

2. (a) [diagram: atom with nucleus containing 2 protons (⊕) and 2 electrons on outer shell, labelled "electrons" and "nucleus"]

   (b) It has the same number of protons (positive charge) and electrons (negative charge).
   (c) helium *(2 protons so atomic number of 2, He)*

3. Both elements have one electron in their outer shells and so belong to the same group.

4.
Particle	Charge	Mass	Where particle found in atom
proton	+	1	in nucleus
neutron	0	1	in nucleus
electron	−	almost 0	outside nucleus

5.
Atom	Number of protons	Number of neutrons	Number of electrons
$^{4}_{2}He$	2	2	2
$^{19}_{9}F$	9	10	9
$^{27}_{13}Al$	13	14	13
$^{31}_{15}P$	15	16	15

6.
Ion	Number of protons	Number of neutrons	Number of electrons
$^{23}_{11}Na^+$	11	12	10
$^{19}_{9}F^-$	9	10	10
$^{24}_{12}Mg^{2+}$	12	12	10
$^{32}_{16}S^{2-}$	16	16	18

Positive ions have less electrons than protons. Negative ions have more electrons than protons.

7. (a) (i) 2, 8   (ii) 2, 8   (iii) 2, 8   (iv) 2, 8
   Remember that electron arrangements of all the elements are given in the Data Booklet.
   (b) When an atom forms an ion, it obtains the same electron structure as a noble gas. Metals lose electrons and non-metals gain electrons to achieve this.

8. (a) $^{35}_{17}Cl$ and $^{37}_{17}Cl$ are described as isotopes. Although they both have the same atomic number, their mass numbers differ. $^{35}_{17}Cl$ has 18 neutrons in its nucleus whereas $^{37}_{17}Cl$ has 20 neutrons.
   (b) The relative atomic mass of an element is the average mass number of all the isotopes. Chlorine is made up of some $^{35}_{17}Cl$ and some $^{37}_{17}Cl$ and has an average mass number of 35.5.

9. (a) CH_4 (b) CCl_4 (c) HF   (d) H_2
   (e) NH_3 (f) H_2S (g) PH_3 (h) CCl_2F_2

10. (a) H − F   (b) F − O − F
    (c) H − N − H
            |
            H
    (d)   H
            |
        H − C − H
            |
            H

11. (a) H ⋅⋅ F̈ :   (b) F̈ ⋅⋅ Ö ⋅⋅ F̈ :
    (c) H ⋅⋅ N̈ ⋅⋅ H   (d)   H
            ⋅⋅|⋅⋅   ⋅⋅|⋅⋅
             H   H ⋅⋅ C ⋅⋅ H
                            ⋅⋅|⋅⋅
                             H

    Hydrogen is unique in that it has only two electrons in its outer level when it forms bonds, whereas all the other non-metals have eight.

CHAPTER THREE

1. (a) NaCl   (b) F_2O
   (c) MgS   (d) Al_2O_3
   (e) CO   (f) CS_2
   (g) N_2O_4 (h) $CuCl_2$
   (i) Fe_2O_3 (j) $HgBr_2$

2.
	Reactants	Products
(a)	sodium, chlorine	sodium chloride
(b)	magnesium, copper(II) bromide	copper, magnesium bromide
(c)	magnesium, oxygen	magnesium oxide
(d)	chlorine, sodium iodide	iodine, sodium chloride
(e)	calcium carbonate	calcium oxide, carbon dioxide

When a substance 'burns' oxygen is added. Decomposing means breaking down into simpler subtances.

3. (a) sodium + chlorine → sodium chloride
   (b) magnesium + copper(II) bromide → magnesium bromide + copper
   (c) magnesium + oxygen → magnesium oxide
   (d) chlorine + sodium iodide → sodium chloride + iodine
   (e) calcium carbonate → calcium oxide + carbon dioxide

4. (a) aluminium + chlorine → **aluminium chloride**
   (b) zinc + hydrochloric acid → zinc chloride + **hydrogen**

(c) lead(II) nitrate + potassium iodide → potassium nitrate + **lead(II) iodide**
(d) sodium + **oxygen** → sodium oxide
(e) **iron** + copper(II) chloride → iron(II) chloride + copper

In (b) 'hydrochloric acid' is also called 'hydrogen chloride'.
You should write equations in one line only.

5. (a) $Zn + S \rightarrow ZnS$
   (b) $Fe + CuCl_2 \rightarrow FeCl_2 + Cu$
   (c) $Ca + Cl_2 \rightarrow CaCl_2$
   (d) $C + O_2 \rightarrow CO_2$
   (e) $2Na + S \rightarrow Na_2S$
   (f) $2Al + 3S \rightarrow Al_2S_3$
   (g) $2Mg + O_2 \rightarrow 2MgO$
   (h) $2H_2 + O_2 \rightarrow 2H_2O$
   (i) $H_2 + Cl_2 \rightarrow 2HCl$
   (j) $Mg + 2HCl \rightarrow MgCl_2 + H_2$

In 5 (a), (b), (c) and (d), no balancing is required. Simply writing the formulae gives a balanced equation. Do not always rush into balancing equations. Often it will not be necessary.

6. (a) $CH_4 + 2O_2 \rightarrow CO_2 + 2H_2O$
   (b) $H_2 + F_2 \rightarrow 2HF$
   (c) $2Mg + CO_2 \rightarrow 2MgO + C$
   (d) $2Al + Fe_2O_3 \rightarrow Al_2O_3 + 2Fe$
   (e) $Fe + 2HCl \rightarrow FeCl_2 + H_2$

7. (a) $Mg(s) + H_2O(g) \rightarrow MgO(s) + H_2(g)$
   (b) $Fe(s) + S(s) \rightarrow FeS(s)$
   (c) $CuCl_2(aq) + Mg(s) \rightarrow MgCl_2(aq) + Cu(s)$
   (d) $CaO(s) + 2HCl(aq) \rightarrow CaCl_2(aq) + H_2O(l)$

CHAPTER FOUR

1. (a) B   (b) E and F   (c) E   (d) A
The more carbon atoms there are in a hydrocarbon molecule the heavier the molecule is. This makes the liquid more difficult to boil, less flammable and more viscous.

2.
Gas	Percentage in air	Chemical test
nitrogen	79%	largely unreactive
oxygen	20%	relights a glowing splinter
argon	less than 1%	totally unreactive
carbon dioxide	traces	turns lime water chalky

3.
Fuel	Combustion products
hydrogen	**water**
carbon	**carbon dioxide**
carbon monoxide	**carbon dioxide**
methane	**carbon dioxide and water**
ethene	**carbon dioxide and water**

A hydrocarbon burns to produce both carbon dioxide and water.

4. (a) B, E   (b) D, G   (c) D, E
   (d) F   (e) C

5. (a) A, C and D
   (b) E   *Not B which is a molecular formula or F which is a name.*
   (c) C   *Not A which is a structural formula or D which is a name.*
   (d) F
   (e) B, E and F

6. (a) butene

   H   H   H   H
   | | | |
   C = C - C - C - H
   | | |
   H   H   H

   You might also have written:

   H   H   H   H
   | | | |
   H - C - C = C - C - H
       | |
       H   H

   (b) (i) C_5H_{10} pentene
       (ii) (cyclopentane structure)

       (cyclopentane)

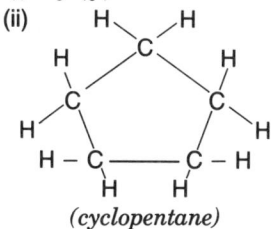

7. (a) A is butene; B is cyclobutane.
   (b) Add bromine solution (bromine 'water') to each in turn. The one in which the bromine is decolourised is butene, the one which is unaffected is cyclobutane.
   When you are asked to 'distinguish' between two substances you should give the effect of the test on both of them.
   The bromine is 'decolourised'. Do not say it goes 'clear'. Bromine water is clear. You can see through something which is clear even although it may be coloured. Substances like water, which have no colour, are described as being 'colourless'.
   (c) isomers

8. mineral wool soaked in paraffin

X

heat

mixture of gases

water

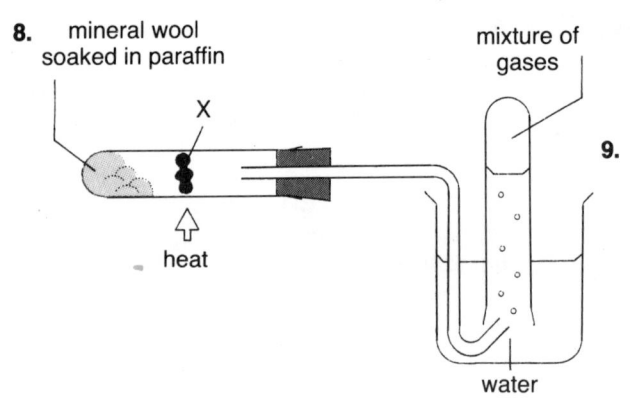

X = steel wool or broken pottery or catalyst

Instead of showing a Bunsen burner, an arrow with the word 'heat' will do. Heat is applied to X and not to the paraffin.

9. (a) C_2H_4 ethene (subtraction: $C_4H_{10} - C_2H_6 = C_2H_4$)

(b) (i)
$$\begin{array}{ccc} & H & H \\ & | & | \\ H - & C - C & - H \\ & | & | \\ & H & H \end{array}$$

(ii)
$$\begin{array}{ccc} & H & H \\ & | & | \\ H - & C - C & - H \\ & | & | \\ & Br & Br \end{array}$$

In (ii) the position of the bromine atoms is not important so long as one is on each carbon atom.
(c) addition reaction

CHAPTER FIVE

1. (a) A, B and I *All metals and carbon in the form of graphite conduct electricity.*
   (b) G and H *D contains ions but does not conduct as it is in the solid state.*
   (c) C
   (d) D

   (c) *In a direct current the electrons always move in the same direction. If this were not the case the blue colour, for example, would move in both directions.*
   (d) *An electrolyte is a better conductor of electricity than water.*

2. Each carbon dioxide molecule, CO_2, is separate from all the others. There are no charges on covalent molecules to attract adjacent molecules. Magnesium oxide is a network solid made up of many millions of positive and negative ions. Each is strongly attracted to its neighbours of the opposite charge, thus making the compound a solid.

6. Oil and water do not dissolve in each other. However, when soap is added they *do* mix permanently, forming an emulsion. It is thought that the covalent part of the soap 'dissolves' in the oil and the ionic part 'dissolves' in the water. The oil droplets formed become suspended in the water.

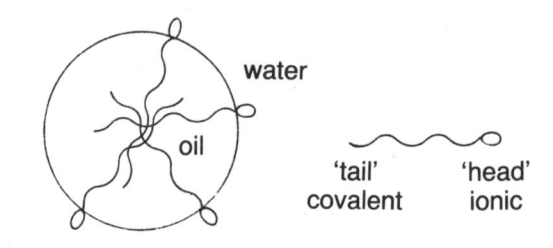

3.

ionic crystal

water
oil

'tail'   'head'
covalent   ionic

(+) positive ion   (−) negative ion

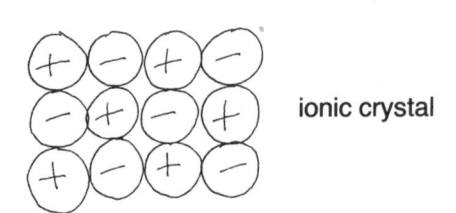

Each positive and negative ion is attracted to its oppositely charged neighbours and is tightly held by them. When melted or dissolved in water this network breaks down and the ions become free to move.

There is a hint contained in the question: 'Diagrams might help with your explanation'. Be sure to make use of these hints.

7. (a) $NaNO_3$ (b) KOH
   (c) NH_4Cl (d) NH_4OH
   (e) $CuSO_4$ (f) Na_2CO_3
   (g) Li_2CO_3 (h) $(NH_4)_2SO_4$
   (i) $Fe(NO_3)_3$ (j) $Al_2(SO_4)_3$

4. (a) $Cu^{2+}(Cl^-)_2$
   (b) (i) $Cu^{2+} + 2e \rightarrow Cu$ (ii) $2Cl^- \rightarrow Cl_2 + 2e$

5. (a) Copper ions have a positive charge, dichromate ions have a negative charge.
   (b) Copper ions, Cu^{2+}, are attracted to the negative charge at A. Opposite charges attract.

8. (a) $Na^+(NO_3^-)$ (b) $K^+(OH^-)$
   (c) $(NH_4^+)Cl^-$ (d) $(NH_4^+)(OH^-)$
   (e) $Cu^{2+}(SO_4^{2-})$ (f) $(Na^+)_2(CO_3^-)$
   (g) $(Li^+)_2(CO_3^{2-})$ (h) $(NH_4^+)_2(SO_4^{2-})$
   (i) $Fe^{3+}(NO_3^-)_3$ (j) $(Al^{3+})_2(SO_4^{2-})_3$

CHAPTER SIX

1.

Acid	Alkali	Neutral
vinegar	baking soda	tap water
lemon juice	sodium carbonate	salt solution
lemonade	sodium hydroxide	
sulphuric acid		

   The headings 'Substance', 'pH' and 'Use' would also be acceptable.

2. B
   All acids have a pH of less than 7. (A)
   All acids produce H^+ ions. (C)
   All acids give hydrogen when electrolysed. (D)

3. C and D
   Potassium hydroxide solution is an alkali. Only acidic solutions contain more H^+ ions than water. (A)
   Oxides of sulphur are part of the cause of 'acid' rain. (B)

4. A and C *Dilution of acid by water does not neutralise it. (D)*

5. A *(hydrogen)* and D *(carbon dioxide)*

6. (a) 42 amu   (b) 56 amu   (c) 100 amu
   (d) 98 amu   (e) 63 amu   (f) 40 amu

7. (a) zinc sulphate
   (b) sodium chloride
   (c) copper(II) sulphate
   (d) copper(II) chloride
   (e) potassium nitrate

8. (a) (i) $Mg(s) + 2HCl(aq) \rightarrow H_2(g) + MgCl_2(aq)$
       (ii) $H_2SO_4(aq) + CuO(s) \rightarrow CuSO_4(aq) + H_2O(l)$
       (iii) $HNO_3(aq) + NaOH(aq) \rightarrow H_2O(l) + NaNO_3(aq)$
       (iv) $2HCl(aq) + CaCO_3(s) \rightarrow CaCl_2(aq) + H_2O(l) + CO_2(g)$
   (b) (i) $Mg(s) + 2H^+(aq) \rightarrow Mg^{2+}(aq) + H_2(g)$
       (ii) $2H^+(aq) + O^{2-}(s) \rightarrow H_2O(l)$
       (iii) $H^+(aq) + OH^-(aq) \rightarrow H_2O(l)$
       (iv) $2H^+(aq) + CO_3^{2-}(s) \rightarrow H_2O(l) + CO_2(g)$

9. (a) H_2O = 18 g
   (b) $CaCO_3$ 100 × 2 = 200 g
   (c) H_2SO_4 98 × 0.5 = 49 g
   (d) HNO_3 63 × 0.1 = 6.3 g
   (e) $NaOH$ 40 × 2 = 80 g

10. (a) $CaCO_3$ 1 mole is 100 g; 10 g contain **0.1 mole**.
    (b) S 1 mole is 32 g; 8 g contain **0.25 mole**.
    (c) Na_2CO_3 1 mole is 106 g; 10.6 g contain **0.1 mole**.
    (d) 100 cm^3 of 1 mol/l of solution contains
       $\dfrac{100 \times 1}{1000} = $ **0.1 mole**.
    (e) 2000 cm^3 of 2 mol/l of solution contains
       $\dfrac{2000 \times 2}{1000} = $ **4 moles**.

    In answers (d) and (e) the name of the substance is not important. 100 cm^3 of any 1 mol/l solution contains 0.1 mole.

11. (a) none
    (b) barium sulphate
    (c) none
    (d) copper(II) carbonate
    (e) lead(II) iodide

12. (a) lead(II) nitrate solution and sodium carbonate solution
       The Data Booklet lists many 'soluble' or 'very soluble' lead compounds and carbonate compounds which would do equally well.
    (b) (i) $Pb(NO_3)_2(aq) + Na_2CO_3(aq) \rightarrow PbCO_3(s) + 2NaNO_3(aq)$
       (ii) $Pb^{2+}(aq) + CO_3^{2-}(aq) \rightarrow Pb^{2+}CO_3^{2-}(s)$
    (c) precipitation
    (d) [diagram of filter funnel above beaker, labelled lead(II) carbonate]

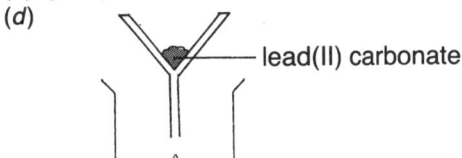

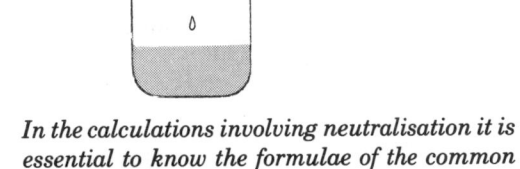

13. *In the calculations involving neutralisation it is essential to know the formulae of the common acids and alkalis.*
    (a) Acid HCl   Alkali NaOH
       volume × concentration × no. of H^+ ions = volume × concentration × no. of OH^- ions
       volume × 2 × 1 = 20 × 1 × 1
       volume of hydrochloric acid = 10 cm^3
    (b) Acid H_2SO_4 Alkali KOH
       volume × 1 × 2 = 20 × 1 × 1
       volume of sulphuric acid = 10 cm^3
    (c) Acid HNO_3 Alkali NaOH
       50 × concentration × 1 = 25 × 1 × 1
       concentration of nitric acid = 0.5 mol/l
    (d) Acid H_2SO_4 Alkali KOH
       50 × concentration × 2 = 25 × 4 × 1
       concentration = $\dfrac{25 \times 4}{50 \times 2}$ = 1 mol/l

14. B

    Remember in all the calculations which follow:
    - *write a balanced equation;*
    - *underline what is to be calculated;*
    - *underline what is given;*
    - *write the numbers of reacting moles (ignore the other substances);*
    - *calculate the masses of the substances underlined;*
    - *calculate the answer.*

15. (a) $\underline{Ca} + \underline{S} \rightarrow CaS$
    1 mole of calcium reacts with 1 mole of sulphur.
    40 g of calcium react with 32 g of sulphur, so **20 g of calcium** react with 16 g of sulphur.
    (b) $2\underline{Na} + \underline{S} \rightarrow Na_2S$
    23 g of sodium react with **16 g of sulphur**.
    (c) $\underline{Fe} + S \rightarrow \underline{FeS}$
    5.6 g of iron react to form **8.8 g of iron(II) sulphide**.

16. (a) (i) $\underline{C} + \underline{O_2} \rightarrow CO_2$
    6 g of carbon react with **16 g of oxygen**.
    (ii) $2\underline{Mg} + \underline{O_2} \rightarrow 2MgO$
    24 g of carbon react with **16 g of oxygen**.
    (iii) $4\underline{Na} + \underline{O_2} \rightarrow 2Na_2O$
    2.3 g of sodium react with **0.8 g of oxygen**.
    (b) (i) $\underline{C} + O_2 \rightarrow \underline{CO_2}$
    3 g of carbon form **11 g of carbon dioxide**.
    (ii) $2\underline{Mg} + O_2 \rightarrow \underline{2MgO}$
    12 g of magnesium form **20 g of magnesium oxide**.
    (iii) $\underline{S} + O_2 \rightarrow \underline{SO_2}$
    16 g of sulphur form **32 g of sulphur dioxide**.

17. (a) $\underline{Mg} + 2HCl \rightarrow MgCl_2 + \underline{H_2}$
    6 g of magnesium form **0.5 g of hydrogen**.
    (b) $CuSO_4 + \underline{Na_2CO_3} \rightarrow \underline{CuCO_3} + Na_2SO_4$
    10.6 g of sodium carbonate form **12.4 g of copper(II) carbonate**.
    (c) $\underline{CaCO_3} + 2HNO_3 \rightarrow H_2O + \underline{CO_2} + Ca(NO_3)_2$
    10 g of calcium carbonate form **4.4 g of carbon dioxide**.
    (d) $\underline{CH_4} + 2O_2 \rightarrow CO_2 + \underline{2H_2O}$
    4 g of methane form **9 g of water**.

18.
$$\begin{array}{c} H\ H \\ |\ | \\ C=C \\ |\ | \\ H\ H \end{array} + Br_2 \rightarrow \begin{array}{c} H\ H \\ |\ | \\ Br-C-C-Br \\ |\ | \\ H\ H \end{array}$$

1 mole of ethene forms 1 mole of dibromoethane.
28 g of ethene form 188 g of dibromoethane,
so 1 g of ethene forms **6.71 g of dibromoethane.**

19. $\underline{CaCO_3} \rightarrow CaO + \underline{CO_2}$
1 mole of calcium carbonate forms 1 mole of carbon dioxide.
100 g of calcium carbonate form 44 g of carbon dioxide.
$\frac{100}{44} \times 0.1$ g of calcium carbonate form 0.1 g of carbon dioxide.
0.23 g of calcium carbonate gives 0.1 g of carbon dioxide when roasted.
As 1 mole of calcium carbonate is 100 g, then the number of moles = 0.23/100 = **0.0023**.

The last questions involve an understanding of the chemistry learned in several chapters. This enables, for example, the correct equations to be written.
A calculator may be needed in some of the questions. You will also require to make use of what you have learned in your maths course to calculate some of the answers. Maths is not confined to the Maths Department!
You may feel thay you can do some chemical calculations in your head and simply put down the answer. The problem about this is that if you make a mistake you will get no marks at all! If you set out your answers as shown above, long winded though it is, it will enable the marker to give you some marks. 1½ marks out of 2 is better than 0 out of 2.

CHAPTER SEVEN

1. C *Electrons (not ions) flow along a metal wire.*

2. D *Consult the electrochemical series. The greatest voltage is given by the metals which are furthest apart.*

3. A *Water is not a good enough conductor. Copper(II) sulphate solution and sulphuric acid both react with iron, zinc and magnesium.*

4. B *'X' is more reactive than all the metals except aluminium which displaces it.*

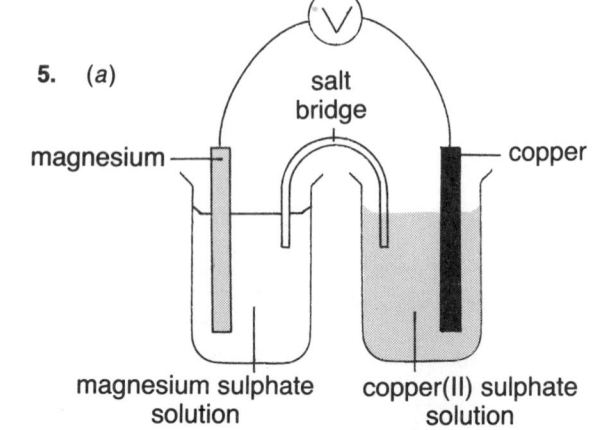

5. (a) [Diagram: electrochemical cell with magnesium electrode in magnesium sulphate solution and copper electrode in copper(II) sulphate solution, connected by a salt bridge, with a voltmeter (V) across the electrodes]

(b)

iron — iron(II) nitrate solution | silver — silver nitrate solution, with salt bridge and V (voltmeter)

(d)

zinc — zinc nitrate solution | copper — copper(II) nitrate solution, with salt bridge and V (voltmeter)

(c)

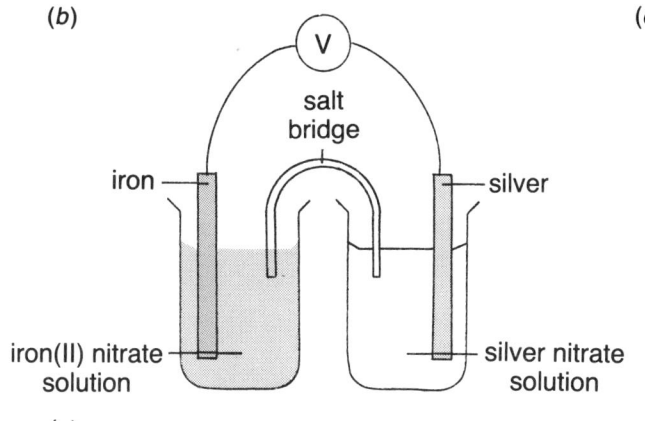

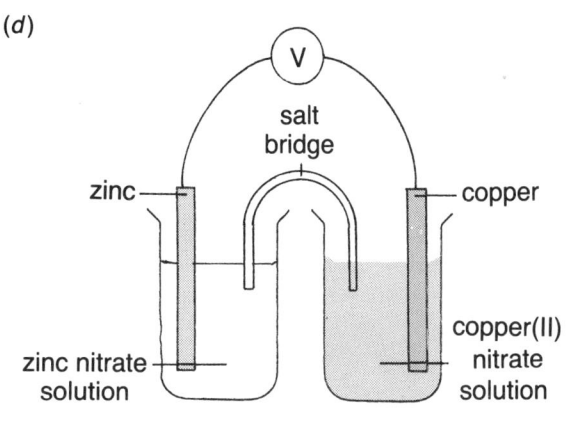

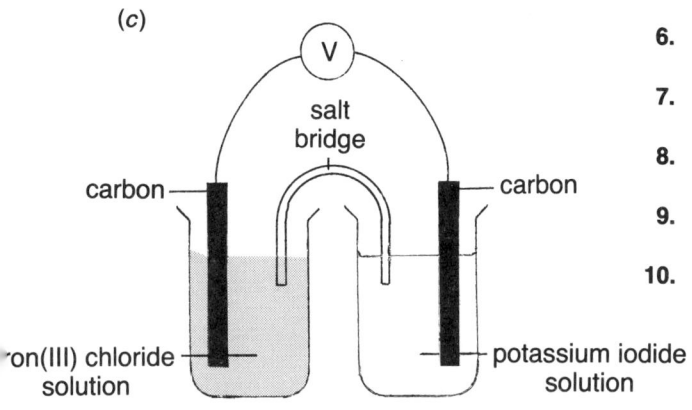

carbon — iron(III) chloride solution | carbon — potassium iodide solution, with salt bridge and V (voltmeter)

In each of the cells (a) to (d), the salt bridge can be filter paper soaked in any one of a number of electrolytes. Solutions of potassium nitrate or of sodium nitrate are best as they react with so few other ionic solutions.

6. C (A neither, B neither, D reduction only.)

7. A, C and E

8. A

9. C and F

10. (a) Reduction $Cu^{2+}(aq) + 2e \rightarrow Cu(s)$
    Oxidation $Mg(s) \rightarrow Mg^{2+}(aq) + 2e$
    (b) Reduction $2H^+(aq) + 2e \rightarrow H_2(g)$
    Oxidation $Zn(s) \rightarrow Zn^{2+}(aq) + 2e$
    (c) Reduction $Cu^{2+}(aq) + 2e \rightarrow Cu(s)$
    Oxidation $Zn(s) \rightarrow Zn^{2+}(aq) + 2e$
    (d) Reduction $Fe^{3+}(aq) + e \rightarrow Fe^{2+}(aq)$
    Oxidation $2I^-(aq) \rightarrow I_2(s) + 2e$
    (e) Reduction $Cl_2(g) + 2e \rightarrow 2Cl^-(aq)$
    Oxidation $2Br^-(aq) \rightarrow Br_2(l) + 2e$

CHAPTER EIGHT

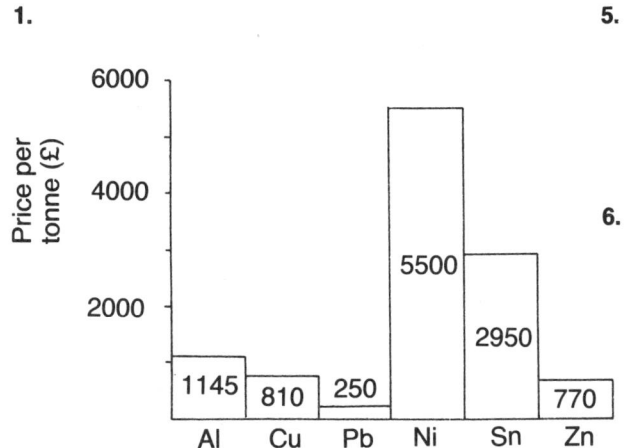

1. Bar chart — Price per tonne (£):
   Al 1145, Cu 810, Pb 250, Ni 5500, Sn 2950, Zn 770

2. (a) E   (b) C   (c) G   (d) A   (e) I

3. (a) E   (b) G   (c) D   (d) B

4. (a) A and C   (b) D and E   (c) B and F

5. (a) Al_2O_3
   (b) Aluminium is light and a good conductor of electricity.
   (c) Aluminium comes just below magnesium which reacts quickly with acids and burns violently.

6.

Metal	Percentage available in earth's crust
Aluminium	30
Iron	20
Calcium	18
Magnesium	10
Sodium	8
Potassium	6
Titanium	3
Other Metals	6

You will be allowed a small error in these values.

7.

Metal	Symbol	Melting point (°C)	Density (g/cm³)	Relative atomic mass
Aluminium	Al	660	2.7	27
Copper	Cu	1083	8.92	64
Iron	Fe	1535	7.86	56
Platinum	Pt	1770	21.5	195
Lead	Pb	328	11.3	207

8. (a) Aluminium is not magnetic; 'tin' cans are.
    (b) A finite resource is a resource whose reserves are limited. Oil, coal, gas and metal ores are finite resources.
    (c) (i) Aluminium 660 °C; copper 1083 °C; iron 1535 °C.
        (ii) Aluminium requires less heat to melt it down again than either copper or iron.
    (d) An alloy is a mixture of metals.

9. For a 'fair' test the three metals should all be in the same form, for example all in the form of lumps. Equal amounts of each should be added to equal volumes of, say, dilute sulphuric acid. The rate at which hydrogen is produced should then be measured.
    In this investigation there are a number of variables: form and mass of metal; concentration and temperature of acid; the same acid should also be used for each metal.
    Burning the metals in oxygen is also possible. In this case powdered metals would be essential. The reaction with water would not be satisfactory.

10. (a) oxygen
    (b) carbon monoxide
    (c) hydrogen
    (d) carbon dioxide
    (e) carbon dioxide

11. (a) copper + water
    (b) lead + carbon dioxide
    (c) copper + zinc chloride
    (d) iron + aluminium oxide
    (e) iron + carbon dioxide

12. *The percentage composition gives the mass of each element in 100 g.*
    Divide each by its atomic mass to get the number of moles of each.

    mole ratio
    calcium : carbon : oxygen
    40 : 12 : 48
    $\frac{40}{40} : \frac{12}{12} : \frac{48}{16}$
    1 : 1 : 3

    The empirical formula is $CaCO_3$.

13. mole ratio
    sodium : oxygen : hydrogen
    57.5 : 40 : 2.5
    $\frac{57.5}{23} : \frac{40}{16} : \frac{2.5}{1}$
    2.5 : 2.5 : 2.5

    The empirical formula is NaOH.

14. mole ratio
    carbon : hydrogen : oxygen
    40 : 6.6 : 53.4
    $\frac{40}{12} : \frac{6.6}{1} : \frac{53.4}{16}$
    3.3 : 6.6 : 3.3

    Dividing by the smallest, the empirical formula is CH_2O.

    It will often be the case that the empirical formula does not seem to obey rules you have learned.

15. The mass of oxygen in 100 g is 100 − 46.6 = 53.4 g.

    mole ratio
    silicon : oxygen
    46.6 : 53.4
    $\frac{46.6}{28} : \frac{53.4}{16}$
    1.6 : 3.3

    Dividing by the smallest, the empirical formula is SiO_2.

CHAPTER NINE

1. (a) C *(no oxygen)*, F *(connected to negative terminal)*, G *(no water)*, I *(sacrificial protection)*.
    (b) A *(water and oxygen)*, C *(no oxygen)*, G *(no water)*
    (c) I *(zinc is more active than iron)*
    (d) B *(ions in the water)*, D and E *(in both cases the iron will sacrificially protect the other metal)*, and H *(the positive electrode will encourage the loss of electrons)*

2. (a) C and H   (b) A   (c) C and E
    (d) B, F and G *(C and E will also fail if the connection is broken.)*

3. (a) B   (b) E   (c) A and E

4. If the coating is broken in either case a cell is set up. In the case of the zinc the electrons flow to the iron protecting it. With tin the electrons flow from the iron, causing rusting.

5. (a) G   (b) E   (c) H   (d) B

6. (a) $Al^{3+}(l) + 3e \rightarrow Al(l)$
    (b) $Cu^{2+}(aq) + 2e \rightarrow Cu(s)$
    (c) $Al(s) \rightarrow Al^{3+}(s) + 3e$
    (d) $2H^+(aq) + 2e \rightarrow H_2(g)$
    (e) $Cu(s) \rightarrow Cu^{2+}(aq) + 2e$

7. (a)

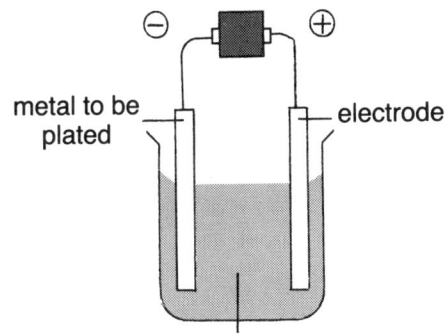

metal to be plated — electrode

solution of salt of plating metal

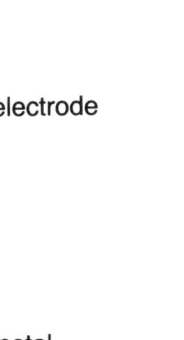

(b)

aluminium — lead

dilute sulphuric acid

(c)

ammeter

carbon — carbon

solution being tested

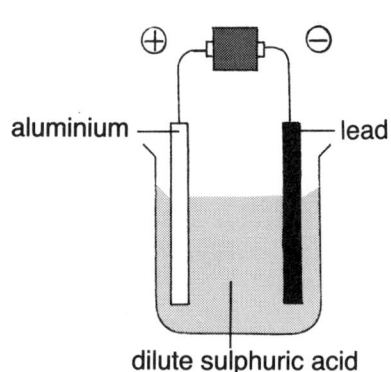

8. (a) A *The copper will be electroplated with nickel.*
   (b) B
   (c) A and C

9.
	Negative electrode	Positive electrode
(a)	$Al^{3+}(l) + 3e \rightarrow Al(l)$	$2O^{2-}(l) \rightarrow O_2(g) + 4e$
(b)	$Pb^{2+}(l) + 2e \rightarrow Pb(l)$	$2Br^-(l) \rightarrow Br_2(g) + 2e$
(c)	$Cu^{2+}(aq) + 2e \rightarrow Cu(s)$	$2Cl^-(aq) \rightarrow Cl_2(g) + 2e$
(d)	$2H^+(aq) + 2e \rightarrow H_2(g)$	$2Cl^-(aq) \rightarrow Cl_2(g) + 2e$
(e)	$Ni^{2+}(aq) + 2e \rightarrow Ni(s)$	$2Cl^-(aq) \rightarrow Cl_2(g) + 2e$

CHAPTER TEN

1. (a) poly(ethene)
   (b) poly(propene)
   (c) poly(tetrafluoroethene)
   (d) poly(styrene)
   (e) poly(monochloroethene)

2. (a) A
   (b) C, D and F
   (c) G and I

3. (a) A and D *(alkenes)*
   (b) C and E *(water will also form)*
   (c) B and F

4. (a) (i) thermosetting
       (ii) thermoplastic
       (iii) thermosetting
       (iv) thermoplastic
       (v) thermosetting
       (vi) thermoplastic
   (b) A thermoplastic polymer softens when heated. The handle of a frying pan should be made of a thermosetting polymer.

5. (a) Thermoplastic means that the polymer will soften and melt when heated.
   (b) Alkene.

(c) The molecular formula of methyl methacrylate is $C_5H_8O_2$. This is written by examining the structural formula which is given.

$$C_5H_8O_2$$

carbon   5 × 12 = 60
hydrogen   8 × 1 = 8
oxygen   2 × 16 = 32
formula mass   = 100 amu

It may seem unfair to be asked a question about formula mass in a topic concerning plastics! You must be ready to deal with any questions in exams.

(d)
```
     H   CH3       H   CH3       H   CH3
     |   |         |   |         |   |
   - C - C    -    C - C    -    C - C    -
     |   |         |   |         |   |
     C   COOCH3    H   COOCH3    H   COOCH3
```

Although you are not asked for it the repeating unit is:

```
     H   CH3
     |   |
   - C - C -
     |   |
     H   COOCH3
```

6. (a) condensation polymerisation
    (b) water
    (c)
    $$HOOC-\square-COOH + H_2N-\square-NH_2 + HOOC-\square-COOH + H_2N-\square-NH_2$$
    $$-CO-\square-CO-NH-\square-NH-CO-\square-CO-NH-\square-NH-$$

7. (a) Choose three names from fuel gas, petrol, kerosine, diesel, lubricating oil, bitumen.
    When you are asked to state a certain number of answers do not give more than this. If you give a greater number of answers including some which are incorrect you may lose marks.
    (b) alkenes
    (c) cracking
    (d) Most plastics are not biodegradable.
    (e) If a plastic is a hydrocarbon, then it will burn (in a plentiful supply of air) to form carbon dioxide and water vapour.
    If other elements such as nitrogen or chlorine are present then poisonous gases will form.

8. (a) A and D
    (b)
    $$\begin{array}{c} F \quad F \\ | \quad | \\ C=C \\ | \quad | \\ F \quad F \end{array}$$
    (c)
    $$HOOC-(CH_2)_4-COOH \text{ and } H_2N-(CH_2)_6-NH_2$$
    These two monomers will form nylon.
    (d)
    $$-CH(C_6H_5)-CH_2-$$

CHAPTER ELEVEN

1. nitrogen, phosphorus and potassium

2. *It is essential to write the formula for each compound.*
    (a) potassium sulphate K_2SO_4
    formula mass
    K 2 × 39 = 78
    S 1 × 32 = 32
    O 4 × 16 = 64
    fm   = 174 amu

    percentage potassium = $\frac{78}{176} \times 100$ = **44.3%**

    The other parts of the question are answered in the same way.
    (b) ammonium nitrate NH_4NO_3 = **35%**
    (c) calcium phosphate $Ca_3(PO_4)_2$ = **20%**

3. Nitrogen can be absorbed by nitrifying bacteria in the roots of plants such as peas, beans or clover.

4. For a fertiliser to be absorbed by the roots of plants it must dissolve in water and be carried through the soil. High solubility may be a disadvantage because very soluble compounds may be washed out of the soil and so pollute lakes and rivers.

5. (a) nitrogen and hydrogen
    (b) iron
    (c) nitrogen and hydrogen
    (d) The process is carried out at a moderately high temperature because: too low a temperature and the reaction is slow; too high a temperature and the ammonia decomposes.

6.
Low temperature	High temperature
slow reaction rate high percentage of ammonia	fast reaction rate low percentage of ammonia

7. ammonium sulphate and soda lime → ammonia (heated, collected in inverted test tube)

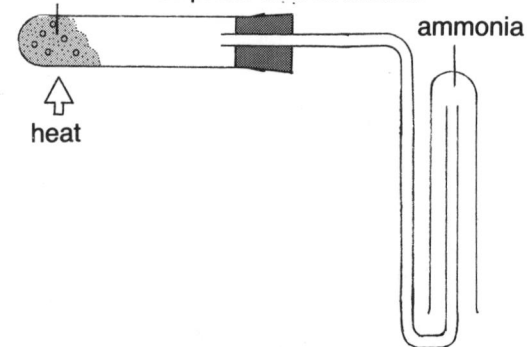

    Ammonia is less dense than air so an inverted test tube can be used.

8. (a) ammonium hydroxide
    (b) ammonia
    (c) potassium nitrate *(and water)*
    (d) ammonia *(and water and sodium sulphate)*
    (e) ammonium nitrate *(and water)*

9. (a) NH_3 (b) N_2
    (c) NH_4OH (d) NH_4Cl
    (e) NH_4NO_3 (f) $(NH_4)_2SO_4$
    (g) HNO_3 (h) $Ca(NO_3)_2$

10. Fill a dry test tube with ammonia, then invert it in a beaker of water.

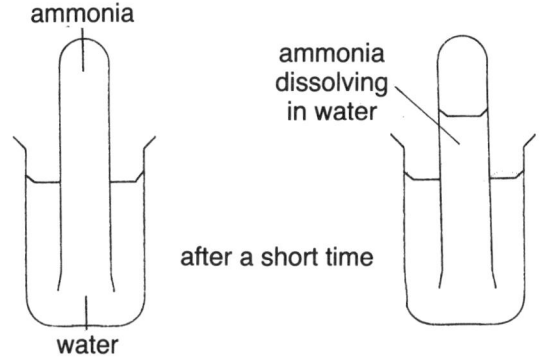

    ammonia

    ammonia dissolving in water

    after a short time

    water

    Alternatively, test ammonia gas with wet pH paper. The pH paper will turn blue showing that ammonia is dissolving in the water to form an alkaline solution.

11. (a) Ostwald process
    (b) Ammonia is made in the Haber process.
    (c) Nitrogen is a very inactive gas. *The only way to combine nitrogen and oxygen is to spark air, a mixture of oxygen and nitrogen. This is a dangerous, expensive and slow process.*
    (d) When energy is given out in a reaction, the reaction is called exothermic.

12. (a) $KOH + HNO_3 \rightarrow H_2O + KNO_3$
    (b) $MgCO_3 + 2HNO_3 \rightarrow 2H_2O + CO_2 + Mg(NO_3)_2$
    (c) $CuO + 2HNO_3 \rightarrow H_2O + Cu(NO_3)_2$
    (d) $NH_4OH + HNO_3 \rightarrow H_2O + NH_4NO_3$

13. Put dilute nitric acid into a beaker and then add calcium carbonate. The mixture will fizz as carbon dioxide gas is given off.
    Continue to add calcium carbonate until the fizzing stops. Filter the mixture to remove excess calcium carbonate.
    The solution of calcium nitrate should be left to evaporate and crystals of pure dry calcium nitrate will form after a few days.

14. (a) D
    (b) E *(produces nitric acid)*
    (c) C *(see table of flame colours)*
    (d) F *(gives ammonium hydroxide)*
    (e) F
    (f) F and G

15. (a)

Soluble	Insoluble
ammonium nitrate	calcium carbonate
ammonium sulphate	calcium phosphate
ammonium phosphate	magnesium phosphate
potassium nitrate	

    (b) Nitrogen compounds are, in general, soluble in water.

16. (a) Experiment A shows compound X contains the ammonium ion.
    (b) Experiment B shows compound X contains the carbonate ion CO_3^{2-}.
    (c) Compound X is ammonium carbonate.
    (d) $(NH_4)_2CO_3$
    (e) Yes! Ammonium carbonate *is* soluble in water as the question suggests.

CHAPTER TWELVE

1. (a) W is H_2O
    (b) X is O_2
    (c) Y is CO_2
    (d) Z is $C_{12}H_{22}O_{11}$
    All of these formulae can be obtained by subtraction, for example in (a)
    $W = 2C_6H_{12}O_6 - C_{12}H_{22}O_{11} = H_2O$

2. (a) Benedict's reagent turns from a blue colour to a red colour when heated with glucose solution. Starch has no effect on Benedict's reagent.
    (b) Iodine solution turns from yellow to black when added to starch. Glucose solution has no effect on iodine solution.
    (c) When a beam of light is shone through water containing starch, it shows up as an intense beam (Tyndall beam). With glucose solution no Tyndall beam is produced.
    When you are asked for a colour change you should give the colours before and after.
    When asked to distinguish between two substances, you should state the effect of the reagent on both of them. This may mean simply saying that the second substance gives 'no effect'.

3. (a) B and E
    (b) F
    (c) H
    (d) A and C

4. The level of carbon dioxide in the atmosphere has risen in recent years owing to:
    large increases in the world population;

large increases in hydrocarbon fuels being burned;
large scale felling of forests.
The first two factors produce extra carbon dioxide. The third factor means that less carbon dioxide is being removed from the atmosphere.
You were asked for two reasons—so you should only give two reasons. Do not get into the habit of simply writing down all you know in questions like this. If part of your answer is wrong or contradicts another part, then you may lose marks.

5. Starch is almost insoluble in water and starch molecules are too large to be able to diffuse through the wall of the gut.

6. (a) In fermentation the temperature and pH must be controlled. In addition the concentration of alcohol produced affects the yeast. Above about 15% alcohol the yeast cells cease to be able to cause fermentation.
   (b) (i) $C_6H_{12}O_6$ carbon $6 \times 12 = 72$
                    hydrogen $12 \times 1 = 12$
                    oxygen $6 \times 16 = 96$
                    fm   = 180 amu
                    mass of 1 mole = 180 g

        (ii) CO_2 carbon $1 \times 12 = 12$
                    oxygen $2 \times 16 = 32$
                    fm   = 44 amu
                    mass of 1 mole = 44 g
                    mass of 2 moles = 88 g

   (c) $C_6H_{12}O_6 \rightarrow 2C_2H_5OH + 2CO_2$
   1 mole of glucose produces 2 moles of carbon dioxide.
   180 g of glucose produce 88 g of carbon dioxide (*see (b) above*), so 9 g of glucose produce $\frac{88 \times 9}{180} = 4.4$ g of carbon dioxide.
   If only 40% of the glucose reacts, then the mass of carbon dioxide formed is
   $\frac{4.4 \times 40}{100} = $ **1.76 g**

Chemical calculations are to be found in Chapter Six.
   (d) Carbon dioxide turns lime water chalky (or milky).

7. (a) (i) 126 °C   (ii) 81 °C
   (b) Liquids with different boiling points can be separated by distillation. When the two liquids are heated, the one with the lower boiling point, cyclohexane in this case, will boil off first.
   Boiling means turning into a gas. In distillation the gas produced is turned back into a liquid by a condenser.

8. (a) A and F
   (b) E and H
   (c) E and G
   (d) H
   (e) D

9. (a) 'Alcohol' is a member of the alkanol family and is called **ethanol**. It is made by the **fermentation** of glucose by **yeast**.
   (b) The formula of 'alcohol' is C_2H_5OH or C_2H_6O.
   carbon $2 \times 12 = 24$
   hydrogen $6 \times 1 = 6$
   oxygen $1 \times 16 = 16$
   formula mass   = **46 amu**
   (c) The concentration or strength of alcohol can be increased by distillation.

10. Alcohol impairs the workings of the mind and body. Manipulation with the fingers becomes clumsy, speech becomes slurred and movements unsteady. Reaction time is slowed down, making people more accident prone. There is a limit to the amount of alcohol allowed in the bloodstream of car drivers.
    In the long term alcohol consumption can cause damage to the liver and increase the chances of heart and other diseases. The disease called alcoholism develops in heavy drinkers who are addicted to alcohol.

CHAPTER THIRTEEN

SELECTING INFORMATION

1. (a) 98 °C   *(remember units)*
   (b) 81 °C
   (c) 1669
   (d) green
   (e) 2.33 g/cm³
   (f) insoluble
   (g) 2, 8, 6
   (h) NO_3^-

2. (a) What is unusual about this reaction is that the temperature increases for a time but then it *decreases*.
   (b) about 40 °C

3. (a) methanoic acid and concentrated sulphuric acid
   (b) Potassium hydroxide solution is an alkali which will react with the carbon dioxide and remove it from the mixture.
   Carbon monoxide gas will pass through the solution unaffected.

(c) X is H₂O
Find X by subtraction: $2H_2CO_2 - 2CO$
$(H_4C_2O_4 - C_2O_2)$
$= 2H_2O$

4. (a) An alloy is a mixture of a metal and other substances, usually other metals.

(b)

Alloy	Percentage of nickel
constantan	40
German silver	15
monel	67
'silver' coins	25

(c) copper and nickel

5. (a) sulphur dioxide and oxygen
(b) sulphur trioxide
(c) It is used in the manufacture of detergents and in the manufacture of sulphuric acid.
(d) Super concentrated sulphuric acid is made by mixing sulphur trioxide and concentrated sulphuric acid.
(e) SO_3

PRESENTING INFORMATION

1. (a)

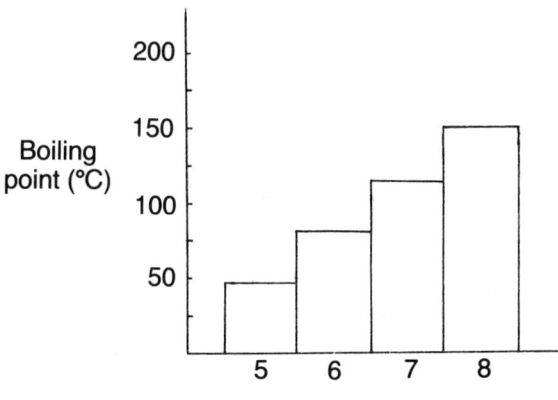

You will be awarded marks for the correct axes, labels and units. You will also get marks for accurately drawing the 'points' in the graph. Be sure to read the question carefully and determine if it is a bar or line graph that has to be drawn.

(b) about 180 °C

2. (a)

Compound	Boiling point (°C)
ethane	−88
butane	0
propane	−42
pentane	36
methane	−164

(b)
1 methane
2 ethane
3 propane
4 butane
5 pentane

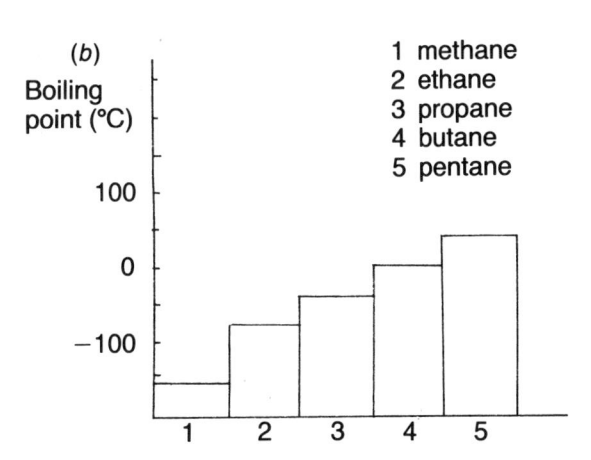

(c) Pentane is a liquid at 10 °C.
*A substance is a liquid above its melting point and below its boiling point.
In this question the boiling points scale includes numbers greater than and also less than zero.*

3. A table is the obvious way to present this information.

Components of glaze	Percentage amount
lead oxide	40
fine sand	30
soda	25
cobalt salt	5

A properly labelled pie chart or a bar chart would also be acceptable.

4. A word equation could be used to present this information.

copper + sulphuric acid → sulphur dioxide + water + copper(II) sulphate

A table with the headings 'Reactants' and 'Products' would also do.

5. A key or flowchart is one way to present the information.

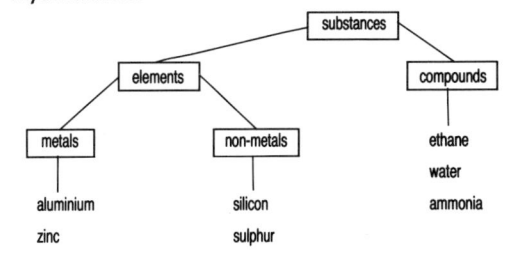

```
                    substances
                   /          \
              elements      compounds
              /      \           |
          metals  non-metals   ethane
            |        |         water
        aluminium  silicon    ammonia
          zinc    sulphur
```

A table with the headings 'Metal elements', 'Non-metal elements' and 'Compounds' is another way to present this information.

6.

Aluminium compound	Use
aluminium oxide	abrasive in sandpaper
aluminium sulphate	water treatment
aluminium hydroxide	antacid
aluminium sodium silicate	food additive
sodium aluminium phosphate	food additive

7.

Temperature (°C) graph showing points rising from about 21°C at time 2 min, peaking around 32°C at 6 min, then declining to about 27°C by 14 min. Y-axis marked 10, 20, 30. X-axis: Time (minutes) 2, 4, 6, 8, 10, 12, 14.

Marks will be deducted if the points which you draw are not accurate. The graph paper provided will be convenient for the figures which are given. Make use of most of the graph paper and take care in choosing the scale.

SELECTING PROCEDURES

1. (a) C *The value of the voltage gives the position of a metal in the electrochemical series.*
   (b) B *The meter indicates if the solution is conducting electricity or not.*

2. C, E, A, D and B

3. B, D, C and A

4. D *Much of the ammonia will escape from A. In B you cannot be sure that the test tube will be full of ammonia. C will not be very effective for a lot of the ammonia will dissolve in the water. D is the correct, but messy, method!*

5. (a) Use a test tube with a stopper or side arm fitted with a rubber tube. Add zinc carbonate powder to dilute hydrochloric acid in the test tube. Bubble the gas which forms through lime water. The lime water will turn chalky.

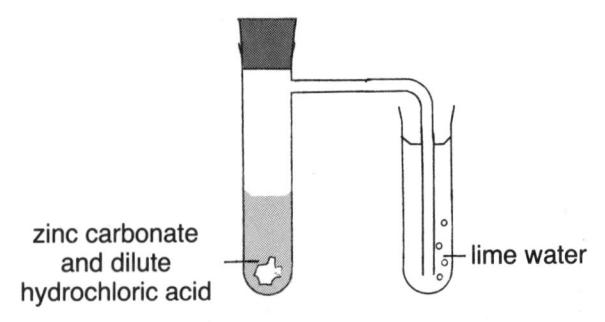

   Diagram: test tube containing zinc carbonate and dilute hydrochloric acid, connected via side arm and tube to another test tube containing lime water.

   When describing an experiment or drawing a diagram the important question is 'will it work?' Learn to draw real pieces of equipment. A stencil may help you. You will see examples of diagrams all through this book. Lines from labels should be drawn with a ruler, and should touch the part of the experiment to which they refer.

   Remember that there are no square-shaped test tubes or pear-shaped beakers manufactured!
   (b) Add the toffee to water so that some of it dissolves. Test the solution formed by heating it with Benedict's reagent. If the mixture turns a red colour, this shows that the toffee contains glucose.

6. The manganese dioxide should be weighed before starting the experiment and its mass noted. After the experiment the remaining solution should be filtered, the recovered manganese dioxide left in the filter paper to dry and then reweighed. The mass will, of course, be the same as it was at the start.

7. Colin should put samples from the three bottles into three separate dry test tubes. A little piece of calcium should be added to each liquid. The one(s) which gave off bubbles (of hydrogen) contained some water. The one(s) which gave no bubbles should be used.

8. (a) Equal concentrations of each solution were used.
   (b) Ammonium sulphate is a salt (made from ammonium hydroxide and sulphuric acid) and does not have a pH of 7.
   (c) For neutralisation:
   volume × concentration × no. of H^+ ions = volume × concentration × no. of OH^- ions
   $25 \times 1 \times 1$ is *not* equal to $30 \times 1 \times 1$
   There is too much potassium hydroxide and so the solution will not be neutral, the pH will be greater than 7. The answer is **A**.
   Perhaps you were able to answer this just by looking at the question.

9. (a) A, D and E
   Each has potassium nitrate solution, and there are two metals more active than iron and one metal less active.
   (b) B and D
   Same metal, copper, in each experiment. One contains water and the other potassium nitrate solution (an ionic solution).

10. Mass of glucose (or concentration of glucose solution), mass of yeast, volume of water and temperature of water.

CONCLUDING AND EXPLAINING

1. calcium and carbon *Look at the names of the elements in the reactants and products.*

2. (a) Substances which dissolve in water and conduct electricity have ionic bonding.
   (b) carbonates
   (c) sodium carbonate *Sodium ions in a compound give a yellow flame colour.*

3. Copper(II) oxide reacts with dilute sulphuric acid to give a copper(II) sulphate solution which is blue. *Carbon electrodes are used in electrolysis,*

so you may have guessed that carbon does not react with dilute sulphuric acid.

If the mixture of copper(II) oxide and carbon is roasted, it will react to form copper and carbon dioxide. The copper(II) oxide is 'reduced' by the carbon, as many metal oxides are.

4. (a) 126 °C
   (b) hexane (*ethanol and propanone are not hydrocarbons*)
   (c) fractional distillation
   (d) The boiling points of the alkanes depends on their formula masses. The fm of heptane comes between those of hexane and octane. This means that its boiling point comes between those of the two alkanes.

5. (a) cadmium(II) oxide
   (b) mercury(I) chloride
   (c) thorium(II) chloride
   (d) chromium(III) oxide
   (e) manganese(II) sulphate
   (f) iron(III) nitrate
   In each compound the valency of the second part in the name is known. This allows the valency of the metal to be found.

6. (a) H_2CO_2
   (b) C
   (c) C_2H_4
   Each answer is found by subtraction.

7. (a) Copper reacts with mercury because copper is more active than mercury.
   (b) Nothing would happen. *Copper is less active than zinc.*
   (c) The boiling point of mercury is so low that it will easily boil when heated. The boiling point of silver is much too high for it to boil when heated.

PREDICTING AND GENERALISING

1. (a) hydrogen   (b) inactive
   (c) hydrogen   (d) oxygen

2. (a)

Soluble in water	Insoluble in water
ammonium carbonate	calcium carbonate
ammonium sulphate	aluminium carbonate
ammonium chloride	calcium phosphate

   (b) In general, ammonium compounds are soluble in water.

3. (a) In general, the solubility of compounds in water increases as the temperature rises.
   (b) 40 g/l
   (c) 29 °C
   (d) Solubility at 60 °C is 40 g/l. At 40 °C it is 20 g/l. The mass of crystals forming is 40 − 20 = 20 g.

4. (a) Decrease. *A gas, hydrogen, is being given off.*
   (b) Decrease. *A gas, carbon dioxide is being given off.*
   (c) Remain the same. *Nothing is being added or given off.*
   (d) Increase. *Oxygen from the air is being added.*

5. (a) The carbonates of the three metals should be heated in turn in separate test tubes.
   The carbonate which gave off carbon dioxide most quickly was the carbonate of the least active metal, etc.
   (b) zinc carbonate → zinc oxide + carbon dioxide
   (c) Copper carbonate would decompose more quickly than zinc carbonate.

6. (a) Experiment 1
   (b) Experiment 1
   (c) It would be less than 2 minutes.
   (d) By heating the acid or by using powdered magnesium.
   (e) Equal volumes ensured a fair comparison.

7. (a) There may be microscopic holes in the skin of the balloon between the molecules of rubber.
   In a question of this nature any scientific answer which is relevant will be acceptable. Answers such as 'The balloon was faulty' will not be acceptable.
   (b) The smaller hydrogen molecules will be able to escape through the skin of the balloon more quickly than the larger oxygen molecules.
   (c) A balloon filled with xenon would go down very slowly because the large xenon molecules would have difficulty in escaping.

Appendix

The Periodic Table

Showing symbol, relative atomic mass and atomic number (of selected elements)

Group 1	Group 2												Group 3	Group 4	Group 5	Group 6	Group 7	Group 0
				1 H Hydrogen														4 He 2 Helium
7 Li 3 Lithium	9 Be 4 Beryllium												11 B 5 Boron	12 C 6 Carbon	14 N 7 Nitrogen	16 O 8 Oxygen	19 F 9 Fluorine	20 Ne 10 Neon
23 Na 11 Sodium	24 Mg 12 Magnesium												27 Al 13 Aluminium	28 Si 14 Silicon	31 P 15 Phosphorus	32 S 16 Sulphur	35·5 Cl 17 Chlorine	40 Ar 18 Argon
39 K 19 Potassium	40 Ca 20 Calcium	Sc 21 Scandium	Ti 22 Titanium	V 23 Vanadium	Cr 24 Chromium	Mn 25 Manganese	56 Fe 26 Iron	59 Ni 28 Nickel	Co 27 Cobalt	64 Cu 29 Copper	65 Zn 30 Zinc		Ga 31 Gallium	Ge 32 Germanium	As 33 Arsenic	Se 34 Selenium	80 Br 35 Bromine	Kr 36 Krypton
Rb 37 Rubidium	Sr 38 Strontium	Y 39 Yttrium	Zr 40 Zirconium	Nb 41 Niobium	Mo 42 Molybdenum	Tc 43 Technetium	Ru 44 Ruthenium	Pd 46 Palladium	Rh 45 Rhodium	108 Ag 47 Silver	Cd 48 Cadmium		In 49 Indium	119 Sn 50 Tin	Sb 51 Antimony	Te 52 Tellurium	127 I 53 Iodine	Xe 54 Xenon
Cs 55 Caesium	Ba 56 Barium	La 57 Lanthanium	Hf 72 Hafnium	Ta 73 Tantalum	W 74 Tungsten	Re 75 Rhenium	Os 76 Osmium	Pt 78 Platinum	Ir 77 Iridium	197 Au 79 Gold	201 Hg 80 Mercury		Tl 81 Thallium	207 Pb 82 Lead	Bi 83 Bismuth	Po 84 Polonium	At* 85 Astatine	Rn 86 Radon
Fr 87 Francium	Ra 88 Radium	Ac 89 Actinium																

Transition Metals

Relative atomic mass (simplified for calculations)
Symbol
Atomic number
Name

Lanthanides

| Ce 58 Cerium | Pr 59 Praseodymium | Nd 60 Neodymium | Pm 61 Promethium | Sm 62 Samarium | Eu 63 Europium | Gd 64 Gadolinium | Tb 65 Terbium | Dy 66 Dysprosium | Ho 67 Holmium | Er 68 Erbium | Tm 69 Thulium | Yb 70 Ytterbium | Lu 71 Lutetium |

Actinides

| Th 90 Thorium | Pa 91 Protactinium | U 92 Uranium | Np* 93 Neptunium | Pu* 94 Plutonium | Am* 95 Americium | Cm* 96 Curium | Bk* 97 Berkelium | Cf* 98 Californium | Es* 99 Einsteinium | Fm* 100 Fermium | Md* 101 Mendelevium | No* 102 Nobelium | Lr* 103 Lawrencium |

Man-made elements

Index

acid rain 45
acidic oxides 45
acids 44
addition polmerisation 86
addition reactions 33
air 28
alcohol 104
alcoholic drinks 104
alkali metals 14
alkalis 44
alkanes 29, 31
alkanols 103
alkenes 29, 31, 86
alloys 64
aluminium 64, 78
ammonia 94
ammonium compounds 95
ammonium ion 96
anodising 78
antacid 46
aqueous solution 8
atomic mass
    (relative) 16
    units 16, 49
atomic number 15
    structure 15
atoms 15

balanced equations 24
base 45
basic oxide 45
battery 57
Benedict's reagent 102
biodegradeable 84
blast furnace 67
bonds 16
burning 28

carbohydrates 100
carbonates 47
carbon cycle 101
carbon dioxide 28, 47, 100
catalyst 9, 34, 65
cells 57, 59, 60
chemical equations 22
    reaction 5
chlorophyll 100
chromatography 8
colloid 103
colours of compounds 40
combustion 28
compost 93
compounds 7, 21
concentration 8, 49
condensation polymerisation 88, 102
conduction 38
conductivity (electrical) 38
copper 64
corrosion 75
covalent bonds 16, 17

solids 40
cracking 33
crystals 39
cycloalkanes 29, 30

diatomic molecules 18
digestion 103
direct current (DC) 38
disaccharides 102
discharge equations 40
displacement 58
distillation 8, 27, 104
dry cell 58

effervescence 5
electricity 57
electrolysis 40, 45, 78
electrolyte 40
electrochemical series 58, 65
electron arrangement 15
electroplating 79
element 6, 14
empirical formula 68
emulsion 41
energy 6, 57, 101
    levels 15
enzymes 103
equations 22
    balanced 24
    discharge 40
    ion electron 40
    state 23
    word 22
essential elements 90
ethanol 103
exothermic 26

fermentation 103
ferroxyl indicator 75
fertilisers 92
fibres 87
filtration 8
finite resources 26, 64
fixation 93
flame tests 96
flammability 27
formula 16, 21, 41
formula mass (relative) 49
fossil fuels 26
fractional distillation 27
fractions 26
fuels 26

galvanising 77
general formula 30
glucose 101
gold 65
greenhouse effect 101
group number 15
groups 14

Haber process   94
halogens   14
homologous series   30
hydrocarbons   26, 29
hydrogen   45, 59
hydrolysis   103

insoluble salts   48
insulators   38
iodine   102
ion bridge   58, 59
    electron equations   40
ions   15, 38
iron   64, 67
isomers   32
isotopes   16

lattices   39
lead   64
leguminosae   93

mass number   15
'mazit' metals   47
mercury   65
migration of ions   40
mixtures   7
mole   49
molecular formula   29
molecules   16
monomers   85
monosaccharides   102

natural fertilisers   93
natural materials   84
network solids   39
neutral solutions   44
neutralisation   46
neutrons   15
nitrates   96
nitric acid   95
nitrogen   29
    dioxide   95
    cycle   97
nitrifying bacteria   93
noble gas   14
nodules (root)   93
nucleus   15
nylon   87

oil   26
ores   64
Ostwald process   95
oxidation   60
oxygen   28

percentage composition   92
periods   14
periodic table   14, 134
pH   44
photosynthesis   100
physical changes   5
plastics   84
platinum   65
pollution   29
polyalkenes   86
polymerisation   85
polymers   85

polysaccharides   102
precipitation   48
products   22
properties of metals   64, 65
proteins   93
protons   15
purification of metals   79

rates of reactions   9
reactants   22
reacting masses   51
reactivity   58, 65
rechargeable cells   57
recycling   65
redox   60
reducing agent   66
    sugars   102
reduction   60, 66
repeating unit   86
repolymerisation   88
respiration   100
reversible reaction   94
rust   75

sacrificial protection   78
salt bridge   58, 59
salts   46
saturated hydrocarbon   32
    solution   8
shapes of molecules   18
silver   65
soap   40
soapless detergents   41
solubility   48, 92
solute   8
solution   8
solvent   8, 40
spectator ions   47
starch   102
state equations   22
    symbols   22
states of matter   5
structural formula   18
symbols   6, 21
synthetic materials   84

thermoplastic polymers   85
thermosetting polymers   85
tin   64
tinplating   77
titration   50
transition metals   14, 22
Tyndall beam   102

unsaturated hydrocarbons   32

valency   17, 22
variables   10
viscosity   27
voltage   58

water   40, 44, 100

word equations   22

yeast   104

zinc   64